BACKYARD MARKET

GARDENING

The Entrepreneur's Guide to

Selling What You Grow

By Andrew W. Lee

Foreword by Jim Hightower

Introduced and Edited by
George DeVault

Cover design and production by Sarah Montgomery
Special cover effects by Phil Laughlin
Cover photo by Ken Burris

Publisher's Cataloging in Publication

Lee, Andrew W., 1948-
Backyard Market Gardening, The Entrepreneur's Guide to Selling What You Grow / by Andrew W. Lee. ; foreword by Jim Hightower ; introduced and edited by George DeVault.
p. 352 cm.
Includes bibliographical references and index.
ISBN 0-9624648-0-5

1. Truck farming--Market gardening. 2. Vegetable Gardening--Guide-books. 3. New business enterprises--United States. 4. Small business--Guide-books. I. DeVault, George. II Title. III. Title: The entrepreneur's guide to selling what you grow.

SB320.9.L4 1992   635
                                                      90-84585

GOOD EARTH PUBLICATIONS
Box 4352
Burlington, Vermont 05406-4352

Published in the United States of America

Acknowledgments

A sincere thank you goes to *The NEW FARM* editors and authors for their contributions. The following materials have appeared previously in *The NEW FARM*.

Ed Shamy: Fitting The Farm To The Climate,

Bob Hofstetter: The Profit Is In The Picking, Mobile Marketing, A Homemade Greenhouse for $100, The NEW FARM'S Greenhouse Guide, Tunnels of Plenty.

George DeVault: The Corporate Connection, City Farm, Irrigation Made Easy.

Craig Cramer: The New Gold Rush, How To Score Big With Consumers.

T.L. Gettings: Higher-Value High-Value Crops, Do What No One Else Is Doing.

A special thanks goes to George DeVault for editing and introducing the book, Jim Hightower for the foreword, Sara Montgomery for graphics and cover design and Mark Schoenbeck for technical advice.

Especially thanks to Patricia Foreman for her encouragement, patience, love and unending support that helped the book become a reality, and to my son, Chris, for all those years of helping me in the gardens and compost piles.

About The Author

photo by Sheldon Ball

Andy Lee owned Natural Lee Farm, a successful market garden near Boston, Mass., and is now executive director of the Intervale Foundation in Burlington, Vermont. He has over 20 years experience as a market gardener and small business owner, and teaches vegetable production and marketing in the University of Vermont's alternative agriculture program. Andy's philosophy of successful market gardening is simply to; *Fix the soil and get close to your customers.*

In Memory of

Robert Rodale and Brian Lee

I never met Bob Rodale, but I feel like I've known him as a best friend for most of my life. I think it is safe to say that for the past three decades he has had a stronger influence on my career than any other human being. My earliest gardening memories revolve around reading and following the advice given in articles printed in the Organic Gardening and Farming magazine published by the Rodale Family.

Three of Bob's books played an important role in my career development as well. In 1971 Bob wrote *The Rodale Guide to Organic Gardening* which gave me the references I needed to learn how to do organic gardening right. Following that, in 1981, he wrote *Our Next Frontier*, which resonated so strongly within my being that I set about creating one of the backyard garden farms that he predicted would become our farms of tomorrow. And his last book, *Save Three Lives – A Plan for Famine Prevention*, started me thinking about how to enrich small plots of land for growing super-abundant crops for local families. From my thinking on this matter came the ideas for creating the obtainable, sustainable integrated garden system which I describe in this book.

Bob and I shared another bond which he never knew about. His son died shortly before my oldest son, Brian, was killed by a drunk driver nearly four years ago. The day before he died, Brian spent five hours helping me spread compost on our market garden. We finished the day tired, happy and satisfied. I can't think of any better way to spend the last day you have with someone you love than to use that time nourishing the soul and building good earth.

In a long-distance, vicarious manner I relied on Bob Rodale's strength to carry me through the most tragic event of my life. He must have suffered terribly, yet in spite of the grief and sorrow of losing his son, Bob continued to bring his message of hope to the world. His passionate desire to help others gave me the courage and inspiration to overcome my own pain and grief and enabled me to learn how to create worth and value in my own life. I am glad that I have been able to bring this book to reality so that I can dedicate it to my son, Brian William Lee, and to my best friend I never met, Robert David Rodale.

Bob Rodale died in an auto accident in Moscow, Russia, September 20, 1990. He was a guiding force in the organic gardening and small-scale farming movement for nearly 40 years, worldwide. At the time of his death he was finalizing plans for the *Novii Fermer* (New Farmer), a Russian-language sustainable farming magazine. He was bringing his message of a sustainable way of life to the Russian people, who have not known freedom on the land for nearly seven decades. I am happy to say that *Novii Fermer* is now in its second year of publication, and that another of my best friends, George DeVault, is the American editor. The following message of hope and inspiration is excerpted from Bob's book, *Our Next Frontier.*

> The highly productive home gardens of tomorrow will, I think, be the sprouts from which many new small farms will grow. The small-scale farmers of the future can hardly learn their craft in the land-grant colleges, which preach bigness in almost every way. These new farmers will start as gardeners and grow from there. I think that we will see the size of gardens increase, so that the distinction between a large garden and a small farm will become blurred.
>
> The new wave of small farms will fill in the chinks of land made available as some of the old-style farmers are driven out of business by ever-bigger farming conglomerates. I think there is room now for many more small farms of the future. Much land that could be used to grow vegetables, beans, specialty crops and fruits is lying idle. Those acres growing up to weeds might be made into profitable farms if the proper plants and cropping systems for efficient small farms are developed by researchers.
>
> I suspect that people displaced by the trend to consolidate farms into ever-larger units, as well as those who don't want to fit into city life, will return to the land and make these small spaces productive. Large farms today aren't suited to produce the fresh, natural foods that are in growing demand. They will be even less suited for that task in the future, as agribusiness turns more and more to the manufacture of

semisynthetic foods from bulk commodities like soybeans, cornstarch, and even petroleum.

The garden-farms that are a growing part of our food future have another important value. They can be operated as closed systems. Organic wastes of both the community and the farm itself can be collected, composted and returned to the land. By doing that, the vitally important minerals and nitrogen in those wastes can be preserved and used over and over again.

The recycling of minerals in that way is more than just a step toward greater commercial and ecological efficiency. It is a significant movement toward the creation of a permanent human society on this planet. Our present system of production is in reality a bleeding process in which the riches of the earth are drained away to create the things we need to support ourselves. As long as we allow that bleeding to continue, we are imposing on ourselves a time-limit for survival.

There need not be a limit to our tenure. We can learn to live happily, producing all the food and other goods we need, without wasting the resources that are going to be needed by future generations. There, in the concept of the creation of a sustainable way of life, is our next frontier.

BACKYARD MARKET GARDENING

The Entrepreneur's Guide to

Selling What You Grow

CHAPTER 4

Foreword

by Jim Hightower

Market Gardening Can Be Very Rewarding To The Soul, The Soil, And The Flow Of Capital

The greatest opportunities can sometimes be found in our own backyards. This is true for the small-scale agriculturist who dreams of selling the fruits of his or her labors to an appreciative public. It also applies to communities and even entire states that are looking for ways to diversify their economies.

In *BACKYARD MARKET GARDENING* Andy Lee shows the tenderfoot how to sell quality garden produce to the public for fun and for profit. Small-scale agriculture as described by Andy can be very rewarding to the soul, the environment, and the flow of capital.

We know this to be true here in Texas because we have had great success in linking small-scale farmers with urban consumers through a revitalized system of farmers markets.

Our experience in marketing the produce grown on small farms in Texas is worth mentioning here. Innovative family farmers have shown that they can make good money by looking for creative ways to market their produce in nearby urban centers. They provide an object lesson in what Andy is talking about in the pages of this do-it-yourself marketing guide.

Texans have plenty of nearby urban markets to sell to. Though we have 200 rural counties, we also have 54 urban counties, more than any other state. These major urban markets are spread fairly evenly across Texas, with a number of good-sized towns between. That puts almost all our small-scale farmers within easy reach of urban consumers. A resource like this cries out to be developed, and it has been.

Our small farmers and market gardeners have teamed up with the Texas Department of Agriculture and local governments. We have created a network of 100 farmers market sites in more than 80 cities and towns. From inner cities to county seats, these markets are helping move Texas toward a safer, environmentally sound and consumer-oriented agriculture.

Texas consumers obviously like what they find at farmers markets, judging by the explosion in demand for new markets. In 1984 the Texas Department of Agriculture introduced a farmers market development program. Within six years the number of farmers markets jumped from only four to an even 100.

Texas farmers obviously like the returns they are getting for their efforts. Statewide direct sales to consumers through Texas farmers markets earned $30 million in gross sales in 1990. This is a 20 percent increase over 1989. A total of 3,500 participating farmers will average more than $8,500 each in sales through farmers markets during 1991.

The ability of Texas farmers to sell their goods directly to consumers has produced other benefits besides better cash flow. Consumers now have the chance to find out how and where their food is grown by talking to the people who produce it. People concerned about pesticide contamination can talk directly with growers to find out what production practices they use.

Farmers markets tend to support diversification of farming operations and to encourage producers to use local resources to sustain their production. Having nearby outlets for their production allows farmers to experiment with alternative crops and to test consumer preferences directly and immediately.

Products sold at farmers markets aren't hauled long distances, and don't need expensive and environmentally damaging preservatives or packaging. These markets make ideal outlets for beginning farmers, especially those who use organic and sustainable methods. Consumers now view these markets as reliable sources of fresh, locally grown organic produce.

Many of our smaller agricultural communities have eagerly embraced farmers markets because they draw weekend visitors from nearby cities, bringing badly needed tourist dollars that spread beyond the marketplace. These new visitors have added vigor to local festivals and promotional events planned around harvests, holidays and market days.

Texas farmers markets are also providing healthy and safe food to those who need it most. Elderly and low-income families are buying fresh produce through innovative programs. One is the Women With Infant Children (WIC) project. Others are food stamp recipients, and participants in the senior citizen coupon programs. These pilot programs made $50,000 in benefits available at 39 farmers market sites in 1989. It is a good trade off – food for the hungry and sustainability for small-scale farmers.

The decision by thousands of individual Texas farmers to begin direct marketing their produce has generated a wide range of benefits on and off the farm. We are all better off in Texas today because of these pioneering small farmers. What we did in Texas can be done elsewhere. Andy's book gives management, marketing guidance and encouragement that will help many pioneering agricultural entrepreneurs become successful.

Jim Hightower, Austin, Texas

§

Introduction:

by George DeVault

You CAN Do It

"The greatest fine art of the future will be the making of a comfortable living from a small piece of land," Abraham Lincoln once said. Truer words were never spoken. You can save tens of thousands of dollars and pay off your mortgage years ahead of schedule with the help of a little piece of land. Or, depending upon your needs, talents and ambitions, you can:

- Build up your savings account
- Pay for your dream vacation
- Reduce the financial risk of an uncertain economy
- Save money to help pay for college
- Make a down payment on a new car
- Get out of debt
- Start a second career

The list of possibilities goes on and on. How can you do all that? Very simply, and by using many of the tools that you probably already have lying about your basement, tool shed and garage. All it takes is a little imagination, some hard work and putting your back yard to work for you.

Before you know it, you can become a successful backyard market gardener. Andy Lee did it. He earned $36,000 in a single year from less than one full acre. You can do it, too.

That's not just marketing hype meant to get you to buy this book. Everything Andy Lee says is true. I know, because I have done the same thing myself, only on a smaller scale. In more than 15 years of writing about food and farming, I have met hundreds of bright, energetic people who are successful "backyard market gardeners." They come from all walks of life, from throughout the world. Each one has taught me something very special about growing and marketing. Most important, though, they have shown me how to lead a fuller, more meaningful life by becoming a more active participant in my local community. But you don't have to wait years and scour the world for such teachers. You now hold many of their stories in your hands in the pages of this book.

The real beauty of a book like this – and the backyard market gardening concept in general – is that you can use as little or as much of this practical information as you want, when you want. Most of you, upon reading Andy's book, will not rush right out and quit your steady jobs to become full-time market gardeners. Instead, you will carefully pick and choose the growing and marketing ideas that seem right for you and your circumstances. Then you will try them out in your own back yard and your own community to discover what works best – for you.

That is what my wife and I have done on our small farm in southeastern Pennsylvania. We bought 20 acres of vacant farmland just outside of a small town about 10 years ago, and immediately began experimenting to learn what crops we could grow and sell well. After we paid off the land in three years, we built a house on the farm and increased the size of our plantings. It was great not having to haul irrigation water from town anymore. All we have to do now to go to work in the garden is walk out our back door.

Most years, we cultivate about half an acre. Some years we farm more, some years less. It all depends upon the demands of our family and our regular jobs. That is one of the very appealing things about working part-time – for yourself. You can scale things up or down as you wish. Except for planting, picking and performing other field operations in a timely manner, you're not locked into a rigid schedule. We already own the land and equipment, so we don't have to work ourselves to death to pay off an operating loan or the other overhead that is such a heavy burden for many larger, full-time growers.

We still make money, though. Most years, we earn several thousand dollars from our small plots of organic vegetables. Melanie and I do that in our spare time, working mostly on weekends and before or after our full-time jobs as journalists. Some of our friends earn much more money from their market gardens. That bothered us at first, until we came to the realization that we have something our friends do not – two children to raise.

Our most important crop is our two children, Donald, 14, and Ruth, 12. While friends are hoeing weeds, picking peas and selling at farmers markets, we are more apt to be chauffeuring kids to diving or swimming practice, piano lessons or a friend's house. Time is our most precious and limited resource. That is why I have been known to pick peas in the rain and at night by the light of a Coleman lantern. Market gardening is our golf and our therapy. Of course, it also drives us crazy sometimes. When that happens, we simply cut back on the amount of stuff we're growing. After all, we can always gear up again when the pressures of daily life ease somewhat.

We have also changed our crop mix to favor crops that are less demanding of our time. A few years ago, we grew a wide variety of fruits and vegetables that demanded almost daily attention throughout the growing season. Then I got transferred to the Russian front – *Novii Fermer* (New Farmer), the Russian-language farm magazine that Bob Rodale was starting when he was killed in an auto accident in Moscow on Sept. 20, 1990. Working on *Novii Fermer* has meant more and more trips to the former Soviet Union and many weeks adding up to several months away from home. I should be planting green beans and other summer crops today. Instead, I'm packing to catch a plane for Moscow this afternoon.

So, what do we have in the market garden this year? "Keeper crops," at least that is what I like to call them. Garlic, potatoes, horseradish, leeks and a few other things that will more or less wait for us to come back to them in our "spare time."

'Our Veggies Sell Themselves'

We don't work very hard at marketing, either. In fact, we like to say that our vegetables sell themselves. Most of our produce is sold to a nearby country club. The long-time chef there is an avid organic gardener. He appreciates freshness and quality. His two most common questions are:

"How much do I owe you?"

"When can I get more?"

Most years, our main crop is sugar snap peas. We plant both spring and fall peas. In fact, we're about the only growers around here who plant fall peas. In the dead of winter, I also give the chef a copy of my favorite seed catalog and ask him to pick out what he would like us to grow for him next season. It is a beautiful relationship. We have a guaranteed market that is just the right size for our schedule, and the chef gets first dibs on top quality, specialty produce.

'The Corporate Connection'

Our other best customer is Rodale Press, where I have worked since 1981. I don't mean the Rodale Food Service, which provides meals for all of the Rodale cafeterias around Emmaus. Tom Ney, director of food services, does buy a lot of our veggies. He loves beets, sugar snap peas, savoy cabbage, spinach and lettuce. But the biggest customers are my co-workers, the employees themselves. At first I thought it would be difficult to sell vegetables around Rodale. After all, it is the company that pioneered organic gardening and farming in America more than 50 years ago. Everyone who works here is sure to have a large, beautiful, well-tended garden just overflowing with organic vegetables of all kinds, or so I thought.

Boy, was I wrong. Like most other companies, many people at Rodale are just too darn busy to do as much gardening as they would really like. Their lives are just as hectic as ours, often more so. So, while many of my co-workers have gardens, they don't really grow all that many vegetables, and certainly not in any kind of quantity.

On my lunch hour or on days off during the season, I go from building to building offering people fresh picked sugar snap peas. My usual price for a one-quart box (about one pound of peas) is $2.50. The peas disappear as fast as I can haul them into the office. Most days, I will walk into a building with four flats of peas (containing six quarts each) and walk out with $60 in my pocket and four empty flats. That's not bad pay for a few hours of pea picking.

It wasn't always this way, though. Our first year growing for market, I was bashful about asking enough for our produce. Some of the local grocers and restaurateurs I tried to sell to expected my prices to "be competitive" with the trucked-in produce they were buying from wholesalers. In other words, they wanted to buy things as cheaply as possible, so they could mark them up as much as possible. They didn't care much about freshness or the fact that this food was grown organically. All they wanted was produce that looked good and cost next to nothing. It didn't take me long to figure out that I was a whole lot better off by skipping these middlepeople and dealing directly with consumers.

It was also tough at first for me to even approach people with something to sell. Guess I felt embarrassed asking them for money. To get around that, I set out a few boxes of "self serve" veggies with a deliberately low price sign in several Rodale buildings. That was a big mistake. Oh, I sold one or two boxes of peas at each location. But the bulk of my produce was just ignored. And without refrigeration, that spelled disaster. My peas quickly wilted. By the end of the day, they were fit only for the compost heap.

'Have You Seen The Pea Man?'

After throwing out my peas a few times, I decided there had to be a better way. That's when I decided to try selling produce desk-to-desk. Hey, home- and office-delivery works for pizza! Why not produce? People were not offended when I told them that I had fresh vegetables for sale. In fact, they were downright delighted that I would ask. No one regarded me as a money grabber, either. Instead, they felt I was paying them a compliment by coming to them individually at their offices. Many are now regular customers with standing orders for at least a couple of quarts of peas whenever I have them.

"It saves me time," everyone says. "I don't have to stop at the grocery on the way home. My family just loves your peas. Bring them by anytime." It even earned me the nickname: "The Pea Man."

"Hey, have you seen the Pea Man this week?" they say around the various publishing offices here.

"Yeah, I just bought his last two boxes."

"Darn!"

"Oh, don't worry. He said the peas are really coming in strong. He'll be back with more in a day or two. And he said he'd probably have spinach, lettuce and garlic greens."

"All right! That's just what we need for our big picnic this weekend. If you see him before I do, tell him to be sure and track me down next time. Nah, on second thought, I'm going to call him right now and put in an order for what I want."

Of course, it helps that I work here and know everyone from the corporate officers to the janitors on a first name basis. But even if I didn't, I think folks around the office would still go for my vegetables. That's because people just can't find this kind of freshness, quality and taste in the supermarket. Often, the produce doesn't even make it home. One time, a woman bought a quart of sugar snap peas, took them back to her desk and began "just snacking." In less than an hour, she polished off the whole box – and developed quite a stomach-ache. That didn't stop her from buying more peas the next time, though. "The Pea Man's" sugar snaps are so popular that Food Service Director Tom Ney measures them into Dixie cups and sells them with dip in company cafeterias as snacks.

Growing A Market

In fact, there is so much demand for fresh produce at Rodale that for the last few years three co-workers (Bob Hofstetter, Frank Pollock and Skip Drake) and I have operated a small farmers market every Friday during the growing season. The market is set up in a small parking lot behind Fitness House, one of the many Rodale office buildings around Emmaus. All we did was ask Chairwoman Ardie Rodale for her blessing. She not only agreed, but decreed that, henceforth, employees in nearby Rodale buildings shall not park in the Fitness House lot on Fridays. Using a 2-page weekly newsletter, we take advance orders from Rodale employees and a growing number of townspeople. Telephone orders are discouraged.

You name it, we sell it: all kinds of vegetables, blueberries, raspberries, apples, peaches, baked goods, fresh apple cider, cut flowers, bales of hay and straw and even bundles of wheat for use in home decorating. In addition to the items in the newsletter, we offer a wide array of what we call "impulse" items that are not advertised in advance.

It's not a big market. We only gross $300 to $500 a day, $150 on a rainy day. Total sales for a season run about $5,000 to $7,000. "We have not fully tapped it as effectively as we can," explains Frank. But it's not bad for a small, part-time operation that basically serves as an outlet for our excess production. Many of the growers you will read about in this book started out the same way.

Putting Your Back Yard To Work

We all know that money does not grow on trees, but many modern Americans seem to have forgotten that it can grow in your backyard. "There is money in *your* backyard," E.L.D. Seymour wrote in his book *Garden Profits, Big Money in Small Plots.* "Perhaps you thought there was only a varied collection of rubbish, weeds and unsightly mud, and no particular hope for anything else," he said. "Or, if you *are* a bit neater and more particular than the majority, it may have meant a smooth grass plot, dotted with clothes poles, perhaps relieved by a flower bed or two.

"But have you ever thought that *every square foot of that ground is worth money to you?* Dollars and cents? Vegetables and fruits for your own use and sale; fresh, tender, delicious and instead of your paying the grocer for them, they are bringing *you* a profit?"

When did Seymour publish that book? Here are a few hints: William Howard Taft occupied the White House, Czar Nicholas II ruled the Russian Empire and the first Model T Ford was just three years old. The year was 1911.

The idea of backyard market gardening is not unique to North America, either. Fred Oerther of Clackamus, Ore., who is featured in Chapter 5, saw his first raised bed garden in Vietnam, while serving as a military physician there in 1968. He brought the idea of intensive, small-scale production home with him and now has 40,000 square feet of raised beds that can gross $1 per square foot.

This spring, I saw much the same thing near Lubnya, a village north of Moscow in Russia. From barely one-third of an acre of vegetables and flowers, Alexie Nicholaivich Kositsyn and his wife Tatyana Ivanovna earned more than 20,000 rubles in one year.

The Kositsyns are some of the most clever and persistent growers I've ever met. They have to be, because northern Russia is not a great place to grow vegetables. In latitude, Lubnya is about 125 miles north of Edmonton, Alberta. Because of the harsh climate, virtually all Russian gardeners make intensive use of season extenders. These devices are nothing elaborate or expensive. They're just workable. Greenhouses are built from scrap wood and plastic sheeting. Many are heated by coal/wood stoves. Crops are grown in permanent raised beds made of old boards and stakes. Next to no fertilizer is available, so everyone uses manure from nearby state and collective farms or small, private livestock operations. Labor is provided entirely by family members.

They have only about three percent of the land in the former Soviet Union, yet private gardeners there produce nearly one-third of the entire food supply. In fact, throughout the former Soviet Union and Eastern Europe, the majority of many food items such as potatoes, some meats and even milk comes from the "backyard farmers."

It is the small, private farmers – backyard market gardeners like the Kositsyns and the many other growers in this book, people like you and me and Andy Lee – who will cure much of what is wrong with agriculture today, not just in the former Soviet Union and the United States, but in countries throughout the world. Of that I have no doubt.

Be careful as you go, though. Next thing you know, you'll be tilling up your front yard, too. It may be the best thing that ever happened to you.

George DeVault

Pheasant Hill Farm

Emmaus, Pa.

May 30, 1992

CHAPTER 1

How I Built A $36,000 Business In My Backyard

In my spare time using everyday tools I had lying around the house (including my two sons)

I thought my success in growing $36,000 worth of vegetables per acre was unique. Now I know that gardeners and farmers all over America are doing just as well and even better. According to the National Gardening Association gardening survey, the average American gardener tends 505 square feet, spends $40 for seeds and materials, and reaps a harvest worth $400. It is possible that an acre of good land can have 86 of these plots and yield $34,400. That equals 80 cents per square foot. Some experienced market gardeners are doing even better than that.

What's important here is to show you that it is fun and profitable to have a market garden in your backyard. It is possible to make $36,000, even $40,000 per acre. Not just by me but by countless other vegetable growers and garden farmers. There are tens of thousands of us across America making a satisfying and rewarding full- or part-time living from our backyards and small-scale farms.

I grew up on a dairy farm in Missouri and learned the basics of gardening from my mom. There were eight kids in my family, so the garden was huge. Each year we raised two or three acres of cucumbers and tomatoes for the local food processor, too. Mom must have been among the first subscribers to the original *Organic Gardening and Farming* from Rodale Press. I can remember sitting with her and reading those little magazines as far back as grade school.

I began gardening in earnest in 1979. Following the old-time recipe for rabbit stew that starts by telling the cook to catch one rabbit, I bought a one-acre house lot. Then I built a house, put in a lawn, bought a lawnmower, and set aside a 20-by 35-foot plot for kitchen gardening. My two sons, Brian and Christopher, were just the right age (10 and 7) to be excited about growing things. They helped me a lot after school and on weekends.

I became a gardener because I like to work in the soil, and I don't like supermarket produce. I became a market gardener because I wanted to buy a rotary tiller.

I wanted to buy a rear-tine rotary tiller made by Kubota of Japan. It cost about $1,200 at that time. Figuring out ways to pay for the rotary tiller started me thinking about selling vegetables for extra income. The craving for new equipment and tools experienced by many of us is *Gardener's Equipment Excitement Syndrome*. GEES has probably caused more than a few otherwise satisfied and fulfilled kitchen gardeners to expand into a backyard business just to justify their tool habit.

It is possible to start a part-time backyard market garden business for just a few hundred dollars, especially if you are good at scavenging materials and supplies. You can barter or rent big ticket items such as a rotary tiller and a greenhouse. For a full-time endeavor you might have to invest several thousand dollars to start a business large enough to support you on a year-round basis.

In my case I grew into the business of market gardening gradually, over a period of five years. During several years of table gardening I had already accumulated most of the equipment and supplies I needed. There were no major up-front expenses involved, at least during the first year as a market grower. Had I started as a commercial grower from scratch I probably would have spent less than $2,000 on start-up expenses during the first year. Budgets in the following chapters will give you a better idea of what your equipment and cash needs might be at different levels of productivity and income needs.

Here's what I did to start a $36,000 business in my back yard.

For me to find a market garden site was easy. I simply used what I had available in my backyard. The part that wasn't so easy was getting the land in shape to grow abundant and profitable crops. The house lot I bought is on the side of the only hill in Pembroke, Mass., that has enough gravel and rocks to make a gravel pit. That's just what it was when I bought it – a gravel pit.

There were rocks everywhere, with very little soil in between. Garden writer Gene Logsdon never saw my place, but he described it perfectly in *The Gardener's Guide To Better Soil....you couldn't raise an umbrella on that kind of land if you were standing on a sack of fertilizer.* We built a driveway and two stone walls with rocks pulled out of the garden beds. Sharpening tools and replacing broken shovel handles took up a good bit of the rest of our time.

The gravel pit came complete with three old rusty cars that I sold to the junk dealer for $50. I used the money to have two dump-truck loads of seasoned goat manure delivered. Wonderful stuff, goat manure. Within days I started seeing weed seeds sprout and grow vigorously. The goat manure was loaded with earthworms, too. These little soil builders survived and proliferated, eventually populating my whole garden and yard.

I advertised for local landscape crews to bring me their leaves and grass clippings. Local stables were happy to deliver horse manure and sawdust, all for free! They gave it to me instead of trucking it all the way across town to the landfill. The first year I simply spread the raw materials about six inches deep and rented a rotary tiller to incorporate them into the soil. After that, we started building compost piles. Turning the compost piles with pitchforks provided an excellent chance for my sons and me to learn the fresh food business from the ground up.

We used compost and green manure cover crops to reclaim the soil. Sometimes we just used weeds that were mowed before they set seed. For eight years we made an average of 110 cubic yards of compost per season. We used the compost to build a layer of loam 14 inches deep in the old gravel pit. The proliferation of earthworms in this new soil is heartwarming. Digging a five-gallon bucket full of that soil today can yield as many as 20 fishing worms.

Getting enough manure to make a well-balanced compost wasn't always possible so I decided to grow our own. One acre isn't much land, but I figured there was room for at least some small livestock. So we started keeping pigs. Their pen was 175 feet from two neighbors, and I never had a complaint about odor. Neighborhood kids came by in the evenings with table scraps for the porkers. We raised three pigs each summer and sold two to get one free. There is usually enough meat on one pig to provide pork through the winter for a family of four.

We also raised chickens, both for the freezer and for eggs. I never did like supermarket eggs. The ones from our flock had bright yellow yolks that stood up in the frying pan. Sweet, homegrown eggs and hickory smoked ham make a wonderful breakfast.

Irrigation water came from the faucet on the side of the house. We used overhead sprinklers for the first few years, but I never cared much for them. There was too much water in some places, and not enough in others. Then the town passed a water ban that didn't allow outside watering. That's when we switched to drip irrigation.

When I started market gardening I didn't have enough money to build a greenhouse. Instead I bought transplants from the nursery, but I was often frustrated at the lack of variety available in local garden centers. I started hardier crops in a homemade cold-frame that I made from a sheet of plastic and some boards salvaged from a construction site dumpster.

Later, I built a 9- by 12-foot lean-to green house on the living room end of the house. Even with new 2 x 4s and new plastic sheeting from the hardware store, the materials only cost $200. That included a little electric heater. In the first year of using the greenhouse we grew 600 tomatoes, 1,700 brassicas, 2,300 lettuce starts and lots of flowers. That many transplants purchased at the garden center would have cost nearly $700, wholesale.

Also, it was really relaxing to sit in the living room and have the two windows open to the greenhouse. The smell of damp potting soil and plants growing is delightful, especially on a bitter March evening.

A small fan blew heat from the house at one window. Another fan blew air back from the greenhouse at the other window. This circulated the air nicely and kept the temperature of the greenhouse pretty close to 70 degrees most of the time. I started hardy crops on the floor, and tender crops on shelves at mid-level. During really cold nights, an electric space heater on the floor kept the temperature well above freezing.

For years I had been using Sea Mix, a fish emulsion and seaweed mixture, for foliar feeding the gardens. I thought it worked well outdoors, so I decided to spray it on the greenhouse seedlings as well. The fish odor stunk up the whole house for a week. It made the cat's tail twitch a lot, too.

I had a lawn chair under the shade tree at the edge of the garden. Did all my future planning there. The deck off the kitchen overlooked the garden. It offered a wonderful place to sit in the evenings with a glass of iced tea and look out over my little Garden of Eden.

But, there was a "serpent" in my garden, too. All the manure and leaves we were putting on the garden contained weed seeds. Weeding got to where it was almost a full-time job, so we started using black plastic mulch. Ugly stuff, but it works well to keep weeds down. For an environmentally concerned vegetable grower it is hard to overcome the psychological discomfort of using plastic mulch. I learned to tolerate it because it helps the soil stay moist and the earthworms seem to like it. That surprised me, since I had always thought the temperature would get too high for them under the black plastic.

I couldn't afford to hire anyone to work in the garden with me at first, and my sons could only help infrequently. So I always looked for more efficient ways to do things by myself, and ways to mechanize. Buying the rotary tiller and building the greenhouse were a couple of my better choices.

It makes more sense to me to have gardens instead of lawn. Vegetable gardening takes more work and time, but you can't eat or sell grass clippings. So I turned the front yard into garden beds of cutting flowers for fresh bouquets to sell at market.

Acid soil has always been a problem here in the Northeast. When I began the market garden the soil pH tested at 4.3, about the same level as vinegar. Continuous applications of dolomite lime and compost brought the pH up to 6.5 within three years.

When the soil is unhealthy or has a mineral imbalance, pests and diseases are often a serious problem. I cleared a part of the pine forest next to the house to put in potatoes and got potato beetles the first year. Potatoes had never been in this soil and I could never understand where the beetles came from. The same thing happened with cucumber beetles. Pests seemed to come out of nowhere, but they became less of a problem as the soil became healthier.

I didn't use enough fertilizers those first couple of years. The plants were anemic and wilted easily. Yields were terribly low, often only one or two fruits or tubers per plant. During the first year my best tomato plant only produced two pounds of tomatoes. After the soil became healthier we were averaging 14 pounds per plant. We could get 20 pounds per plant when we protected the plants with season extenders during spring and fall.

My first year marketing efforts in 1984 were a bit of a false start. I opened a card table roadside stand for a few days in the front yard. It didn't work out too well because there wasn't a good place to park. Plus we were on a side street location, and I didn't think to put up signs at the cross roads to attract people to me. My customers were mostly my next door neighbors and people who used my street as a short-cut to the highway. Sales averaged about $15 per day, so I closed the stand after a week.

Then, I tried selling produce to a couple of local restaurants, with mediocre results. I'd only racked up $1,700 in sales by the end of the first market garden season, but it was enough to pay for the new tiller. This small profit whetted my appetite for the future.

Each year I would add another 5,000 or so square feet to the garden. I tried different crop mixes and varieties, and just kept plugging away, learning the business of selling fresh food. In the summer of 1985 I made $3,000 as a part-time vegetable grower.

In 1986 I decided to start selling produce in the city. My plan was to cash in on the new farmers markets that were opening in Boston neighborhoods. In four years the number of farmers markets in Massachusetts rose from 12 to 67. This created a shortage of vegetable farmers. The new markets were all crying for vegetable growers to sell produce. Within 36 miles of my garden were 10 markets I could choose from. I could attend a different market each day of the week, May through October, but I didn't have enough produce, so I settled on only four market days per week. That left me with three days each week to take care of the gardens.

My first day at the farmers market I only sold $17.20 worth of produce. That was discouraging, to say the least. What was really encouraging, however, was to see the other, more established and well-known farmers selling several hundred dollars worth of vegetables. I figured if I kept working hard, studying, talking to and learning from these other growers I could do as well as, or even better than they did.

That proved to be very true. By the end of 1986 I had grossed $9,000 from my half-acre garden. In 1987 I increased the gardens to three-quarters of an acre, and grossed $17,000. In 1988 I had nearly one acre planted, and grossed $36,000. This gave me a net income of over $17,000 for seven months of work. Since I was working about 50 hours per week, that averaged out to about $12 per hour, for doing work I dearly love to do.

Why Start a Market Garden Business?

Making the switch from home gardening to market gardening isn't all that difficult. It is mostly a frame of mind, combined with a management and technical shift to a larger garden. Most home gardeners grow vegetables for fun, satisfaction and to save money. It is fun to grow things, and even more fun to eat them. The satisfaction of being partially self-sufficient can't be overlooked. As for profits, everything you can grow in your backyard will cost less than similar yet inferior food at the supermarket.

Market gardening can be fun and satisfying in ways not available to the home gardener, especially the profit part. It's very gratifying to use your specialized knowledge and skills to do something that not many of your neighbors are doing. Growing food as a way to make a full- or part-time income can be very rewarding.

The market for fresh food is growing rapidly. You can cash in on it the same way I did. Learn the trade and practice the techniques outlined in the following chapters. Within a short time you'll be well on your way to creating and enjoying your profitable backyard business.

How would you describe the perfect business for your personality, talents, interests, abilities, and goals? Do you want a business that will be fun and profitable, easy and relatively inexpensive to start up? Do you have a backyard, and do you want to create a business there? Will your new business deal with regenerative products, and a repeat customer base? Do you want it to be satisfying both physically and intellectually, and not take an inordinate amount of time away from your other pursuits? And, will your new business

29

work with nature to provide a truly beneficial service to your community?

Perhaps your primary goal is to earn a living independently, doing something for which you have a passionate interest. Ultimately, you may want to achieve a sense of cooperating with nature to create something beautiful and useful, physically satisfying and spiritually fulfilling.

Beginning a market garden has proven to be all these things for me, even more than I had anticipated. First, of course, is the fun. How thrilling it is to till the earth in the new spring, plant the seeds and watch them grow as if by magic. Then harvesting the bounty of my labor and sharing it with responsive and appreciative customers who give me continual feedback of approval. Having their friendship is the final satisfaction.

I feel a tremendous sense of excitement when learning new growing techniques, trying new varieties and watching the soil and vigor of the plants improve from year to year. I enjoy the positive reactions of pleased customers when they try my organically grown and freshly picked produce for the first time. This has all been very gratifying for me, just as it will be for you.

The profit motive I talked about earlier has become almost secondary to the real joy. Formulating a garden plan, nursing the plants from the greenhouse to harvest, and sharing this bounty of the good earth with my many friends and customers is exciting and satisfying. I sometimes fail to follow through on good business planning and implementation simply because I get caught up in the wonderful world of plants and people around me. Fortunately the market garden has been sufficiently profitable to maintain my standard of living while enjoying life to the fullest.

"Walk To Work . . . Go Home For Lunch"

Wanting to work closer to my home played an important role in my becoming a market gardener. Like most of you, I don't like commuting long distances to a work place. Driving to work is expensive, frustrating and time consuming and it takes me away from more enjoyable activities.

A backyard business avoids the up-front costs normally associated with starting an enterprise. Keep overhead low by

30

not having to rent an office or warehouse space. Commuting costs are nil, and you can go home for lunch. The best part about lunch of course, is that it grows right in your backyard.

Labor requirements, at least for part-time market gardeners, can usually be filled by yourself and members of your family or circle of friends. As your market garden becomes larger, however, it may become necessary to add hired help, or apprentices, especially during the peak growing season. Having friends or family members working alongside can add to the fun and satisfaction of gardening. Interacting with like-minded individuals and sharing the heavier and more laborious tasks with other willing hands adds enjoyment to each day.

Much of the enjoyment I find in market gardening comes from teaching and sharing experiences with the people who work with me, especially those who have a sincere interest in what is taking place, both in the garden and at the market. I have had particularly good results in hiring college students who are majoring in agricultural sciences, environmental studies, or in natural resources. They seem to have a better understanding of the inter-relatedness of plants, animals and humankind to the environment. They are willing to learn faster and work harder. This is especially true if they feel they are a part of the new natural-farming movement that has swept the country over the past several years.

If possible, organize your market garden so that apprentices can be hired and trained. Solicit apprentices who will want to go on in following years and start a market garden or farm.

Don't be afraid of creating too much competition by training new market gardeners. We are only serving about 1 percent to 3 percent of the market right now with organic foods. The number of acres dedicated to growing organic produce amounts to less than 1 percent of the national agricultural land base. There is very little chance that we will ever meet, let alone exceed, the market demand for locally grown organic vegetables and fruits.

Most people considering the merits of different home businesses pay close attention to how future ups and downs of the economy will affect profitability. In this category, a market garden is a winner. Despite how badly the economy slumps or what whimsical path the stock market takes, market gardeners will still find willing buyers for their produce. Food is a necessity for the continuance of life, not a luxury. This is especially true when food is picked at the peak of ripeness and is full of delightful flavor and vital energy.

Many at-home businesses provide a one-at-a-time or one-of-a-kind product, such as real estate sales, carpet installations and even books. These companies have to find a continuing clientele of new buyers to make their business profitable. This is not true in market gardening. If you satisfy your customers they will come back week after week, year after year.

Creative skills and entrepreneurial urges are two big reasons why many people start home businesses. They also have a sincere interest in and passion for their product. Most of us would feel trapped and smothered in a business, even a highly successful one, if we weren't creatively and passionately involved in the growing of the product and the business.

The sameness or monotony of manufacturing widgets is never going to be a problem in the market garden. It has many facets; more than 200 varieties of vegetables, 1,000 varieties of flowers, close to 100 different herbs, several distinctly different growing methods, and at least 10 prime marketing methods. Plus, the variability of the market, the seasons, weather, and the gardens themselves make it unlikely that you will ever get bored as a market gardener.

One satisfying and stimulating result of starting a market garden business will be the new friends and interesting people you will meet. There is often a wonderful sense of community between market gardeners and appreciative customers. Work hard to develop and maintain this rapport. It will serve you well.

WANTED: More Market Gardeners

Sure there is competition between food growers and marketers in any given area, but for the most part it's healthy for the industry. It can be fun to be challenged by your peers. I've gained knowledge, inspiration and assistance from other growers in my area, and have always gone out of my way to reciprocate.

Many of my customers frequent more than one farm stand or specialty store, choosing special varieties or unusual items from each. I'm confident that there is room for many more growers in most areas of this country. The real problem is not competition among growers. It is that 97 percent of the population doesn't buy from us. They buy from supermarkets instead. We can add more business for all food growers by working together to change the buying habits of this 97 percent of the marketplace.

There are aesthetic rewards in market gardening, too. Establishing a market garden has improved my property tremendously by making a fertile field out of a former gravel pit. It has helped my community by creating and preserving farmland. It provides training opportunities and employment for people in the area. It provides a real community service with fresh produce and the market garden offers consumers a visually exciting destination for what otherwise might be a dull and uninteresting trip to the supermarket for groceries.

One important aspect of establishing market gardens has been my improved physical vigor and mental well-being. This has come about through increased exercise and a sure supply of healthful and nutritionally valuable food. I find great pleasure and satisfaction in working with nature. This pride of accomplishment, having created something from nothing, has been a major contributor to my interest in writing this book. I feel so good, and am so thankful for this new lifestyle, that I want to share it with everyone I possibly can.

When asked why I would recommend that anyone start a market garden as a home business I offer the following reasons. It's fun, relaxing, healthful and generally helpful to the environment. It offers a very real possibility for a satisfying part-time or full-time income and fulfills many creative desires and entrepreneurial urges.

The most important benefit of owning and operating a market garden is to enhance the quality of your life. Market gardening offers an arena for individuals and families, friends and neighbors to work, learn and have fun together – in your neighborhood and in harmony with the natural world around you.

Today, this is a far different industry than the one our parents saw. Over the next decade the innovations and improvements will be fast and intense as interest and research in sustainable food systems increases. The supply side continues to decentralize, allowing more niche opportunities for beginning and expanding small-scale farmers. The demand side continually asks for more locally grown fresh-picked fruits and vegetables. There is an ever-expanding need for more market gardeners to fill these gaps.

CHAPTER 2:

Sites and Soils

Do what you can

with what you have

where you are.

-Teddy Roosevelt

Before you can be a successful backyard market gardener you need a good site, and good soil. My first market garden was in a former gravel pit where three junk cars were the most prominent feature. The soil was in terrible condition, but it was a good site because I already owned it. All I needed to do to turn this "good" site into a "great" site was to improve the soil.

We know that nature can heal herself. We witness the process all the time. Weeds are continually reclaiming exposed soil and natural reforestation is taking place where land has been abandoned. It's a process that can often be expedited if we use common sense and are willing to work hard to help nature out. So, don't let a worn out piece of farmland or even a gravel pit scare you off. If you have raw organic materials, you can make compost that will bring almost any soil up to levels of fertility to grow good crops.

For example, the verdant and luxurious community gardens at the Findhorn Community in Forres, Scotland, were started on the worst possible beach soil. Sand dunes and thickets of thorny gorse are the most prominent features of the landscape. The climate is one of the least attractive for successful vegetable and flower growing. Yet they make it work, with compost and innovative growing techniques. Findhorn is often described as *the garden where 40-pound cabbages are average and roses bloom in the snow.*

Certainly, it is easier and more profitable to start out with fertile soil, but this isn't always possible. Even if you do have good soil it can always be made much better with compost, soil amendments and proper management. In humans it is possible to test the health and disease resistant capabilities of the body with blood samples and hair tissue tests. These can be used to gauge the value of a person's diet. The same thing applies to soil tests and plant tissue tests. With these it is possible to know almost instantly if the soil you are farming is healthy or if it is deficient in one or more essential elements.

Plant tissue tests are particularly useful in explaining why many people have to take nutritional and vitamin supplements, even if they eat a well-balanced diet containing sufficient quantities of fresh fruits and vegetables. If a person's diet is primarily made up of conventionally grown food it may be deficient in many of the vitamins and minerals required by the human body.

Tests at Rutgers University offer a comparison of the highest versus the lowest mineral levels found in organically and conventionally grown vegetables. There are often enormous vitamin and mineral deficiencies in foods grown on nutritionally depleted soils. For example, in the Rutgers test tomatoes grown organically contained five times more calcium and 2,000 times more iron than conventionally grown tomatoes. It is also true that conventional produce grown in healthy soil with chemical inputs can be far superior to produce grown organically on soil that needs to be restored.

To understand these differences in nutritional value it helps to look at proper mineral structures in healthy soil. There are 92 different micro and macro nutrients and trace elements that may be essential for optimal plant growth, vigor, and nutritional value. Of these, 16 of the more commonly known are: boron, calcium, carbon, chlorine, copper, hydrogen, iron, magnesium, manganese, molybdenum, nitrogen, oxygen, phosphorus, potassium, sulfur, and zinc.

Commonly available chemical fertilizers normally only supply the three basic nutrients: nitrogen, phosphorus, and potassium. Even the most highly complex of the conventional synthetic fertilizers will contain no more than 12 of the essential elements. In fertile native soil, the plant can often extract all the other nutrients it requires, but only in the presence of sufficiently high levels of humus. Humus is naturally decomposing organic matter.

Sometimes, however, even with the addition of natural fertilizers containing many different nutrients, the goal of complete soil fertility may not be quickly or properly achieved. Without a sufficiently high level of humus in the soil to capture and hold these added nutrients many of them will never become available to plants. Without the proper balance of soil pH, moisture, naturally occurring soil minerals, and biological activity, the nutrients may remain locked in the soil, unavailable to plant roots or soil microbial life.

At other times, the nutrients will be so loosely bound in the soil that heavy rains or excessive irrigation will cause leaching. The nutrients pass through the layer of biologically active soil and make their way into the ground water. Not only is this a waste of fertilizer and money, it often poisons our water supply.

Vigorous root systems can metabolize the elements they need from the soil if a sufficient amount of rock powders and organic matter are present for biological stimulation. Biological activity will eventually form humus. Yet the usual soil test doesn't even address humus unless you ask for it and pay extra to test the level of organic materials available. It is a good idea for you to send your soil samples to a laboratory equipped to test for organic matter. Land grant universities and colleges of agriculture can do these tests. Private testing labs often are more expensive, but usually give more useful recommendations on the test results.

These recommendations from private testing labs usually come in the form of a written report or soil audit that will accompany the results of your soil test. This report will give recommendations for organic soil amendments and fertilizers instead of the chemical recommendations offered by most conventional university testing laboratories.

Soil organic matter levels even as high as 5 percent will not always guarantee that your plants will get a healthy diet of the things they need. But, a high percentage of organic matter with a large portion of it in humus form promotes soil health. A healthy soil can grow healthy plants. That makes healthy people.

The grower needs to first test the soil, then make any initial adjustments with lime and natural minerals. Apply plenty of organic matter, use good crop rotation and cover crops and keep tillage and traffic on the soil to a minimum. This will help the soil become healthy and vibrant, able to sustain healthy and high-yielding crops.

The best, quickest and potentially least expensive way to increase your soil organic matter and available humus level is to use compost. A well balanced compost with appropriate levels of animal manure and plant residues will contain all the elements your plants will be looking for. If not, you can add supplemental soil amendments and minerals.

Once enough organic matter is available in your soil it will encourage the proliferation of soil life such as microbes, fungi and earthworms. As these organisms feed on the organic matter they will turn it into humus from which your crops can extract the various essential elements.

Another benefit of having a proper level of organic matter is to enhance the friability and tilth of the soil. Compost can loosen clay soil, or it can bind sandy soil. This provides a healthy, nutrient-filled environment for the plant roots. It also controls erosion and compaction and aids in the retention of water, either from natural rainfall or from irrigation.

Is it possible to have too much organic matter (OM)? At OM levels of more than 12 percent you may see your plants having difficulty maintaining a root hold. The soil is just too loose. This is especially true if too much partially composted organic matter is applied without sufficient time for complete decomposition to occur before planting. When this happens the soil balance swings in the wrong direction and a nutrient depletion will occur, usually causing a nitrogen deficiency.

Use natural fertilizers and soil amendments and apply them heavily during the first years of your market garden so the soil life can concentrate on building good soil. This will help the plants grow and give you better crops. It will also help you to get a faster return on your investment.

Spend the money up front to guarantee success. Don't wait years to improve your soil slowly. Buy a semi-truck load of compost if you have to, but get that soil in shape! Borrow the money from some other place to put in the compost and soil amendments *now*.

If you don't have access to compost during the first year then go out to the country and buy some aged cow manure. We measure cow manure in cubic yards, and buy it in truck loads. Sometimes a farmer will deliver the manure to you and charge a flat fee for the manure and the hauling. Otherwise, you can pay a trucker separately for the hauling. Dry cow manure averages 2 cubic yards per ton (2,000 pounds).

The dump truck will deposit the loads of manure anywhere you want them, providing the truck can get to the point you have chosen. If the truck can't get into your garden then you will have the chore of moving the piles of manure from wherever they are dropped to your garden. Use wheelbarrows and forks, or a rented tractor with a bucket loader. If you have neighbors close by it's important that you work the cow manure into the soil as soon as possible to eliminate the odor.

Here's how to figure out how much cow manure you need to cover a 1,000 square foot garden. A good annual application rate for most garden soils is one inch deep. There are 144 cubic inches per square foot. Multiply that by 1,000 square feet and you need 144,000 cubic inches of manure.

There are 1,728 cubic inches per cubic foot, and 27 cubic feet per cubic yard. Multiply 27 cubic feet times 1,728 cubic inches. That equals 46,656 cubic inches per cubic yard. Divide 46,656 into 144,000. That comes out to 3 cubic yards per 1,000 square feet of garden.

So, if your garden is 10,000 square feet, you will need 30 cubic yards of cow manure. If the garden is 20,000 square feet you'll need 60 cubic yards, and so on.

If farmers near you are selling cow manure for $10 per cubic yard, and the trucking cost is $10 per cubic yard, then to cover a 1,000 square foot garden with a one inch layer of manure will cost $60. The cost for one acre would be $2,580. This amounts to 65 tons of cow manure per acre. If your soil is loose sand or heavy clay and in poor tilth, then you may want to double the amount of cow manure.

Where is the pay back on this cost? It will likely *double* your yields during the first year. For example, if you grow tomatoes, each plant will take up 10 square feet (if they are in cages). A common yield in poor soil is 5 pounds per plant. At a retail price of $1.20 per pound, each plant will yield $6. Divide that by 10 square feet and your yield is worth 60¢ per square foot. This may be well below the average value per square foot needed to have a profitable tomato crop.

However, after you have added the cow manure, rock powders, fertilizer and lime if needed, you can expect each caged tomato to yield 10 pounds or more. On the same 10 square feet you then have a value of $1.20 per square foot, well above the profit-making line.

On 1,000 square feet of fertile soil you can grow 100 tomato plants that have a potential value of $1,200. The manure only cost you $60. That makes manure one of the best possible investments for the backyard market gardener. Cow manure is available in most areas of the country. In some locations it may be more expensive than others. But, if you want to get a fertile garden instantly this is probably the fastest and least costly way to do it.

There's nothing new about this idea of using livestock manure to build super-rich garden soil. In 1867, Peter Henderson, a New Jersey seedsman and market grower, wrote GARDENING FOR PROFIT; A Guide To The Successful Cultivation of the Market and Family Garden. (see bibliography for new edition available from The American Botanist). In Henderson's budget of production costs he allowed $100 per acre for manure, and $300 per acre for hired labor. Other costs brought total expenditures to $605 per acre. This allowed him to reap a typical harvest of 12,000 cabbages, 14,000 lettuces and 30,000 celery plants, for a gross income of $735 per acre. Manure costs amounted to nearly one-seventh of his income.

In today's marketplace, growers can expect gross incomes ranging from $10,000 to $30,000 per acre. Using Henderson's ratio, we can therefore afford to spend anywhere from $1,400 to $4,300 per acre for manure or compost, and still get an excellent return on our investment.

After the manure application you will see a much greater yield. Other things you will see are healthier soil, healthier plants, fewer pests and fruits and vegetables that look better, taste better and sell easier. The soil will hold more water, and there will be less dust. The plants will have fewer diseases. You will get more good looking produce to put on your display at the farm stand or farmers markets.

How much greater can the yields be? When I first started my market garden in Massachusetts, the tomatoes yielded 2 pounds per plant. After three years of manure and compost applications, the average yield had increased to 14 pounds per plant. At a average retail price of $1 per pound, the value of my 1,000 square foot crop increased from $200 to $1,400. Just the improved tomato yield alone was enough to pay for the cost of dressing the entire one acre with a 1-inch layer of cow manure.

Potatoes are another example. In unenriched soil a yield of less than a half-pound per plant is normal. In super enriched soil the yields can scoot way up to 5 pounds per plant, 2.5 pounds per square foot. At my garden in the Intervale section of Burlington, in compost enriched soil, I have been able to average 5.75 pounds per plant. These have very little scab (a soil borne fungal disease) and excellent flavor.

Potatoes that are certified organic are selling at retail here in New England for 40 cents per pound. In poor soil the grower will earn less than 20 cents per square foot. In the super enriched soil the crop value increases to $1 per square foot or more.

Homemade Fertilizer

How can you get super yields when you don't have access to cow manure? Make compost. It takes half as much compost to accomplish the same task as cow manure. The composting process concentrates the nutrients and enables biological activity to take place, thus making a more vital soil amendment. Fortunately, it only takes three to six months to make good compost.

Making your own compost is easy once you have gathered the raw materials. Over the years I've used various kinds of materials: leaves, grass clippings, food waste, spoiled hay and straw, wood chips and spent plants from the garden. Manures I've used include chicken, goat, cow, horse and pig. For most backyard market gardeners the easiest materials to obtain will be leaves, grass clippings and horse manure.

To get leaves just ask neighbors and people on your street to bring them to your garden. Or if there is a community pick-up of leaves, you can ask the street department to deliver a few loads to you.

Also, call the lawn care contractors in your area and let them know you will accept leaves and grass clippings free of charge. These contractors usually have a hard time getting rid of leaf and yard waste. Even if the landfill will take the material, the contractor still has to pay a tipping fee. They will be happy to bring them to you for free, instead. Just be sure the material is free of contaminants such as plastic and glass bottles, cans and stones. If they do deliver junk or trash to your garden make them pick it up and take it away. Be sure, too, that there aren't any local ordinances that prohibit you from receiving these materials.

A really good source of compostable material is from horse stables. They often use sawdust or straw for bedding in the stalls. This soaks up the urine and is full of nutrients and trace elements for the soil.

Horse stables abound in every area of the country. Often, the horse stables cannot spread their horse manure and used bedding back on their pastures because of stomach parasites that are deposited in the fields. This is particularly troublesome for stables near cities where land is very limited. They need to haul their manure and used bedding to someplace, and it often goes to the landfill for disposal. To find stables in your area start by checking the phone book. Also, stables usually have to be permitted by local animal inspectors. Call your town hall and find out how to get a list of stables in your area, then call them up. Chances are they will be happy to haul the manure to your garden rather than to the landfill where they have to pay a tipping fee.

Nutrients in horse manure with sawdust or straw bedding are not as immediately available to your soil as those in cow manure. Cows have four stomachs and do a better job of digesting food than horses do. The big advantage of horse manure is that you can often get it free of charge, especially if you volunteer to do the hauling. If you can spare your pickup truck or trailer for a few days just park it at the stable and let them fill it up for you, no charge.

Beware however, that horse manure is loaded with weed seeds. You will be introducing a whole new family of weeds to your garden. Also, the sawdust bedding takes a long time to break down in the soil. It is very high in carbon and is apt to rob the soil of nitrogen during decomposition. One application of horse manure and sawdust is all you would want in the first year, unless you can compost it before applying it to your garden.

Using horse manure and sawdust bedding as a sheet compost is a quick way to start building fertile soil and good tilth. Just spread the material in a 3-inch layer and till it in immediately. Wait for the weed seeds to germinate, then spread cover crop seed. Till the soil lightly again to kill the weeds and incorporate the cover crop seed.

Sometimes, I've let the weeds germinate and grow as a cover crop. They are vigorous, many are deep rooted and they all add a tremendous amount of green matter to the soil when you plow them down. Just be sure to till them under before they set viable seeds. Do this the year before you want to start your garden so that the soil will be balanced by the following spring.

Green + Brown = Black Gold

Here's How I Make Compost in my Backyard Market Garden

Making compost is as much an art as it is science. The idea is to mix materials into the pile that are combinations of brown (carbonaceous) and green (nitrogenous). The goal is to achieve a mix of materials (recipe) that is close to 30 parts carbon to 1 part nitrogen. Then make sure the pile is large enough to create an insulative mass (one cubic yard minimum) and damp enough (like a wrung out sponge) to support bacterial life. The microorganisms that live in the compost pile can grow and reproduce easily in this environment. They will quickly turn the raw materials into nutrient rich humus that has approximately 10 parts carbon to one part nitrogen. This becomes a valuable food supply for soil microbes and plant life in your garden.

Achieving the correct carbon to nitrogen ratio (C/N) in your compost pile is easy once you understand the relative value of the different materials that are available. I've included a list of commonly available materials:

All you have to do is mix appropriate quantities of the carbon materials and nitrogenous materials to achieve a blend (recipe) that is about 30 to 1. This mix is the ideal range for composting to take place. For example, mix 1 part leaves and 1 part grass clippings (50 + 20 = 70). Divide by two and you have a mix that is 35 to 1. In reality, getting the proper mix *exactly* is only necessary when you want to make compost quickly. With the proper conditions it is possible to make good compost in only two or three weeks, although this isn't usually necessary in the market garden.

Table 1. Carbon/Nitrogen Ratios

Carbon Materials (Brown):	Carbon/Nitrogen ratio:
Sawdust	500-1
Paper	170-1
Straw	80-1
Dry cornstalks	60-1
Leaves	50-1
Nitrogen Materials (Green):	
Grass hay	25-1
Grass clippings	20-1
Manure	20-1
Fresh clover	15-1
Food Scraps	10-1

Any of the organic materials mixed together will make compost, some just take longer than others. My favorite recipe is 1 part horse manure, 1 part sawdust, 1 part leaves and 1 part grass clippings. Taking into consideration the relative values of these materials, I get a recipe of about 150 parts carbon to 1 part nitrogen. This is not ideal, but nonetheless will make compost within six months to a year.

As the leaves are delivered in the fall I windrow them about 4 feet high in a pile 10 feet wide, and as long as I need it. Each lineal foot of windrow is roughly 1 cubic yard. As the raw materials decompose they will shrink in volume. An example, our leaf piles at the Burlington Leaf Composting Project shrink by 80 percent before stabilizing. Sawdust will not shrink nearly as much, but will take longer to break down unless you have a really good nitrogen source to mix with it.

A pile of horse manure and sawdust is then lined up beside the leaves. Then, during the following summer I ask lawn care contractors to bring me their lawn clippings. When they bring in the grass clippings I simply mix the windrows together using a long-handled pitchfork. When you mix these materials in a 1-1-1 ratio the resulting mix will heat up quickly and begin to decompose into fertile humus. The original pile will shrink during the composting process. Final yield will be about one-third of what you started with. To get 65 yards of compost to treat a half-acre market garden will require about 200 cubic yards of raw materials. This will take a pile of fresh materials that is 4 feet high, 10 feet wide, and 200 feet long. Or, two 100-foot piles.

It isn't really necessary to shred the materials before composting, but it speeds up the composting process by at least 50 to 75 percent. This grinding action will reduce the pile immediately by half or more. I've had best luck with a Lightning chipper/shredder. They are available through Gardener's Supply and cost $800 to $1,200, depending on the size. As I feed the materials into the machine I mix the different materials in equal pitchforks full. This thoroughly mixes the different materials and makes a smaller particle size that bacteria and microbes can start working on immediately. To keep the shredder from plugging with wet materials I just take out the screen and bar grate.

The refuse from the garden and left-over vegetables from each market day can be shredded and mixed with the other compost materials. Occasionally, I sprinkle on a shovel full of garden soil to inoculate the pile with bacteria. They begin to colonize the pile immediately, which expedites the composting process.

This makes a nice combination of materials that can be left in the windrow to compost slowly. When time is available, the windrow can be turned by hand with a pitchfork. The best fork I've found for hand turning compost is a long handled 5-tined manure fork available for about $35 from farm and garden centers.

You can also rent a skid steer loader or a tractor with a bucket loader to turn the windrows mechanically. Whenever possible, I prefer the pitchfork method because I can manipulate the pile better, mixing various materials and breaking up clods, and adding moisture when needed. The mechanical loaders tend to lump everything together and even cause compaction in the windrow if the turning is not done carefully.

Compost piles should be in the garden or at least at its edge. It's always better if piles are in the garden so they can be rotated each year with the cropping plan. The ground underneath the compost piles will be well supplied with the nutrients that are washed out of the piles by rain.

Another benefit of having the compost pile in the garden is to take advantage of the bacterial life in the soil. Bacteria can easily move upward into the compost pile and colonize it. Also, with the compost pile so close by, it is convenient to take weeds and spent plants from the garden to add to the pile. Plus, when you go to spread the finished compost you won't have to travel so far and there will be less work involved.

If you don't have easy access to your garden for the trucks that are bringing the material then you will have to pile the materials nearby. Then carry them by wheelbarrows or buckets. This is a huge amount of work, so try to get it in the garden if possible.

As you manage the compost piles the ground around them will become compacted. This will be especially true with trucks coming and going and foot traffic around the windrow. This is OK; just rotary till the area next year and plant a deep-rooted cover crop such as rye to break up the compaction. This cover crop will help the soil life to assimilate and metabolize the nutrients from the compost pile, and will help interrupt any cycles of diseases or pests.

A properly constructed compost pile will heat up to 140° F or more, and will stay there for several days. As the heat starts to decline it's time to turn the pile. This turning accomplishes three things. It lets oxygen back into the pile, loosens compacted materials, and moves the outer layers of the pile to the inside. This way the material can be evenly heated. If the heat cycle can be held in the 140° F to 150° F range for three weeks or more it will also kill all the weed seeds and disease pathogens in the material.

The turning process involves moving the outer layers into the center of a new pile that is just ahead of the old pile. Begin at the north end of the windrow. One forkful at a time, turn the outer layers of material into a new pile that is 3 feet north of the old pile.

Use the damp and partly decomposed materials from the center of the old pile to cover the new pile. As you progress down the windrow it may be useful to alternate between sides of the pile so you can reach the middle easier. Then, the next time you turn the windrow just start at the opposite end and move the pile three feet in the other direction.

Moving compost to your garden can be time consuming and laborious.

My sons and I used this method to turn nearly 1,000 tons of compost in eight years. It is excellent exercise after work or after school and it's a lot more fun and productive than jogging or many other forms of recreational exercise.

Making agricultural-grade compost doesn't require any rigid turning schedule. Just do it when you have time. If you notice an ammonia smell from the pile or if you see flies gathering on the pile it's time to turn it. In a stretch of dry weather, you may want to turn the pile and add water with a garden hose as you go along. I've also watered compost piles by stretching a soaker hose or drip irrigation tape along the top of the windrow and leaving the water on for a few hours. The pile needs to be damp, but not wet. If it gets too wet, the composting process will slow down or stop and odors will occur. In an especially wet year you may want to cover your compost piles with plastic to keep them from getting waterlogged.

A way to introduce compostable materials to your garden without all the work of making piles is sheet composting. This is sometimes called sheet mulching. Use any of the raw materials you would use in a compost pile and simply spread them on the ground you intend to turn into a garden. It isn't even necessary to till the ground first, just spread the materials and let them rot. This is an excellent way to reclaim land that has perennial grasses such as quack or crabgrass. It can even kill poison ivy if you get all the plants covered with a thick enough layer of organic materials. The disadvantage, of course, is that it takes several months for the material to decompose to a point where you can plant your garden.

Cover Cropping for Soil Improvement and Smother Cropping for Weed Control

Another way to improve garden soil is to grow a series of green manure cover crops on the garden before growing vegetables. This is not an instant improvement, as is the case with cow manure or compost. However, even one season of cover crops will go a long way toward improving the tilth of the soil for super yields.

This all starts the year before you plant your market garden, of course. Rotary-till the market garden space in the spring and plant it to buckwheat or millet. They will grow in poor soil in most climates and will help break up the hardpan and smother the weeds that germinate in the tilled soil. This will give the soil microbes a chance to break down the sod that you are tilling under, too.

When the cover crop has flowered or is starting to form seed heads, turn it under and plant another crop. Let it grow for a few weeks, then mow it, spread your compost or cow manure, and till everything down. Wait a week or so until the weeds germinate, then plant winter rye and hairy vetch for a fall and winter cover crop. Rye and vetch together are a good cover crop mixture. The rye has an allelopathic affect on some weeds, helping to suppress them. The vetch will grow in most climate zones under wide conditions and will fix nitrogen in the soil. Just broadcast the cover crop seeds and till them in lightly. The tilling action will kill the newly germinated weeds and cover the rye/vetch seeds so they will germinate. By the following spring, the rye/vetch mix will be ready to till under as you prepare your garden beds for spring planting.

Other green manure cover crops you might consider using are legumes such as alfalfa, Austrian winter peas, crimson clover, white clover, white lupine, yellow lupine, cowpeas, velvet beans, and soybeans. These are all good smother crops having the added benefit of helping to fix nitrogen in your soil. Non-legume cover crops don't fix nitrogen but they are usually easier to establish and have a shorter growth period while still supplying plenty of biomass and nitrogen if they are still green when plowed under. These include annual ryegrass, oats, winter barley, winter rape and winter wheat. Most of these grass or grain cover crops will winter kill and will leave a nice mulch on the surface that will help smother germinating weeds and will protect the soil during the winter months. Different climates have different plant requirements, so check with other growers in your area and follow the seeding rates listed on the seed bags.

A Cash and Cover Crop

A really neat way to earn a small income from your garden while you are growing cover crops on it is with a pumpkin patch. Begin in the spring of the year with buckwheat or millet. After the cover crop gets about knee high, till it down and prepare a seed bed. Plant rows of pumpkin seeds one foot apart in rows six feet apart. Use the rotary tiller and hand hoes to keep the weeds under control until the pumpkins have started vining and setting flowers. Then, under-sow a cover crop of white clover. Broadcast the seed and rake it in lightly for good germination. The raking action will destroy any newly germinated weeds. The clover will only grow a foot or so tall and will not interfere with the pumpkins.

The combination of clover and pumpkin leaves will help keep weeds under control. In late September, harvest the pumpkins and store them under cover until time to sell them for Halloween. Rotary till the field to turn under the clover and the pumpkin vines. Wait a few days for weed seeds to germinate then broadcast winter rye and hairy vetch. Till the field lightly to kill the sprouted weeds and to cover the rye and vetch seeds.

49

Come next spring you should have a lovely cover crop stand, with only a few weeds and plenty of biomass to till under before you plant vegetables. If the top growth of the cover crop is more than a foot high you may want to mow it first before tilling it under. Be sure to wait a couple of weeks after tilling it under before planting vegetables. This will give the soil a change to recover from the tilling. The allelopathic effect of the winter rye, which inhibits seed germination, will not affect your vegetables after this 2-week wait. Also, the wait gives you a chance to get weed seeds germinated and tilled under again before you put in vegetable seeds.

The pumpkins will sell for enough to cover the costs of cover cropping and your time. You can also plan on selling the pumpkins as pick-your-own. This is a wonderful way to introduce new customers to your market garden and it will encourage them to come back next summer for fresh vegetables.

§

Fitting The Farm To The Climate

Coaxes $25,000 out of 2 cold and rocky acres.

by Ed Shamy

RANGELEY, Maine – Planting conditions deep in the Maine woods just 20 miles south of the Quebec provincial border are far from ideal. The growing season is short and temperamental. Frosts in each month aren't uncommon. The topsoil is thin and rocky, barely covering boulders which render conventional plows useless. Moose trudge through the open land, leaving broken plants in their wake. Spruce seedlings sprout quickly in open soil, trying to reclaim it for the forest.

Only an active imagination could conjure up a successful produce farm in such an inhospitable setting. Certainly no serious vegetable grower would ever really try it. Maybe that's why Kit and Linda Caspar have prospered up here. When they purchased First Farm in 1976, it was a motley collection of roughly 6 cleared acres and several run-down buildings. Neither of them was serious about farming. Yet the Caspars' interest in gardening motivated them to breathe new life into the land. In the years since, their ingenuity has turned it into a successful operation that sells organically grown vegetables, small fruits, cut flowers and herbs.

"We started selling very casually, just to friends," Linda recalls of the summer of 1977. "But in mid-August there were six cars parked along the road," says Kit. "We said, 'You know, this might be a business.' "

Until their arrival only 1,200 square feet of First Farm had ever been cultivated. Today about 2 acres are used to produce peas, six kinds of beans, potatoes, strawberries, blueberries, squash, carrots, spinach, endive, arrugula, broccoli, cauliflower, garlic, leeks, shallots and six kinds of onions as well as 10 varieties of lettuce.

"In our second or third year we had our first $100 day (in gross sales)," says Kit. "Now we regularly do $400 in a day without a blink. In 1989 we even had a $600 day, and that did make us blink."

Total farm income has tripled since they began keeping complete records in 1985, going from $8,500 that year to $25,700 in 1989. The share contributed by fresh vegetables also has risen in the same period from half to more than 60 percent. Sale of starts for perennial flowers earned the couple $3,600 in 1989. Also contributing were fresh-cut flowers, homemade jams and vinegars, strawberries and raspberries, maple syrup made on the farm and custom rotary mowing.

Labor needs also have increased to include one full-time and two part-time workers during the peak selling and production periods. Recently, the Caspars chose to have fewer people working longer hours. Reasons for the shift include the availability of qualified help and the desire to have all personnel on the farm more knowledgeable and therefore better able to serve customers' needs.

Piles and Pigs

The Caspars grow their crops without chemical fertilizers or pesticides. Rather than view nature as a limiting factor they use the area's daunting climatic and geologic conditions as an incentive to intensify their efforts and add value to their crops.

"There's 8 inches of soil in good spots, some clay and a lot of compact gravel, real hardpan. It's rugged ground," says Kit. He went at it with his tiller after finding a neighbor's plow was useless, and used a back hoe to move boulders "as big as a Volkswagen." He brought in animal manure, combed the town for bags of leaves, and used compost to boost the soil's organic matter content. And he hired some swine.

"Our pigs work here," boasts Linda, explaining the role of the porcine soil builders. In 1990 the farm had four hogs, purchased as feeders, on their way to slaughter weight. Turned into an area targeted for crops after the boulders have been removed, the hogs root about, repeatedly turning the soil better than any machine, Kit believes. They chew or trample woody items that wouldn't normally decompose for many years.

After a year the hogs are moved and Kit adds rock phosphate. Potatoes and strawberries are planted first. Then he adds wood ashes and plants two years of peas and beans to add nitrogen. By the fourth year, the plot is ready for any crop. "It gets so mucky it looks like Iowa soil," says Kit.

Even with newly vitalized soil the Caspar's crop selection is limited. They recognize that the short, unpredictable growing season – often only 60 days – means long-season crops just won't work. So they select short-season varieties and pick them before maturity, turning conventional crops into gourmet miniature vegetables that they can market at premium prices.

Rolling with the punches, they add specialty items – Chinese cabbage, bok choy, radicchio, corn salad, baby beets, mustard greens and others – to their crop list. Harvesting young crops allows for a quick turnover of the limited space to make way for new crops. Further, demand for baby carrots allows a profit on 6-inch roots. If grown to full length the carrots would be mangled by the underlying hardpan.

Stretching It Out

Just how short is the summer season in Rangeley? "If we haven't had a killing frost by September 10, it's really a long season," Kit says.

Crops at First Farm are grown in beds up to 3 feet wide. Kit seeds carrots up to seven rows per bed at two-week intervals eight times during the season. Floating row covers of white, spun-bond polyester protect early crops and those direct-seeded in late summer. The covers provide a warming margin of 5 to 20 degrees, depending on the intensity of sunshine, and offer the Caspars a jump start on the growing season come spring, a necessity for northern commercial gardening.

Informing The Loyalists – 20 Percent of the Customers Buy 80 Percent of the Produce

Customers can't seem to get enough of First Farm's produce. "They want lettuce faster than I can clear land," says Kit. "We can't keep peas in the shop," says Linda. "I have to buy my onions at the grocery store because customers have stripped the garden beds clean."

First Farm's regular customers call ahead to reserve their peas and other produce. Linda pays special attention to these loyalists, who make up 20 percent of the farm's customers and provide four out of five dollars of its income. Regular customers also receive Linda's newsletter twice each growing season. It tells what crops should be expected at what time, valuable information when weather is such an important factor.

One season for example, hot and dry weather combined to hastily ripen their strawberries in late July. "We got so sick of picking strawberries so fast we could cry," says Kit. Regular customers were made aware of the shortened season, and Kit and Linda made sure each had some berries. In particular they made sure that Sue Carpenter had some berries. Carpenter is chef at the Rangeley Inn, a restored inn and restaurant just a mile down the road. She buys one-quarter of First Farm's produce.

"She's one of the few people who understands when we say, 'you'll have strawberries today and tomorrow they'll be gone.' She'll take anything we can grow, whenever we can get it," says Kit.

Carpenter explains why, "They have the best produce I've ever had. There's no time wasted in transportation. There's no spoilage, so it holds up longer." First Farm's produce arrives at her restaurant washed and cleaned the same day it is picked. "They get me nice young carrots and all kinds of lettuce – iceberg is basically history. What I get from Kit and Linda is more flavorful."

"I get 100-percent yield. Every piece of lettuce I buy is useful," she adds. "You pay more for it, but it's a lot better. I don't believe in the cheap route. It pays in the long run to pay more for something better."

Carpenter says she also appreciates the close communication with Linda. They talk about features of new vegetables and Linda often passes along culinary tips on using the new varieties of produce coming from the farm.

Forming the core of their clientele are up-scale seasonal vacationers from further south – New Jersey, New York and Philadelphia. They bring interest in quality and gourmet vegetables, and the willingness to pay the going price. "Most of the people come from a background where they spend to get what they want. People are always telling us we don't charge enough. We like that, because it gives us some leeway to gradually increase prices if we need to," Kit says. Ideas for use often are handed out with a sale, especially for specialty vegetables new to many cooks.

Walk-up customers may not get the same red-carpet treatment as the regulars, but Linda and Kit know that taste will lure them back. Kit says these customers seem particularly fond of his carrots, which are sold in bunches of six – each no more than 6 inches long – and in clusters of 20 young fingerlings. Both sell for 80 cents each.

"They'll buy a bunch and eat them while they walk around the farm," he says. "Then they buy another bunch and drive around for a while. Then they come back to buy a bunch to take home."

Pest-Free Plants

While customers keep coming back, pests seem to stay away for the most part. Colorado potato beetles and cutworms can usually be picked off by hand and the floating row covers keep flea beetles and other pests away from young plants. Cabbage worms are treated with a bacterial insecticide based on Bacillus thuringiensis (Bt), while frequent cultivation and incorporation of rye and clover cover crops keep weeds in check.

As for the bigger, four-legged pests, the Caspars are experiencing more visits as time goes along, but no devastating losses. Moose occasionally make an appearance, walking through 4-foot woven wire hung on well-anchored posts as if it were paper. The fearless half-ton intruders don't eat vegetables, but wreak havoc on their strolls when $85 row covers are torn by their feet. Deer go for the hearts of late-season salad crops, but don't bother covered rows, Kit has found.

The Caspars have not sought certification as organic growers due to their decision to use transplants not grown organically, and seaweed, fish emulsion and bagged fertilizer that Kit feels wouldn't meet strict state certification standards. Other farm practices would qualify as organic, he believes.

The Caspars have learned to count their blessings – big and small – and say they are lucky to be farming successfully under such rugged and forbidding growing conditions.

"In a big sense, we make up for our drawbacks," Kit says. "If everybody could do it, we wouldn't do it. I'm kind of a contrary person. If it were easy I probably wouldn't be here."

Should You Pay Rent for a Market Garden Site?

What if your backyard isn't big enough? Worse, what if you don't even have a backyard? In this event you can rent or borrow land from someone else in the community.

Should you pay rent for that land? Not if you can help it. Try to get the land free-rent in exchange for improving the value of the soil, or for safeguarding or maintaining the premises. To add land rent to your already long list of expenses will not normally be necessary. A token payment, say $25 or $50 per acre is probably all you should ever have to spend. Avoid sharecropping proposals altogether. Sharecropping has never done much to improve the lot of most farmers, and usually only benefits the landowner.

Convince the landowners that the improvements you will make in the soil with organic gardening practices will benefit them greatly. I once had a landowner decline to rent land to me because she felt that vegetable gardening causes weeds. She is absolutely right, poor gardening practices will cause weeds, lots of them. But a well-managed garden is clean, attractive and leaves the soil in far better health than it began with.

If you want to start out fairly small you can rent one or several plots in your community garden, if there is one. In Burlington, Vt., we have five community gardens, totaling 250 individual plots. Roy Dedama is one of the market gardeners renting plots in these community gardens. He pays $25 per year for each 25- by 30-foot plot, and rents 10 plots. This totals 7,500 square feet. In exchange for his $250 rental fee the city provides spring tillage, compost or cow manure, irrigation water and bulk straw mulch purchases. Roy grows edible flowers, gourmet tomatoes and fancy lettuces for sale to local restaurants. He lives about six miles from the site, and this is only a part-time job for him.

The Intervale Foundation currently rents 20 acres of good farmland from the Burlington Electric Department for $1 per acre per year. We manage this land organically and have increased the fertility and productivity of the soil tremendously. This justifies the low rent. The Electric Department rents adjacent land to a dairy farmer for $25 per acre per year.

In your search for free or low-cost gardening land don't overlook the obvious. Factories, churches, schools, hospitals, apartment and condominium complexes, even retail stores, often sit on larger parcels than they need for buildings and parking. Usually, the grounds maintenance crew spends many hours each year mowing large areas of lawn that might very well be available for organic gardening. Landscaped areas are expensive to maintain, so maybe you could work out a deal to manage some of this land in exchange for rent.

Establishing a market garden at such a location can immediately give you a ready-made market, too. This can be the employees of the company, residents of housing developments or whatever organization shares the site with you.

A good example of putting unused land to good use is the farmer who rents a 3-acre market garden site from Instrom Electronics near Route 128 just west of Boston. The market garden thrives next to the headquarters building. Instrom personnel have access to a wonderful selection of fresh fruits and vegetables during the season.

Instrom employees take full advantage of the nearby harvest, and even consider it somewhat of a "perk" for working where they do. Maybe it's not as attractive as company paid health and dental insurance, but it's a good source for vegetables, herbs, and flowers. It's also a nice place to stroll during coffee breaks and lunch hours.

The farmer has a ready-made market. He can sell everything he can grow. He doesn't have to truck his produce anywhere, and can look forward to building up a solid rapport with the long-term employees of the company. I'd really like to see more of this type of urban garden farming taking place throughout the country.

Examples could go on and on. Recently, for the Farmland Stewardship Program, the Massachusetts Department of Food and Agriculture identified nearly 11,000 acres of state-owned land that could be available for farming. More than 3,000 of these acres are suitable for vegetable, herb, and flower crops. Tremendous opportunities abound in this program for beginning farmers to get a start or for established farmers to expand their acreage.

Look around your community, talk to community leaders and other farmers and growers and your state department of agriculture. Ask anyone you can think of for leads on sites you can rent or borrow. If you grow organically it will help you get an interview with many landowners who are just as concerned about chemical contamination and ground water pollution as you are. Often, they will consider leasing their land to you *only* if you are organic.

It is becoming more common for towns and counties to get involved in long term land rental or lease arrangements with farmers. Burlington, Vermont, is one example, Duxbury, Massachusetts, is another. The town of Duxbury owns several acres of high-value cranberry bogs that are leased to a local cranberry grower. The town is working in harmony with the farmer to preserve open space, support local employment, enhance tax value of agricultural property and create business ownership opportunities. This helps keep more food buying dollars in the local economy, too.

What To Look For If You Do Rent Land

Once you have located a suitable piece of land to rent or borrow, work out a mutually beneficial agreement with the owner. Outlining the details of your understanding with the landowner is a good idea. From the landowner's point of view they want to make sure that you don't unnecessarily damage the land with excessive drainage ditches, continuous corn cropping or similar destructive practices. They will also be concerned that you pay the rent, if any, on time. They will ask you to carry sufficient liability insurance to protect their interests in a calamity.

From the grower's point of view, you want to make sure that the zoning allows you to grow and sell crops. Try for as long a lease as possible. That will give you more time to build up the soil. Other improvements such as fencing and buildings, will require capitalization over several years. So, plan on having enough time in your lease to recover your investment.

You also need to be assured of getting enough irrigation water, and easy access to the site. Irrigation water is critically important for successful market gardening. If you have to drill an irrigation well, it could easily cost you $2,000 or more. Check it out carefully before you sign the lease. Even with the modern and highly efficient drip and soaker irrigation systems you will still use a great deal of water. You'll need water for washing produce and containers, too.

Don't try to be an intensive, *quality* grower without irrigation.

On the other hand, you don't want too much water. If the site you are considering is low-lying and drains slowly after a heavy rain it may be too wet for a successful and profitable market garden. You can't work the soil soon enough to get your early crops started in the spring. Any crops you do get established here may be at risk of flooding during a wet season.

Don't discount this type location entirely, though. Such sites sometimes make excellent ground for late crops of sweet corn, pumpkins, and squash. If the site requires mechanical drainage, stay away from it completely unless it is the only outstanding retail site in your community. By the time you wade through conservation restrictions to drain farmland you may wish you hadn't started. The environmental damage you may cause with such practices might also outweigh any benefits you may get from the site.

Stay away from steep and easily eroded sites, too. You want your market garden to appear pretty and well-groomed, not filled with runoff ditches and unsightly mud puddles.

If you want to market your crops through a farmstand, it's important to rent or borrow land with the best retail site you can find. Pay attention to accessibility and roadside market potential. Don't be too concerned about the soil type. Inferior soil can be improved to obtain maximum yields. But a poor marketing location is just that, poor.

If the land you are about to rent is on a state highway, call the highway department to see if you will be able to get a "curb cut" approval to build a driveway leading to a farmstand. If there is a serious curve or hill near your site check with zoning authorities to make sure they won't prohibit you from having customers enter and exit onto a busy road. For the safety of your customers and employees you need safe ingress and egress to your site.

If you don't need or want a roadside retail sales location then your land search will be much easier. There are thousands of small parcels all over this country going begging for someone to use them. Drive down main streets and back roads, ask around and start making a list of possibilities. Look at each site carefully, first for its limitations, then for its potential.

A useful visual aid in your land search will be a copy of the topographic map of the area. These are commonly available at sporting goods stores. These maps show open areas and fields, back roads and cart paths, streams, wetlands and elevation lines of changing terrain.

Another handy aid is the county soil maps. These are available from your Cooperative Extension Service or area Soil Conservation Service office. Most counties in the United States have maps showing soil types and current or potential uses. These maps come in manuals that you can borrow. These manuals give a description of each soil type and its drainage characteristics. They also show potential crop uses, open fields versus wooded or developed areas, and soil limitations for housing development.

The soil maps are often taken from aerial photos. They are useful for searching out former hay fields and crop land. A site that rates excellent for field corn or alfalfa hay is also good for mixed vegetables.

Some soils are just not suitable for efficient and profitable vegetable production. The ones you want to watch out for include those that stay wet because of hardpan or tightly packed gravel just below the surface. These will neither drain well nor will they let deep-rooted vegetables develop good root systems. If the hardpan is not too deep or too extensive you can break it up with a sub-soiler plow pulled behind a large tractor. If you run across a situation like this though, you might want to check with your county Extension soils specialist before proceeding.

The .i.ideal soil is a fine or very-fine sandy loam with a high organic matter level, underlain by loose gravel or sand for good drainage. This is also the best soil for constructing housing septic systems. Don't be surprised when you find housing developments now cover much of the good farmland, not only in the heavily developed coastal regions, but throughout the country.

When you are looking at a site, check out the neighborhood. If it has mostly middle class or higher priced homes you probably won't have more than a small amount of vandalism and theft. If a huge housing project is nearby, the opposite may be true. Having lots of people nearby will have an impact on your crops, buildings and equipment. One advantage of a large nearby housing project, of course, is the potential market provided by those residents. Because of their modest income level it may be necessary to sell your crops for lower prices, but this might easily be offset by reduced transportation and marketing costs.

At most sites you need to be concerned about installing electric varmint fencing to keep the raccoons, deer and rabbits from raiding your goodies. This fencing is expensive, ranging from $400 to $600 per acre, but well worth the investment in obtaining a marketable crop from your land.

Throughout this discussion I've avoided talking about purchasing land for vegetable farming. In most areas near major population centers the average land prices are just too high for profitable farming enterprises. Even if you can buy land for as little as $1,000 per acre, the carrying costs are an extra burden on your budget, especially during the critical start-up period.

For more in-depth information on rebuilding soil fertility and tilth I recommend *The Soul of Soil* by Grace Gershuney and Joe Smillie, available from Necessary Trading. Also, *Rodale's Guide to Composting* and *The Gardener's Guide To Better Soil* by Gene Logsdon (see bibliography).

CHAPTER 3:

Tools Of The Trade

As a beginning business enterprise the first tool you need is a telephone listing. Don't make the customers guess how to get in touch with you; they won't. For the smaller enterprise use your home phone, but as you get larger it's better to have a separate listing for your farm name. This is important for three reasons. First, if you have a common last name such as Brown or Smith, there may be several listings in the phone book and customers won't know which one to call. Second, with an easily recognizable farm name, such as Natural Lee Farm, customers will be able to locate you in the phone book easily and quickly. Finally, with a business listing it is easy to install a recorder to give customers updates on your crops without having to answer the phone at all hours of the evenings and weekends, and your teenagers will still be able to use the home phone without fear of having you yell at them for tying up the line.

Car or Truck?

For the first two years as a farmers market vendor I hauled the produce in a Subaru station wagon. That was really an odd sight. I had sawhorses and two sheets of plywood tied to the roof rack. They assembled into a very sturdy bench for market days. With the Subaru's back seats folded down I could load in $500 or $600 worth of veggies. The car had air conditioning, which helped get the vegetables to market without wilting.

During my third year as a market gardener I rented a van for the season. It had air conditioning, too. To help keep veggies cool I put a used 4,000 BTU window air conditioner in the back door of the van and blocked off the upper doorway opening with a piece of plywood. This gave me a cool place to store veggies until I was ready to leave for the market.

This temporary refrigeration set-up held temperatures about 30 degrees cooler than outside air. On a 90 degree day it would hold temperatures down to about 60 degrees. That was enough to keep everything but lettuce from wilting. Because an air conditioner also acts as a dehumidifier it tended to dry out the air, so I put wet burlap bags and wet towels over everything.

Inexpensive banners can help dress up a truck and attract attention at the same time. This banner cost less than $30. The canopy rolls up for easy storage on the roof racks and can be mounted at rear or side of van. photo courtesy Mass. Department of Food and Agriculture

I fashioned a canopy for the van out of 1-inch PVC piping and a blue polypropylene tarp. It was designed to mount from the roof racks, either for the back doors of the van or the side doors. Two of the markets I attended had head-in parking slots, the other was a side-delivery slot.

Trellising

Trellising was a problem until I learned how to do it properly. The first year I got free sawmill slabs, thinking they would make good posts. They all broke when the vines got too heavy and my cucumbers and tomatoes collapsed. Now I use steel fence posts and #9 galvanized wire to build a support trellis for each bed. The steel posts are set every 15 feet and the galvanized wire is fixed to the top clip on the posts. The wire is anchored with fence posts set at an angle at each end of the line. Slack is removed using ratchet type fence tighteners available at farm supply stores.

I plant two rows of tomatoes on 24-inch centers in each bed. The posts and wire are installed in the middle of the bed. I use untreated binder twine, available from farm supply stores, to tie each individual plant to the support wire. Each week as the plants grow we remove all but the central leaders and wrap them around the twine. This keeps the tomatoes well supported off the ground, and makes it easier to tend the plants and harvest the ripe tomatoes. The tomatoes that are held up off the ground are cleaner, have a better shape and ripen more evenly than if they are allowed to sprawl.

Marketable yield from trellised tomatoes is greatly improved, too. Tomatoes that are allowed to sprawl on the ground are often not salable because of uneven ripening, being misshapen and subject to fungal diseases and other soil-borne diseases. In one experiment I did, nearly 40% of the fruits that were not trellised weren't salable.

Sun screen

One summer I tried leaning salvaged wooden pallets in a pyramid over the lettuce and broccoli plants to cool them off and keep them from bolting. It didn't work worth a damn, and the neighbors questioned my lack of concern for community aesthetics. They were especially unhappy because that particular year the lettuce and broccoli were in my front yard. The following year I bought wire hoops and shade net, and added a trickle tape and straw mulch to cool the soil. This method for growing crops in hot weather works much better. We also now use varieties bred for warm-season growing.

There are other ways to obtain sun screen for heat-sensitive plants. One is to plant the lettuce and cole crops in the shade of nearby trees, or tall growing garden crops such as sweet corn, or trellised crops such as cucumbers or tomatoes. With increased concern about ozone depletion and skin cancer, sun screen or sun block is a good idea for gardeners, too.

Walk-In Cooler

Yes, you should have a walk-in cooler for storing vegetables between sales days. If you do your garden farming in your spare time you don't want to have to get up at 4 a.m. on market day to pick veggies. It doesn't work to pick them early in the week and try to hold the flavor, either. This will lead to composting more wilted produce than you should. It's better to pick and store, even for a day or so, in a good cooler.

During my first year as a market grower I relied on a used refrigerator in my basement to hold modest amounts of produce. This was a frustrating solution because the space was so small. I later used the refrigerator to cool lemonade and apple cider that I sold in paper cups at the markets.

The cooler can be fairly simple. One year I used a window air conditioner set in the back door of the van. A better plan would be to construct an 8- by 8-foot building, insulate it with cellulose and insert the air conditioner through the wall. Since the air conditioner also dehumidifies as it cools you may want to add an inexpensive humidifier to keep from dehydrating the vegetables.

Special refrigeration package units are available, but they sometimes cost considerably more than a used 4,000 BTU window air conditioner. Richard Wiswall at Cate Farm in Plainfield, Vt., built a 10- by 10-foot cooler room, complete with used refrigeration equipment, for less than $600. If you have mechanical abilities and access to used equipment you may be able to do that, too.

For a larger market garden, shop around for a used refrigerated truck. You might get the refrigerated body, without the truck, for less than $1,000. These units have an independent diesel engine. Some also have electrical standby that you can plug into your house. This might require running a 220-volt outlet to an area where you can plug in the unit. These units are fairly noisy, and the diesel engines produce smelly exhaust fumes. So, it's a good idea to check the options carefully before building a cooler too close to your house, or your neighbor's house.

At Intervale Community Farm we have a unique answer to the cooling of garden produce. Our cooler is a used refrigerated truck box mounted on a farm wagon frame. We bought it used for $1,500. It has a diesel powered refrigeration unit with electric back-up.

For quick cooling we tow the cooler/trailer directly to the field and operate it with the diesel engine. As soon as they are picked, vegetables go right into the cooler. For night storage we move the cooler back to the barn and plug in the electric back up unit.

§

The Profit Is In The Picking

High-value harvesting hints that help your produce look good, taste good and sell better.

by Bob Hofstetter

He probably doesn't know it, but the strawberry grower I visited a few years ago near my southeastern Pennsylvania farm taught me a valuable lesson about how *not* to market high-value crops.

His half acre of berries looked great in the field. Every rich, dark green plant was loaded with fruit so large and red I wanted to just pop one in my mouth. You couldn't ask for a better selection of varieties. Even his field location was perfect. Well-drained soils. Plenty of air movement to minimize fungal diseases. "This guy has done his homework," I said to myself, fighting feelings of jealousy. "He'll do well."

I was wrong. When I talked with some friends who had just bought berries at the farmer's roadside stand, they showed me fruit that wasn't even suitable for processing. Most of it was muddy. Some was unripe. Some was starting to rot.

The only reason these folks had bought the berries in the first place was that they were friends of the grower. And they still are, but mainly because he has made several improvements in how he harvests his fruits and vegetables.

There's no telling how many customers or how much money this farmer lost before he learned to pick and handle his high-value crops properly. You can avoid such an expensive lesson by paying as careful attention to harvesting and handling as you do to other aspects of production.

Careful picking and handling is important with berries, and equally so with vegetables. Any farmer who has ever grown sweet corn, for example, knows how meticulously customers will evaluate this summer favorite – and how willingly they'll recommend you to their friends if they like your crop.

To keep them coming back for more, harvest your corn at dawn when temperature is at its lowest point of the day. Coolness slows the conversion of sugars to starches, which helps your corn retain that sweet taste customers crave.

Take the ears to a shaded area and immediately remove excess husk and cob shank. This unwanted growth will draw moisture from the kernels if you leave it on the ear.

Put the ears into baskets or mesh bags (no more than 50 or 60 cobs per container), and hose them down with ice cold water. Let them drain for a few minutes and put them into a cooler. I've held super-sweet and sugar-enhanced hybrids in my walk-in cooler for seven days at 32 degrees F with excellent results. Standard hybrids should be sold the same day they're picked.

If you don't have a cooler, avoid picking any more sweet corn than you can sell within eight hours. Stack bags of wet ears four or five high in a shaded area. Cover each individual layer with wet burlap, and keep the layers wet by hosing them occasionally. The ears should be well-cooled before you stack them. Otherwise, left-over field heat won't be able to escape, and will ruin the flavor of the kernels.

If sweet corn has any rival in the summer produce market, it's red, ripe tomatoes. Trouble is, the tomatoes your customers buy should not be picked red. They should be pink and just starting to turn red, because they are much less susceptible to damage at this stage. (Don't worry, the tomatoes will turn completely red in a day or two – sometimes less.)

Red tomatoes that aren't sold within 24 to 48 hours will have to be dumped. If you're lucky, you may be able to sell them for processing – at half price.

Like raspberries, tomatoes must be packed with care. Use containers that hold no more than 8 or 10 pounds of fruit. If you're picking into half-bushel baskets, fill them only two-thirds of the way.

Gently wipe off soiled fruit with a damp cloth right after harvest. *Don't refrigerate tomatoes* – it ruins the taste and slows reddening. Display ripe fruit for immediate sale, and keep it out of direct sunlight to avoid flesh-softening heat buildup.

Pick Peppers As Needed

Peppers, beans and peas can tolerate rougher handling. You can keep them in bushel baskets or even larger containers without fear of damaging them. But they still require some care.

When picking peppers, for example, be sure a portion of the stem remains on the fruit. That will protect the flesh from exposure to air and bacteria, which can cause rotting. For the same reason, be careful not to bruise or lacerate the skin when you're placing peppers into containers or dumping them into display racks. Pepper damage isn't always noticeable right away. Sometimes it's on the inside, and shows up in a day or two as soft spots or rotten fruit.

Without refrigeration, peppers have a storage life of about two or three days. You can store them in a cooler for 10 days or more. Peppers also hold well on the plant. I simply pick them as I need them.

Fresh asparagus is a quick-selling item when handled properly. Rapid moisture loss and wilting will be a problem if you don't cool the spears right after harvest. For display, place asparagus spears upright in containers lined with wet, absorbent material like sponges. Some farmers put them in buckets filled with ice water, but that's a mistake. The spears will absorb moisture and start elongating. Taste and nutrition won't suffer, but appearance will. Customers don't want thin, spindly asparagus.

Yellow wax and green beans must be harvested when they're firm and meaty. They should snap freely when bent. Also, never pick wet beans. Moisture promotes fungal diseases and causes beans to russet.

It's a good idea to cool beans after you pick them. But like muskmelons, beans are susceptible to chilling injury. Storage temperature should be in the range of 40 to 45 degrees F. If refrigeration isn't available, pick early in the day, before field temperature rises but after dew has evaporated.

Remove beans to a shaded area. And when displaying them, sprinkle them occasionally with very cold water to help retain freshness.

Cooling is even more critical with garden and sugar snap peas. They will lose sugar content and become tough rapidly if you don't remove field heat immediately after harvest. Rinsing in cold water for 15 to 20 minutes is effective.

Drain the peas well and keep them out of direct sunlight. Spray them occasionally with a mist of cold water while on display.

Same goes with leafy greens like lettuce, spinach and endive. Harvest early in the morning. Then remove them from the field and place them into a cooler right away. If you don't have a cooler, *don't pick more than you can sell in a day*. And, keep them damp when you display them for sale.

With today's appearance-conscious grocery shoppers, anything you can do to give your crops eye-appeal will set you apart. Of course, there are plenty of sprays, waxes and other assorted potions for doing that.

So why worry about careful picking and packing? Because people are fast learning that the best-looking produce may not always be the best-tasting (or the healthiest, for that matter).

Put it this way: Produce makeup, such as waxy coatings, can get anybody to buy a tomato – once. Careful picking and handling will bring them back again and again.

And After You Pick....

Table 2. Recommended storing times and temperatures for common fruits and vegetables.

Crop	Relative Temp. Deg F	Humidity (%)	Approx. Length Of Storage
Asparagus	32-36	95	2-3 weeks
Beans, snap	40-45	90-95	7-10 days
Beets, bunched	32	95	10-14 days
Beets, topped	32	95	3-4 months
Blueberries	31-32	90-95	2-4 weeks
Raspberries	31-32	90-95	2-3 days
Strawberries	32	90-95	5-7 days
Broccoli	32	90-95	10-14 days
Brussels Sprouts	32	90-95	3-5 weeks
Cabbage, early	32	90-95	3-6 weeks
Cabbage, late	32	90-95	3-4 months
Carrots	32	90-95	4-5 months
Cauliflower	32	90-95	2-4 weeks
Celery	32	90-95	2-3 months
Cucumbers	45-50	90-95	10-14 days
Eggplant	45-50	90	1 week
Lettuce	32	95	2-3 weeks
Melons - Muskmelon	32-35	85-90	5-14 days
Crenshaw	45-50	85-90	2 weeks
Honeydew	45-50	85-90	3-4 weeks
Watermelon	40-50	85-90	2-3 weeks
Parsley	32	90-95	1-2 months
Peas	32	90-95	1-3 weeks
Peppers	45-50	90-95	2-3 weeks
Radishes, spring	32	90-95	3-4 weeks
Spinach	32	90-95	10-14 days
Squash, summer	32-50	90	5-14 days
Sweet corn	32	90-95	4-8 days
Tomatoes*	45-50	85-90	4-7 days

Table #2 Source: Adapted from USDA Agriculture Handbook No. 66, "The Commercial Storage of Fruits, Vegetables, and Florist and Nursery Stocks."

* Editor's note; Even though tomatoes are listed, it is not a good idea to cool them below 55 F. It degrades flavor and delays ripening, leaving an off flavor.

15 Super Garden Tools Let You Whistle While You Work

Most market gardeners I've met over the years complain of sore backs, necks and knees. The continual bending and kneeling we do is hard on the body. Also, there is the problem of speed and efficiency. With time at a premium it's important to chose tools that pay for themselves quickly by reducing your labor costs.

1. Scoot-N-Doo

My favorite working platform and garden seat is the "Scoot-n-Doo" offered by Gardener's Supply Co. This has wide plastic wheels that don't sink in soft ground. The seat is low to the ground, and it's padded. The manufacturer says the unit will carry 300 pounds but I've never tested it. I weigh nearly 180 pounds, and haven't had a problem with the tool in the five years I've used it. The price tag is nearly $60, but the scoot is well worth it.

It has a rope pull cord for moving around the field. I use this tool anytime I have to pick strawberries or bush green beans or do extensive hand weeding. It's really fast, too; just use your feet to push yourself backwards along the rows. In the bed system you can pick half a bed on each side as your feet push you along the path.

Behind the seat is a work surface large enough to carry a flat of seedlings or a harvesting box. There is also a tray under the seat useful for holding tools. The rim of the work surface has three holes for holding hand tools. The middle hole is just the right size to hold insect spray, or a soda can.

The Scoot-N-Doo is a comfortable seat and efficient work platform.

2. Multi-Dibble

Another useful tool that will ease your work and speed up seeding and transplanting is the multi-dibble. We use the dibble for making holes for transplants or large seeds. The single dibble comes either with a short pistol grip handle, or a longer handle for making individual holes while you are standing up. The multi-dibble is merely a bunch of single dibbles sharing a common carrier.

I made my multi-dibble from a 36-inch long piece of plastic sewer pipe that is 15 inches in diameter. It looks like a lawn roller with studs. It has a frame attached for pulling behind the tractor. I've seen other examples that have old lawnmower handles attached. David Miskell, a market gardener in Shelburne, Vt., made his multi-dibble from an old lawn roller.

The multi-dibble pulled by hand or tractor gives instant, exact spacing, soil firming and prepared holes for seedlings.

The multi-dibble is pulled or pushed along the bed and will leave perfectly spaced planting holes. The studs that make the holes can be made from almost any material. Mine are 3-inch sections of old hoe handles, bored lengthwise and bolted to the pipe. They can be spaced any way you want them. Mine has three rows at 12-inch spacing, with the studs 14 inches apart in the row.

This gives three rows per bed, for crops like lettuce. Or you can use the two outside rows for 24-inch row spacing for crops like broccoli or tomatoes. For squash and melon seeds or transplants we use just the center row. After the holes are made just walk along and drop the seedlings in the new holes. Use a small hoe to firm the soil around the seedlings, and that's all there is to it. These rows are laid out just right for cultivating with the wheel hoe or the cultivating tractor.

We also use the multi-dibble to mark rows for hand seeding crops like pumpkins and winter squash. Just drop the seeds in the center row of holes, then walk along with a hoe handle pulling dirt to cover the seeds.

73

Market Gardener David Miskell made his multi-dibble from a derelict lawn roller.

The parts for this multi-dibble were free, except for the bolts. It took me a full day to build, but it pays me back every week during the season.

3. Push Seeder

For planting smaller seeds we use three Earthway push seeders. These are bolted together on a common axle at 12-inch spacings. The common axle is 5/8-inch threaded rod. We can plant three rows of carrots or other small seeds as fast as we can walk. Or, use the two outside planters for wider spaced crops like sweet corn. To get a single row of cucumbers or squash down the middle of the bed we just use the middle planter. The outside seeders have marking rods installed. As we are planting one bed, we are marking the next bed. For drilling cover crop seeds we make two passes on the bed, with the seeder spaced over 6-inches on the second pass. This gives us six rows spaced 6-inches apart.

Three Earthway seeders with a common axle can plant 3 rows 12-inches apart easily and efficiently while marking the next bed. To plant rows 6-inches apart simply make two passes, with the second pass measured over 6 inches from the first.

Another feature of the Earthway seeder is the detachable fertilizer hopper. This has a manual metering device to allow the operator to chose the proper rate of application for side-dressing the row as it is being seeded. The side-dressing can take place at the time of seeding, or at any time before the seedlings get too high for the seeder to clear. For example, we use the 3-row rig to sidedress sweet corn when the corn plants are about 6 inches high. After the corn is too high for the common axle to clear, we unbolt one outside Earthway seeder and use it to sidedress single rows of corn.

The aluminum and plastic Earthway seeder sells for about $70. Its fertilizer attachment costs about $25. Adding the common axle and support brace to build a 3-row rig costs another $20.

The Earthway comes standard with six plastic seed plates good for planting at least 16 common vegetables, including peas, corn, carrots, beans, radishes and beets. Five optional plates that cover everything from brassicas to popcorn are available for about $17. You should buy the extra plates, because this extremely versatile and economical planter will cut your planting time to next to nothing, while increasing the quality of your planting.

The Earthway's seed plates drop seed at precise intervals in the row, eliminating time-consuming thinning later on. Its adjustable depth shoe positions seed at just the right depth in the soil, from one-quarter inch to 1.5 inches. A simple drag chain covers seed with soil, which is then firmed by the rear press wheel to assure proper seed-soil contact for good germination.

In design, the Earthway is similar to the classic Planet Jr., a thoroughly dependable wooden and cast metal planter, which has been around for nearly a century. Today, a new Planet Jr. costs more than $300. Sometimes you can find an old one for much less at farm auctions or yard sales.

4. Wheelbarrow

Another necessary tool is the wheelbarrow. It is useful for all the things it was intended, and more. Fill it with water, add a chunk of ice or a frozen plastic jug and it becomes a hydrocooler for picking lettuce. Bore holes in the handles for a cross brace, pin it to the tractor drawbar, and it becomes a light trailer. Put your backpack sprayer in it, tape the spray wand in the proper orientation, and push the wheelbarrow along as you spray your crops. Fill it with sand and carry your children into the garden with their favorite sandbox toys. These are just a few ways to make your work fun, faster and a lot less tiring.

5. Tool Shed

The Green Mountain SunShed is manufactured by Gardener's Supply Company, Burlington, Vermont.

Probably one of the more irritating things about gardening is not being able to find the right tool when you need it. Over the years I've kept them in the basement, in the barn, in my car, in the cooler, in the greenhouse and under the porch. When I need something I often can't remember where the dickens it is, and waste a lot of time searching. The obvious solution is to build a tool shed. It doesn't have to be large or expensive, but it does need wall space for hanging tools, and a bench for potting and repairing tools. A simple vise to hold hoes for sharpening is nice, too.

Gardener's Supply Company has developed what I feel is the ultimate tool shed. It's called the Green Mountain SunShed, and measures either 8- by 8-feet or 8- by 10-feet. The front wall has a sloped roof with plastic panes installed so the shed can be used as a cold frame or greenhouse. There is a window and a door to let in air and light, and the back wall has plenty of space for hanging tools. It's big enough to hold your rotary tiller and shredder, and much more.

6. Washstand

An old bath tub makes an excellent washstand at Intervale Community Farm.

A washstand can be made by mounting an old bathtub or laundry double-sink at waist height, and filling it with a garden hose. A canopy overhead will keep rain and hot sun off your back and off your veggies while you are washing them. Fit another garden hose to the bathtub drain and run the hose to the top of your garden, assuming you are on a slope. The water will follow the paths alongside the beds as it drains back down the slope. This water will contain some of your richest garden soil and plant nutrients, so don't waste it. If nothing else, plant some flower or herb beds around your buildings and use the wash water to irrigate them.

Also, at the washstand have a drying rack made from a wooden frame and wire screen so you can dry veggies before packing them. Most veggies will go in crates or waxed boxes. Tomatoes go into untreated cardboard boxes, though. If tomatoes are wet they will soak through the box. Of course, if you are selling from a roadside stand or to a membership club, these boxes are not as necessary.

7. Giant Cart

Intern Dylan Zietlan pulling the giant cart with his bicycle at Intervale Community Farm.

Efficiency in the garden demands the right tools, and that includes harvesting carts. When you are using the wide row or raised bed system there isn't room to get a normal garden cart between the beds. Then you wind up doing everything with buckets and baskets and make a lot of unnecessary trips to carry produce to the washing-packing shed.

Hauling stuff around the garden such as compost, seedling trays, vegetables and kids requires a good sturdy garden cart. I built my first cart with scrap bicycle tires, scrap plywood and a threaded rod for the axle. It took three prototypes to create a working model. The result is my "giant" cart. It has 24 inches of ground clearance, can straddle 4-foot beds and hauls up to 300 pounds of produce. We can add attachments to hold rolls of plastic mulch and drip tape, which makes unrolling them on the beds much easier.

We can pick produce and pack it in boxes right on the giant cart, then wheel it right to the cooler or delivery truck. This saves walking back and forth with buckets or baskets.

We move this cart down the row, picking as we go. When it's full, we just push it to the washstand. We plant our tall-growing trellised crops in beds beside low-growing varieties and pull the giant cart along the adjacent bed, while harvesting the trellised crops.

If you buy all new parts to build your giant cart the cost will run approximately $200. The most expensive parts, of course, are the axle and wheels. Here's how to build a giant cart. Purchase a set of garden cart wheels from any of the mail order catalogs in the appendix. Also ask them for an 8-foot section of axle material, this is 3/4-inch treated steel rod. Take this rod and the wheels to a welding shop. Ask them to heat and bend the rod in 4 places, with 90 degree bends. Leave room for a hole to be bored at each end of the axle. This is for the keeper pin outside each wheel.

After the bends are complete, have a 2-inch steel angle iron welded to the top of the axle. The floor of the cart will sit on this plate. Have holes bored in the plate so the cart floor can be bolted to the plate.

Next, buy a 4- by 8-foot sheet of 5/8-inch exterior grade plywood to make the floor, sides, and front. The box floor will measure 48-inches square, with 12- by 48-inch sides and front. Use 2-inch angle iron as the corner bead for sides meeting front board, and floor meeting sides.

The 2-inch angle iron that forms the corner bead along each side of the floor can be extended 18 inches to the rear. A 1-inch square tube bolted crosswise to the corner bead extensions makes the handle.

Two separate pieces of 1-inch square tube can form the legs. These are bolted to the cart sides about 6 inches from the rear of the cart box. Center the cart box over the axle and bolt it in place.

For carrying hoes and shovels, bolt two "Y" brackets on the right sideboard. Tools can be cradled in these brackets. Bolt another "Y" bracket at the rear of each sideboard. This will hold a rod for unrolling rolls of drip irrigation tape. Just position the cart at the end of a bed, take the loose end of the drip tape and run it underneath the handlebar. Tie the drip tape to a hoe handle and hold it just above ground level as you walk to the other end of the bed. Suddenly, laying drip tape becomes a simple, one person operation that is quick, easy, effective and very satisfying.

You need a separate attachment for holding and unrolling 48-inch wide rolls of plastic mulch and 63-inch wide rolls of Reemay floating row covers. Mount this attachment underneath the handlebars. Have a 1-inch square tube resting across the handlebars just behind the box. This tube is 72 inches long. At each end have a loop of wire hanging down that can cradle another 72-inch tube. Insert this lower tube through the holes in the cardboard tube that the Reemay or plastic mulch comes on.

Now, all you have to do is move the cart into position at the end of the bed. Take the loose end of the material and walk to the other end of the bed. The roll of plastic or Reemay hanging down from the handle bars has plenty of clearance, yet it is low enough to the ground so that a little breeze won't disrupt the laying procedure. A stiff wind, however, will blow things all over the place, so delay your mulch or Reemay application till later in the day when the wind dies down.

This system can also be used for rewinding drip tape and Reemay at the end of the season. Just reverse the process. It will take two people to keep the material rolling back on the spool without kinking or getting tied in a knot. Make sure the Reemay and drip tape is clean. Use duct tape to mark the row numbers so that the proper length can be identified for reinstallation the following spring. The plastic mulch, of course, cannot be reused unless you buy the heavier duty grade.

If weeds are allowed to get out of control, then the largest amount of the backyard market gardener's time will be spent hoeing and weeding instead of growing and selling. Weeding is without doubt the least glamorous of the market gardener's tasks. The only way to keep weeds from wasting a lot of your time is to stay ahead of them. Cultivating when the weeds are tiny, and doing it more often, will cut down on total hoeing time. One thing that really makes hand-hoeing easier and more enjoyable is a sharp hoe, so keep a flat file handy and touch up your blade each time you stop to rest.

8. Weeding Tools

Intervale Community Farm manager Tim Laird uses the colinear hoe for in-row weeding while Dylan Zietlan uses the REAL wheel hoe for pathways and between rows.

It takes about 20 minutes to hand hoe a 4- by 50-foot bed using a single-edge tool such as the swan neck or collinear hoe. With exact spacing it is possible to hoe both along the bed and across the bed in long, smooth strokes. Exact equidistant planting is very easy with the multi-dibble hole-maker; still, you have to lift the hoe and reposition it for each stroke. This is an up-and-down motion combined with a reach-and-pull that requires time. The hoe isn't very heavy, but the position of the body is tiring, sort of stoop-bend-stand-stoop. The advantage of the long-handled collinear hoe, developed by master gardener Eliot Coleman, is that you can stand upright while moving backward down the row, and hoe as you go.

In the beginning years of your market garden it may be necessary to hoe everything about every two weeks. That's 10 times per year. For a half-acre market garden that can take up to 120 hours total for the season. At $10 per hour, just weeding will cost $1,200 annually in labor per half-acre. This time can be cut by half, even two-thirds, with a combination system using a hand hoe, wheel hoe and the rotary tiller.

These efficient weed control systems rely on equally spaced, straight rows. It may be true that you can grow more corn in a crooked row, but it will take longer to hoe it. Determine the row spacing you want to use, then design your cultivation system to match.

The diamond-shaped scuffle hoe (my personal favorite of the hand-held cultivation tools) is a single-blade "push-pull" tool with cutting edges on both sides and sharpened tips. Use it like you do a vacuum cleaner, just scoot it back and forth just below the soil surface. It's good for getting under foliage and very close to plants. Keep in mind though that the tip is below the surface and out of sight, so it's very easy to nip a plant accidentally along with the weeds.

A similar push-pull tool is the stirrup hoe, sometimes called the oscillating hoe or scuffle hoe. This has two cutting edges so that you can run it just below the surface and sever weeds on the forward and back strokes. The hoe doesn't have to be lifted from the ground for repositioning, just drag it where you want it.

The stirrup hoe has a single blade that wraps in a U, like a stirrup. It is an "oscillating hoe" because the blade attaches to the handle with a fitting that allows the blade to swivel slightly in forward and reverse strokes. The practice is to scrub the hoe back and forth with the blade just below the soil surface. This nips off the small weeds without disturbing the soil too much. Weed seeds resting deeper in the soil are not brought to the surface where they can germinate.

The uprights of the stirrup U are not sharpened. These sides move foliage out of the way so the cutting edge can be brought close to young seedlings without injuring their roots.

The stirrup hoes and the diamond-shaped hoes are about 40 percent faster than the single-edge hoes. This is because of their ability to cut on the forward and reverse strokes and get close to the seedlings quickly.

For maintaining our field edges we use a combination of tools. In confined areas and around crops we use a gasoline-powered backpack type string trimmer. These are available at hardware stores and chainsaw dealers. For larger areas, especially for mowing cover crops, we use the DR Trimmer, the DR Brushcutter, or the BCS cutter bar mower. The DR Trimmer and Brushcutter are available from Country Home Products, Box 89 Ferry Road, Charlotte, VT 05445. They have large wheels and are fast, maneuverable, safe and easy to maintain. The BCS front mounted cutter bar fits on the BCS walk-behind tractors. They are available from BCS dealers nationwide. It is slower, but it will cut bigger materials and mow a wider path. It is also less expensive that other options, provided you already own the BCS walk-behind rotary tiller.

9. The Wheel Hoe

The REAL wheel hoe can be equipped with dual wheels for straddling rows. Photo courtesy Johnny's Selected Seeds.

The time for weeding can be reduced dramatically by investing in the ultimate market gardeners weeding weapon, the wheel hoe. One wheel hoe system is built around the REAL (pronounced ray-al) frame. It's a wheel hoe with a tool bar for attaching different cultivating tools. Manufactured by Berg in Sweden, the REAL system is designed for rapid weeding in loose, stone-free soil. They are available by mail-order from Johnny's Selected Seeds in Maine, or Peaceful Valley Farm Supply in California.

In its simple form it is a wheeled frame that holds a stirrup hoe that can be 5-, 8- or 13-inches wide. With attachments it can be converted to a dual wheel hoe that will straddle a row of small seedlings. Offset hoes can be attached for weeding two rows simultaneously.

The center-mounted stirrup hoe can weed a pathway up to 13 inches wide. Remove the center hoe and add the second wheel to straddle the rows. Use the 5- or 8-inch offset stirrup hoes to weed a path on each side of the row. The dual-wheeled version can be used until the plants are up to 6 inches high.

The stirrup hoe attachments on the REAL frame can be removed and replaced with either the goosefoot or the chevron hoe. These are useful for hoeing between rows of larger plants that are leafy near the ground such as lettuce.

The REAL Professional Wheel Hoe comes with adjustable handlebars to fit your height. The handlebars can be swung left or right, so you can walk beside the area you are cultivating. One disadvantage of the REAL stirrup hoe is its tendency to "plow" soil onto adjacent vegetables as the soil and weeds build up on the blade. To prevent this you need to use a push-pull action, clearing the build-up on the backstroke.

The complete REAL Professional Wheel Hoe system for market gardening costs nearly $500, but will pay for itself in the first season. This includes a hiller-furrower for trenching for potato planting, or laying irrigation drip tapes and plastic mulch or Reemay. With this system you will save time, weeding is easier and more enjoyable, and the increased yield will be very satisfying.

10. Maxidyne Speeder-Weeder

If you can't afford the $500 REAL Wheel Hoe system, you can still get wheel hoe speed and versatility with the Maxidyne Speeder-Weeder. It has a 9-inch hoe, fully adjustable handlebars, really light weight, and low price, about $90. An optional furrowing attachment adds about $20 to the price.

The unique shape of the cutting blade allows the operator to push forward smoothly without plowing soil on adjacent vegetables. This machine is very well crafted and an absolute delight to use. It is available from A.L. Johnson Mfg., Rt. 1 Box 815, Dept BMG, Pine River, Minnesota, 56474.

The author uses the Maxidyne Speeder Weeder in his Burlington garden. For low cost, light weight and super fast weeding between rows you can't beat it.

11. Rotary Tillers

There are nearly 100 companies world-wide that make rotary tillers and two-wheeled miniature farm tractors. The better ones can cost up to $5,000, with the less expensive ones being only a few hundred dollars.

Rotary tillers that cost less than $1,000 are usually front-tine tillers, meaning the tines are in front of the engine. They are not very effective in soil that is rocky or has heavy sod. They usually have a tilling width of nine to 16 inches. They usually have trailing wheels, and are very maneuverable, which is important in intensively planted gardens. With the trailing wheels it is easy to cultivate very shallowly between rows by pushing down on the handlebars to lift the tiller tines.

Left to right, Lightening chipper/shredder, Gardener's Supply rotary tiller and BCS rotary tiller in the test gardens at Gardener's Supply Company, Burlington.

Some rotary tillers have the tines mounted under the engine, with a parking and transport wheel in front. Most of these designs are Japanese. The Kubota and Honda models can till a path up to 36 inches wide. I used a 5-horsepower Kubota mid-mount for two years until I could afford a larger and more robust tiller. The smallest of these mid-mount tillers is the Gardener's Supply model, with a tilling path of only eight inches. It is my favorite in this size range and sells for less than $300. It is very useful for working inside the greenhouse or for cultivating narrowly planted rows.

Larger, mid-mounted models in the $1,000 to $1,500 range usually have a tilling width of 16 inches. Some of them can till up to 36 inches, with add-on tine sets. They are useful in the market garden, especially if the outer tines can be taken off to narrow the tiller for cultivating between rows. They are not particularly good at tilling rocky or sod bound soil. Often, you need several passes to prepare a fine seed bed. Because of the mid-mount configuration, the operator can't control the tilling depth. They usually dig in to their maximum depth of five or six inches. This limits their use for light cultivation. When you are cultivating you don't want to turn up the soil that deeply because it will often bring ready-to-sprout weed seeds to the surface.

For the market garden larger than 10,000 square feet, yet smaller than one acre, I'd recommend one of the more expensive and more powerful rear-tine tillers in the $1,500 to $2,000 range. I've used several different makes and models over the years. The American-made rear-tine tillers are not as expensive as the foreign makes, but often aren't as robust or sophisticated. Unlike the American models, almost all of the foreign models have multiple gears in forward and reverse and adjustable handlebars.

Most of the better rear-tine tillers have swinging handlebars, too. This allows you to walk beside the bed you are tilling. Also, you will need the hiller-furrower attachment. You will use this for making raised beds, furrowing for potato planting, hilling potatoes, sweet corn and leeks, and laying drip irrigation lines or making watering furrows.

Most of the rear-tine tillers I've owned or used have an annoying inability to till a clean path. The center of the path, between the inside tines, will not be tilled. This is particularly true with the Troy-Bilt, but it is noticeable in the Honda and Kubota rear-tine tillers as well.

You can improve their performance by having a 2-inch or 3-inch goosefoot plate welded to the depth gauge of the tiller. This add-on plate acts like a cultivating sweep as the tiller moves through the soil. It will plow the middle area, but won't leave it as smooth as you would like for planting fine seeds. The BCS tillers have a flanged depth gauge that automatically compensates for the spacing between the inside tines.

Another feature I like in the larger rotary tiller models is the steering clutches. These hand-operated clutches remove power from the wheel so you can guide the tiller more easily. They are especially useful for turning the tiller at the row ends. If you want to turn the tiller to the left, just remove power from the left wheel and let the right wheel power the turn. This is really helpful at row-end turnarounds and when you are tilling alongside crooked rows or plastic mulch.

After several years of moving through the ranks of power tiller sizes, I've graduated to the ultimate market gardener's companion, the BCS walking tractor system. The BCS walking tractor can handle any implement the gardener needs, with power to spare. It is manufactured in Italy and is available in this country through more than 1,500 dealers.

Tim Laird uses the BCS model 725 rotary tiller for fast weeding in 5 acres of mixed vegetables.

The BCS rotary tiller and walking tractor system is ideal for the backyard market gardener up to one full acre. Beyond one acre, the BCS makes a good companion tool to a farm tractor. We use our BCS almost daily for cultivating, bed forming, mowing field edges and preparing seedbeds.

The BCS Model 725 that we use has five forward speeds, and two reverse. The retail price is about $2,000. It has infinitely adjustable handles to fit the body size of everyone who works in our gardens. It has a lower center of gravity, and is very well balanced. It's easy to maneuver, and has more than enough power in its 8-horsepower gasoline engine to handle every chore we have given it.

We separate the growing beds with 24-inch paths. After the crops get too high for the cultivating tractor we use the BCS walk-behind tiller for cultivating paths. Early in the season we set the tiller to its maximum 26-inch width. As the crops grow we can narrow the tiller by removing the outside tines and readjusting the tiller hood. Spacing positions on the tiller are 16, 20, 24 or 26 inches. The 16-inch width is just right for cultivating between 24-inch rows of vegetables such as potatoes, sweet corn and leeks. After these crops are about 12 inches high we put on the hiller-furrow that pushes dirt up around the plants to anchor them and provide room for root growth.

With the tiller set at 1-inch depth we can cultivate in fourth gear. This is as fast, about 4 mph, as the average person can walk in soft ground comfortably. When the weeds get ahead of us and get too large for faster gears we can slow down to first or second gear. This slower speed, in the 1 or 2 mph range, allows the tines to really macerate the weeds.

It's a good idea to use a hood on the tiller. The more expensive tillers come with a hood, but you can easily make one from canvas or plywood. This will keep dust from kicking up on your vegetable crops. Many of the soil-borne fungal diseases can be spread this way. Also, it takes extra effort to wash produce that has had dirt pitched on it, especially lettuce.

In soft soil it's hard to keep the tiller from tilling too deeply. This pulverizes the soil needlessly, and brings buried weed seeds to the surface. To correct this problem we have a gauge wheel that fits into the depth gauge. This holds the tiller tines at about 1 inch depth, ideal for cultivating tiny weeds.

This gauge wheel is actually a transport wheel sold by the manufacturer. It's purpose is to hold the tiller off the ground while you are transporting the machine. To make the transport wheel into a gauge wheel just use a hacksaw or cutting torch to cut several inches out of the middle of the shank. Then weld the top and bottom back together. The gauge wheel will then position the tiller about 1-inch into the soil and prevent the tines from digging deeper.

The BCS system includes a wide range of implements that can be attached to the power take off (PTO) shaft. This PTO shaft runs from the engine, and provides power to the attachments. These attachments can be used for mowing, spraying, snowblowing, cutting brush, and chipping/shredding. There is a riding sulky for mowing, and for moving the machine long distances. We use this sulky to go from the barn to the fields and back.

Be careful with this sulky, though; there aren't any brakes on the machine. In fifth gear the tractor travels at 9 mph, even faster going downhill. BCS also makes a riding trailer you can use for transporting supplies and produce from the field to the barn. The trailer has brakes. A second, more expensive trailer is gear driven by the power take off (PTO) on the tractor. This unit equips your walking tractor with four wheel drive and is very useful in hauling heavy loads in soft soil or on slopes. It even has a dump bed for easy unloading.

In our gardens we use the BCS with the tiller attachment, the hiller-furrower and the 44-inch cutter bar. The cutter bar mows our roadways and keeps the saplings at bay around the field edges. There is a lot of power in that cutter bar, enough to cut 1-inch hardwood saplings. It even cuts irrigation hose and extension cords if you've a mind to use it for that.

The BCS Model 725, with the 26-inch adjustable tiller, 44-inch cutter bar, riding sulky, and hiller-furrower costs more than $2,500. In the small market garden it will take two or three years to recover this cost. If you amortize the machine over several years it will pay for itself each season. The unit is very well-built and will last for many years with proper care.

In a larger market garden the BCS system and the REAL Wheel Hoe system or Maxidyne Speeder-Weeder will pay for themselves in the first year. If you can eliminate one field worker the payroll savings alone will cover the cost of the equipment. Even if you don't eliminate a field worker you can be doing other things that are more profitable than hoeing weeds by hand all day.

12. When Your Garden Outgrows the Rotary Tiller

Once your backyard market garden grows beyond an acre or so in size you will want to buy a tractor. Tractors are a lot of fun. They are expensive, but in a larger market garden they will pay for themselves each season in not having to hire extra field workers.

They make tilling, cultivating and compost turning pleasant and less time-consuming. With a tractor-mounted sprayer you can get the bad guys easily and in a timely manner so you don't suffer crop losses. The mower can keep field edges from cropping up with weeds that will send seeds into your vegetable beds. Some of these weeds harbor pests, too.

91

Here in the Intervale we have two tractors for our 10 acres of vegetables. One is a 25-horsepower Kubota L2550 four-wheel drive, with a front-end loader. This unit costs about $15,000 new. We use it for tilling, brush hogging, mowing cover crops and weeds, laying plastic mulch and floating row covers and pulling the wagons. We also use it for turning and moving compost, and chasing our neighbor's cows out of our fields when they jump the fence.

We use the front bucket on the tractor for picking vegetables. We fill the bucket with water, add a jug of ice and turn it into a portable hydrocooler. A pallet-sized platform on the rear 3-point hitch is also a handy work and harvesting platform, smaller and more maneuverable than pulling a trailer or wagon for small jobs.

With this tractor we use a 48-inch rear-mounted rotary tiller to make raised beds. They are only raised about 4 inches, but it gives us a smooth planting surface and helps keep the bed spacing correct. This is important for using the tractor for cultivating. By reversing the wheel rims we are able to increase the wheel spacing to 45 inches. This works for straddling the beds until the vegetables are nearly full grown.

Our second tractor is a 20-horsepower Tuff-Bilt, made in Georgia. It's a modernized version of the Allis Chalmers Model G that was discontinued in 1956. These tractors have the gasoline engine mounted behind the seat. The framework for the tractor is very minimal, just enough to hold the wheels and seat and implements. This gives the operator an unobstructed view of the rows and plants.

Author and farmer Gene Logsdon describes these little tractors as looking like an arthritic spider. They are incredibly quick and efficient for high-speed cultivation, though. As an example, it takes four workers about half a day to hoe an acre of broccoli that is planted in 24-inch rows. The Tuff-Bilt can cultivate that acre in less than an hour. It sells for about $10,000.

Gardener's Supply president Will Raap using the TuffBilt to cultivate crops up to 24" high. Cultivator tines are adjustable for various row spaces.

The Tuff-Bilt has rear- and mid-mounted category "0" (garden tractor size) 3-point hitches. The mid-mounted cultivator has 8-inch sweeps. We use it for all of our crops, from 12-inch to 60-inch row spacings. The rear mounted cultivator has sweeps behind the wheels and extending out into the path between the beds. These sweeps loosen the compaction from wheel tracks and hoe the weeds between the beds.

The tractor has a hydrostatic transmission with infinite speed variability, from a slow crawl to a fast walk. The road speed for transporting is about 10 mph.

With its 24-inch ground clearance and 50-inch wheel track we can straddle beds until the crops are nearly mature. For taller crops like corn and trellised tomatoes we alternate beds of low crops and high crops. This way we can straddle a low crop bed while harvesting or spraying the adjacent high crop.

The Tuff-Bilt has a mid-mount 60-inch mower. We use it for mowing cover crops, field edges and driveways. We also have a 25-gallon spray tank with a 3-bed boom and a spray wand for spot spraying. In easy ground the tractor can also pull a single-bottom plow or a 3-foot rotary tiller, though we don't use it for that.

The TuffBilt can be equipped with a 25 gallon sprayer tank and a 3-bed spray boom. In this picture Tim Laird is spot-spraying potato beetles with the hand held wand.

For harvesting we mount two platforms, one on the rear and one on the mid-mounted three point hitches. Each platform is 36- by 48-inches. We can also pull a trailer or hay wagon for larger harvests.

Kubota, John Deere and Ford all make offset cultivating tractors in the 20-hp range. These offset tractors have the engine in front, but off center from the line of view, so the operator can see the crops. All of these companies have stopped selling the offsets in the United States. The market for these specialty tractors apparently isn't large enough to warrant the cost of the manufacturing facility and sales force for these specialty models.

*Platforms mounted on front and rear three point hitches
make the TuffBilt a dandy harvesting rig.*

One manufacturer, Case-International Harvester, is still
making offsets. The Case-IH units are gear-driven. They are
not nearly as fast or nimble as the Tuff-Bilt, with its
hydrostatic transmission and short turning radius. But, the
Case-IH is still a very useful tractor for the market gardener
who has outgrown the walk-behind rotary tillers.

Another alternative for a cultivating tractor is to find a used
Allis Chalmers G or one of the other used offset tractors from
Ford, John Deere or Kubota. The "G" can be purchased for
$1,000 to $3,000 depending on condition. The later model used
offset tractors in good condition will cost around $7,000 to
$12,000.

Used garden tractors such as this Farmall can often be purchased for less than $2,000. However, they often don't have a three point hitch or power take off, thus limiting their usefulness for market gardening.

13-14. How To Install Plastic Mulch and Floating Row Covers

Plastic mulch is lightweight, and easy to install. It needs to be anchored in the ground on each side of the growing bed. Use a twine to get a straight line, and the furrower on the wheel hoe to make a trench about 3 inches deep. The furrower throws dirt in both directions. By bending the left wing parallel to the shank you can turn the furrower into a plow. It will leave a vertical edge on the left and throw the loose soil to the right.

Push the plow down the right side of the bed making the first furrow. Then, measure over 42 inches – this leaves three inches of plastic mulch on each side of the bed to be buried. Reset your twine and make another furrow on the opposite side of the bed. Make the furrow by plowing forward with the bed on your LEFT. The vertical edge is on the left, closest to the bed, and the loose dirt pushes to the right.

After forming the furrows, unroll the plastic mulch to the end of the bed and anchor it. Then walk back and snug the sides into the furrow and backfill the loose soil in several places to hold it tight. Use the wheel hoe with plow attachment to backfill the length of both furrows. Do this by simply plowing forward with the bed on your RIGHT side, thus throwing the loose dirt back into the furrow to cover the edges of the plastic mulch.

We are developing an attachment for our BCS rotary tiller to open the furrows for laying plastic mulch. This is a square tube mounted behind the tiller. It has two plows 24 inches apart. One throws soil to the right, the other to the left. We just drive the tiller down the paths, making two furrows as we go.

Use this retrofitted plow attachment to make furrows along each side of several beds. Then lay the plastic mulch over the bed and walk back along the beds kicking dirt into the furrows to anchor the plastic in several places. Then reverse the plows on the BCS, set them 20 inches apart, and drive back along the pathway throwing dirt over the furrows that are holding the plastic. Two people and a BCS Walking Tractor should be able to install plastic mulch on one acre of beds in less than a day with this system.

Floating row covers are designed to protect plants from cool temperatures but they can also help control insect infestations. To install floating row covers follow the same procedure as for plastic mulch, but leave an inch of space between the buried edge of the black plastic mulch and the row cover. Then when you pull the row cover up in a few weeks it will not dislodge the plastic mulch. The row cover should "float," so don't make it too tight over the bed.

Weeds will grow in the 1-inch space between the mulch and the row cover. When you pull the row cover up you can use the hand-held stirrup hoe to get very close to the edge of the plastic mulch. The rounded side of the stirrup hoe will not tear into the plastic mulch as would happen with open face hoes.

15. 'Flame Thrower'

Another tool you might find useful for weeding is the "flame thrower" which is gaining popularity with larger growers for killing weeds as they germinate. It is used over the beds just before the crop seeds germinate.

These commercial machines require a tractor and they are expensive, often costing thousands of dollars. However, in small areas the backyard market gardener can use a hand-held propane torch. A spreader nozzle flares the flame so you can treat a 4-inch to 6-inch band.

Simply tape the torch to a hoe handle and walk down the rows with the flame held just above ground level. The flame only has to touch the weeds for a split second. Weeds won't die immediately, but within hours they will wilt and fall over. I find this technique most useful in weeding carrot rows before the carrots germinate. The carrots take as long as three weeks to germinate, and during that time you could get two or three generations of weeds and grasses sprouting. The flame thrower will solve this problem.

It's only necessary to flame a 6-inch path along each carrot row. The rest of the bed can be weeded with the wheel hoe. The flame weeder only works when the weeds are small. Anything taller than one inch will not get hot enough to die, or it will take you too long to stand there holding the flame on it.

For larger plantings there is a commercial version of the hand-held flame thrower called the Red Dragon. It comes as a kit containing a 3-foot handle and torch and hose with fittings. All you have to add is the 30-gallon propane tank that you can rent or buy from the local gas dealer.

The tank can be carried in one hand while you aim the wand with the other. Or you can buy or build a small dolly to hold the tank. The Red Dragon puts out a lot of heat, up to 2,000 degrees F. It's available from Vey Sales, Pittsburgh, Pa.

The propane torch has lots of other uses, too. You can sterilize animal cages and thaw frozen pipes. Farmer and writer George DeVault says, "The torch is ideal for destroying wasp nests and zapping multiflora rose sprouts in fencerows. Easy to set house on fire, too. Be careful."

With a pointed flame tip you can walk along the plastic mulch and burn holes in the plastic for transplants. This only takes a split second. With a light touch, you can make 1- or 2-inch diameter holes.

These seared edges are less apt to allow wind to rip the plastic. This method is much faster than making slits for transplants. If you make the holes too large, though, weed seeds will germinate around your plants. This creates extra work for you because these weeds will have to be pulled by hand. If you have installed plastic drip tape under the plastic mulch be sure not to burn holes in it as you are making transplant holes.

CHAPTER 4:

Marketing Is The Fun Part Do It First and Do It Right

We all have competition, that's the nature of things. You can outsmart your competition, though, if you give your customers a really compelling reason to buy from you. One compelling sales tool is the ability to state that you grow everything organically. Each year organic food becomes more popular. Customers will turn down your vegetables for a lot of reasons, but I have yet to have a customer refuse to buy because the product was organic!

Many small-scale agriculturists are growing crops organically. They don't like using synthetic insecticides, herbicides and fertilizers. Reasons include ease of selling contaminant-free produce and a huge market for organically grown produce.

Nationwide, organic growers make up only about 1 percent to 3 percent of the farming population, depending on which survey you happen to be reading. So, in any particular market area you can eliminate up to 97 percent of your close competition simply by being organic.

Why does organic produce command a higher price in the marketplace? One major reason is the lack of chemical contamination from potentially carcinogenic sprays. Another reason is the increasing national awareness of dietary and medical problems associated with eating food that is inferior in nutritional value. This creates a significant degree of demand that so far has out-stripped the supply. Mostly, however, organic food commands a higher price because it's just plain better! Better for the soil, better for the farmer, better for the customer, period.

Within our lifetime it is conceivable that all farmers will grow crops organically. More states each year are passing "chemical ban" laws. I can imagine a time in our future when the word *farmer* will become synonymous with *good* once again.

The same 92 nutrients and trace elements required for healthy soil are also needed to help build healthy plants. Many of these 92 elements help build healthy cells in the human body. We are what we eat. If we have a truly healthy diet, and live in a healthy environment, we will have a healthy body.

What is really compelling about organic food is not only its enhanced flavor, but its ability to help regenerate the human body. A clean diet can help cleanse the body of many accumulated pollutants. According to David Steinman, author of *Diet For A Poisoned Planet* (Harmony Books), a safe diet over an extended period can result in improved health. It can result in a 70 percent reduction in DDT residues and a 90 percent reduction in PCB residues that have become lodged in the human body.

As a general rule, organic food sells for a higher price than conventionally grown food. At some point in the future, organic produce will become more of a mainstream item, and the pricing differences may become less noticeable. For that to happen we need a national shift of interest in large numbers of mainstream markets and consumers.

When this shift occurs, more growers will start producing consistent and reliable supplies of organic fruits and vegetables. The supermarkets will find it an easier task to replace conventional produce on the display shelves. Once consumers see this greater availability and more moderate pricing they will start buying more volume. This shift is already underway. Supermarkets are starting to stock more gourmet items and more organic vegetables and fruits, and even organic and free-range meats and poultry.

Meanwhile, organic growers cannot produce enough to satisfy existing market demand. Therefore, it behooves us to charge as much as the traffic will bear, without gouging. By continually showing the profit potential in organic farming we will encourage others to follow our lead. This will increase consumer awareness, and increase demand for organic produce even further. This trend will continue to gain momentum as we are able to prove a consistently higher degree of monetary sustainability and a significant return on investment for organic farmers.

So, the real difference in price between organic and chemically grown produce is a question of supply, demand and production costs. The organic supplies infrastructure will grow large enough to achieve the economies of scale presently available to chemical food producers. This will allow the higher costs of production for organic farmers to come down.

For example, organic fertilizers are only available from just a few mail order houses. The cost of the fertilizer isn't very high, but the cost of shipping a few bags is quite expensive. In small orders of a ton or less, the shipping costs are apt to be equal to or greater than the actual cost of the fertilizer.

To the average consumer it may appear that organic produce is far more costly. We need to take the time to explain to people the real cost of less expensive chemically grown vegetables.

When you look at the whole picture, you begin to realize that we as a nation of tax payers are footing the bill for massive environmental clean-up projects. Our grossly prohibitive health care costs are partially the result of using chemical pesticides and fertilizers. Only a portion of these costs directly relate to food production practices, but they are still the *real* costs of conventional food production. Thinking in these terms makes it clear that seemingly overpriced organic foods may indeed be a bargain.

Another big reason that organically grown produce can command a higher price is *flavor*. Consumers and marketers alike are becoming increasingly aware that vegetables from organically managed soils taste superior, usually have a healthier sheen, and often last longer in the refrigerator. For example, Don Wilson of Wilson Farms in East Lexington, Massachusetts, claims that his winter squash grown in compost-treated soil will keep up to two months longer before spoiling.

Why this increase in flavor and storage life? Because the successful organic farmer's soil is healthy and well balanced. The plants can extract the nutritional elements they need for optimal growth.

Marketing is the Fun Part – Do It First and Do It Right

You may be tempted to try planting the garden first, then finding customers. That is risky. When your vegetables ripen you want to know, right now, where to deliver them.

Think of market gardening as a system that has three major components; business planning, operations planning, and market planning. Your choice of a marketing system will affect how your business and operations planning will shape up. You need to have some idea of how you will market your crops before you can start planning what crops you will grow.

Growth of any business can only come about by the wise investment of capital. This investment money is only available because you or your financial source have previously earned a profit from a business enterprise. Profit is not a thing to be avoided. It is the only way that any business, large or small, has the impetus to grow to its full potential. If marketing what you grow is not profitable, your business will not be economically sustained.

Your choice of marketing methods will have a direct influence on the continuing profitability of your enterprise. This book describes 11 marketing systems that can be used to create a successful market garden business.

1. Community Supported Agriculture

2. Clientele Membership Club

3. Food Buyers Club – Membership Garden

4. Home Deliveries

5. Farm Stands

6. Roadside Stands

7. Farmers Markets

8. Pick Your Own Farms

9. Restaurants and Specialty Stores

10. Brokers, Supermarkets and Food Processors

11. Producers Cooperatives

Find Your Niche

Some of these 11 marketing options will fit your circumstances, others won't. Most successful market gardeners use more than one marketing outlet, and often cut and paste ideas from one method to another.

To be successful, the small-scale agriculturist needs to avoid directly competing with the large commercial growers. Most market gardens are too small to compete effectively in the wholesale markets. But, each of us has a profitable market niche in our local or regional community that we can fill. All we need to do is find that niche. If we can fill it properly, it will be profitable.

Filling a niche properly often requires us to become marketers. We see examples of aggressive marketing every day as we travel about our daily business. Multi-national conglomerates use elaborate advertisements and catchy phrases or jingles to grab our attention long enough for them to make their pitch. This type of advertising is not usually appropriate for small-scale farmers.

Creative marketing, however, is very appropriate and very valuable. Tastefully done advertising or promotion lets potential customers know that something unusual and potentially beneficial to them is happening and that they should stop in and check it out. A good example would be to dress up like a vegetable or a cute animal, and stand by the farm stand waving at passersby. Yes, a five-foot tall walking tomato is guaranteed to grab people's attention.

The successful market gardener or small-scale farmer will use creative and tasteful promotions to bring in new customers. Do whatever you can to increase demand for your produce, without resorting to flim flam. Fancy marketing gimmicks will not bring customers back a second time. Only superior produce, a friendly atmosphere, and undeniable quality throughout your operation will cause customers to be anxious to return week after week and year after year.

Always impress upon your customers how valuable you feel they are. Let them know how much you rely on them to spread the word about your farm. Word-of-mouth is the best and least expensive means of advertising you can use.

Select your marketing system, build your core group of satisfied and loyal customers, then expand gradually from there. Plan your business for the future. Let each customer feel that you plan to be here for a long time, and that you want them to be here right by your side all the way.

Keep your customers informed about what to expect as the season progresses. Even to the point of modest educational programs geared to teach flavor differences between early, mid, and late season varieties, aas well as preparation and cooking methods.

Frequent contact is useful to keep established customers aware of the changing seasons and new crops. Don't lose touch with your customers over the winter. Use your newsletter, or keep the local newspapers informed of your various activities so they can give you a mention occasionally.

Use community oriented functions to keep your public image alive and of interest. Host school tours for children, and give them a free goodie to take home to mom and dad. You can bet that if the kids like your garden they'll bring their folks back to see it.

Host a cookout each season and invite the press and other community leaders. Enter a float in the local July 4th parade, or enter an exhibit in the county fair. Do whatever it takes to keep your farm or market garden in the public eye from month to month.

Find out where your competition is, but don't spend too much time worrying about how much business they are taking away from you. Whether it's a supermarket or grocery store or the roadside stand across town, they have marketing problems and limiting factors just as you do.

Use them as your best sales tool. Don't speak badly of them, just gently point out the advantages you have to offer. Show your customers the differences in quality, freshness, flavor and freedom from chemicals. Promote what you perceive to be the real advantages of your produce as compared to the competitor's.

Customers really do appreciate these differences, and will pay higher prices to buy something wholesome and good for their families. Just be sure that you don't claim what isn't true. Customers are becoming more well informed each year, so treat them as you would like to be treated and you'll do just fine.

Your marketing strategy may be a card table in the front yard, or a space right in the middle of the busiest farmers market in a major city. Wherever the location, you need to pay attention to pricing. Only display prices directly with the produce, or behind it.

If your customers see a roadside sign listing your dozen ears of sweet corn at 50 cents more than the supermarket, they may not stop. They may think your prices are too expensive. If they see how fresh and tasty and delightful your corn looks, then notice the higher price, they won't be as reluctant to buy from you.

If your prices are higher than your competition you want your customers to know why. Let them justify in their minds that your prices are reasonable. Don't be afraid of pricing your produce somewhat on the high side. If the quality and freshness and flavor are there the customer will pay the price gladly, and come back next week for more.

Give prices by the unit whenever possible. Unit pricing makes the check-out move a lot quicker. The process of weighing each item at the check-out counter is slow. If you have several customers lined up it's important that you handle them quickly and efficiently. Even when there is plenty of time you still want to be free to talk about and show other varieties to the customer. This attention to people and their needs will help you increase sales.

For certain vegetables and fruits, keep the quantities small. Per unit pricing of a pound of snow peas, for example, may be as high as $4. This will cause customers to be reluctant to buy. It is better to offer such items in more manageable units, such as a quarter pound for $1.

Same thing applies to strawberries, blueberries, and raspberries. Sell pints instead of quarts. A very real advantage of this method is that customers will pay more for two individual pints than they will for one quart. Even if the price difference is slight, it will add up over the course of a season. If you are in a market with a lot of single-person households you might even consider selling berries in half-pint containers.

Selling sweet corn by the dozen will allow you to sell more volume, but at a lower price. You will be doing many of your customers a favor by selling items in smaller units. Individuals and smaller families particularly will not be able to use a dozen ears of corn before the remaining few ears turn starchy and lose flavor. Better to have your customers come more frequently for smaller orders each time. Don't sell them so much that they can't use it up before it loses flavor. Besides, if they come more often to your stand you have more opportunities to build a positive relationship with them, and to sell them other things.

Building this special positive relationship with the customer is really what marketing is all about. As you get to know them better you focus on their needs. This gives you the chance to grow specialty crops that are in demand, and to show your customers that you really do care about what they want or need.

The really successful market gardener will want to use a combination of the various marketing outlets described in this book. Individual success will depend on the site-specific circumstances of the garden and the community.

What most of us will wind up doing is selecting the elements from each strategy that best suits our personality, our garden space and our goals. By carefully meshing these diverse elements into a cohesive whole, you will create a program that is successful, profitable, fun and satisfying. It will provide a real service to your community, and help you achieve your personal goals.

As you start to prepare your initial business plan or expand an existing one, you may find limiting factors that preclude certain market strategies. Or, you may want to grow your business in a particular direction for personal reasons.

As you talk to interested parties in your community you may discover a definite need for a particular marketing system. Look for the niche that you feel will be exceptionally fun and profitable for you. Let your imagination roam through the possibilities, and keep an open mind. Be receptive to new ideas. You can create a new marketing system that will give you a tremendous advantage over the competition.

After selecting the marketing strategies that appeal to you, prepare a sample business plan for each system. Make these plans complete with preliminary income and expense budgets. You may find the potential net profits are much more attractive in one system than in others.

Don't be afraid to ask questions, and always canvass people for their input. They may try to discourage you; at least your friends and family probably will. It is normal for our families to want to try to protect us and keep us from making mistakes.

You can rely on strangers to be more objective, and critical, of your plan. If you get six out of a dozen people who are thrilled with your idea and want to sign up right away, then go for it. Let yourself have some fun along the way, too.

You can develop a core group of customers who shop daily or at least weekly at your farm stand or farmers market booth. They will buy a continuing stream of products, week after week and year after year. Concentrate most of the marketing efforts in the first year. The goal is to attract and satisfy a core group of customers for your business. Your core group can be made up of neighbors, farmers market customers, or commercial clients. It just depends on the marketing outlet you are trying to access. Old-time marketing advice is that 20 percent of your customers will buy 80 percent of your produce. Spend your marketing time and money to attract and satisfy that top 20 percent of your customers.

Always remember that the business you are really in is that of building and maintaining relationships. By forming a loyal core group the small-scale farmer can expand his or her business through the simple expedient of word of mouth advertising. This is the cheapest and most effective form of business promotion available to any company, particularly a start-up.

You will need to work hard at locating and maintaining this core group of loyal customers. Pay careful attention to continually satisfying them. Then the business can grow smoothly and seemingly effortlessly. The best part of the garden business from a marketing standpoint is that everybody can become your customer. If they like your produce, your neighbors, friends, and even strangers from across town, can become your best sales people.

There is an unending supply of customers for your business, everybody has to eat, and you are selling food. All you have to do is provide a quality product at a reasonable price. Satisfy your core group and they will help ensure the continued growth and success of your business.

Direct Marketing: Subscription or Retail?

Direct marketing generally means that the producer sells directly to the consumer, without benefit of middlepersons or wholesale outlets. Until recently this term was not normally applied to vegetable growers, but the name fits. If you are producing vegetable crops and selling them directly to the household that will consume them then you are reaping all the value of your productivity. According to the US Department of Agriculture, American farmers are now receiving less than 24 cents of each food dollar. By selling directly, you can get all of it. With no truckers, warehouses, or brokers to pay, you get to pocket all of the profits.

Subscription Direct Marketing

Subscription Direct Marketing occurs when the customer agrees in advance to buy a share of your output for the whole season. In this system the consumer pays a membership or share fee, usually up-front. Often the member helps with the actual farm work at intensive times such as planting or harvesting. Some examples of subscription marketing are:

• **Community Supported Agriculture (CSA) Farms** This is a membership garden or farm in which families agree to pay a seasonal fee to share in the harvest. The families become partners, sharing the risks and the rewards with the farmer. Usually the payment is several hundred dollars and the family will receive enough vegetables to last them throughout the season and sometimes for winter storage. Often, the share price is payable before the season starts, in one or several installments. Calculate the share prices to cover the production costs of the garden, including the salary of the gardener. Usually, food prices are below retail price, but the customers pick up their food weekly at the farm, saving transportation costs for the gardener. "Membership Gardening," the smaller version of CSA, fits in this category, too.

• **Clientele Membership Club** Families pay a membership fee for the privilege of coming to your garden and picking produce when it is ready. Usually, the fee is $25 or $50 annually, and the customers pay by the pound for what they pick.

• **Food Buyers Clubs** Again, families pay an annual membership fee to join, usually $25 to $50. Then the gardener takes the food to a central receiving point for pickup by the club members. Usually the club members fill out an order form each week.

• **Home Deliveries** The garden farmer delivers the groceries to individual homes and gets paid for each trip. Often the customer pays a membership fee, and calls in a weekly order. In some cases this can be a membership garden or CSA farm with individual home deliveries.

Retail Direct Marketing

Here, the grower sells direct to the consumer and can expect to receive retail prices, sometimes even more than retail. Some examples of retail direct marketing are:

• **Farm Stands** They can be as simple as a card table or picnic table in front of your house under a shade tree or as fancy as a large retail outlet, complete with walk-in cooler, greenhouse and outdoor display areas.

• **Roadside Stands** Similar to a farm stand, but often located on a busy street removed from your garden. This can be as simple as selling from the tailgate at a wide spot in the road.

• **Farmers Markets** The garden farmer harvests the produce and brings it to a central location to join with other farmers in selling to a broad audience, usually in a nearby city or large town.

• **Pick Your Own (PYO) Farms** In the PYO system the customer does the harvesting and packing in exchange for lower than retail prices. PYO is not always suitable for the backyard market gardener. Unless you have a large planting, and not enough time or labor to pick crops yourself, you're better off without PYO sales.

Wholesale Direct Marketing

Wholesale Direct Marketing occurs when the grower sells produce at less than retail prices to large-volume buyers. This can be further broken down into premium wholesale and low wholesale. The difference has to do with the price the buyer is willing to pay, and the specialty varieties they are willing to buy. Examples are:

• **Restaurants and specialty stores** – Premium wholesale

• **Brokers, supermarkets and food processors** – Low wholesale

• **Producers Cooperatives** – Low wholesale

Membership Garden Farms

Can a Community Supported Farm Work for You?

Your first reaction to the need to sell excess produce from your garden may be to put a card table and a cigar box in your front yard. Before you dust off the card table and look for a board to make up a sign, though, give a thought to another possibility. Look across the fence, in both directions, and consider what your non-gardening neighbors do when they want fresh vegetables during the season.

Do they drive across town to the supermarket and hope that the vegetables they buy are fresh, tasty and healthful? Do they go downtown and buy from the natural foods store at silly prices? Maybe they drive out to the country to a farm stand once or twice a week.

If you aren't sure, then go ask them. You might find that your neighbors have all but given up the hope of ever tasting fresh, flavorful vegetables and fruits again. They might be delighted to walk over to your place every day or so and buy fresh vegetables directly from your garden.

Because of the convenience, freshness, and flavor, they may even be willing to pay you 10 percent or so *more* than what they would have paid at the supermarket. The market gardener can justify the extra charge. The customer will receive freshness, flavor and lack of chemical contamination. The gardener will make repeated trips daily to the garden to pick things as the customer wants them.

You can generate plenty of profits even if you charge less than the supermarkets. You won't have any spoilage from over-picking. There isn't the expense of running a stand or making deliveries. Considering these savings you will still be well ahead of the game, even if your pricing is 10 or 20 percent less than retail.

Think this idea over for a minute and see if it might fit your situation. What could possibly be wrong with getting a group of your friends and neighbors together to support your new market garden? The name for this marketing system is Membership Gardening. The more sophisticated title is Community Supported Agriculture (CSA). Whatever you chose to call it, it works.

All you need is to get some neighborhood folks together, find out what veggies they want you to grow and in what quantities. Figure out how much it will cost you to grow and distribute these crops. Then divide that cost by the number of shareholders you have recruited. This becomes the individual share price that each member will pay.

Distribution of food from this membership garden can be handled in several ways. The members can pick up their produce at the garden. Or, the gardener can deliver pre-bagged shares to a central receiving point such as a church or community center. Sometimes, the gardener charges a larger service fee and delivers individual shares to the member's homes. The main difference is the final cost to the shareholders. The share cost will be higher when the gardener provides more service.

Sell It <u>Before</u> You Sow It!

From the vegetable grower's point of view the best part of this membership gardening system is that you can ask the members to pay you in advance. This can be in one sum or in payments. This idea is so unusual that I'll say it again. The *customers pay you in advance*, a predetermined amount equivalent to the quantity of produce they expect to receive from you over the course of the season.

It's easy to understand membership gardening. This system can be as small as a gardener and a non-gardener coming together to grow food where they live. The non-gardener pays the expenses of the garden, and the gardener grows the food. They share the produce equally, and both parties benefit.

To understand the theory and principle of membership gardening it will be useful for us to explore the history of Community Supported Agriculture (CSA). This marketing system originated in Switzerland and first arrived in the United States in 1985. There is not yet a national or world directory of CSA farms, so it's hard to tell just how many are in operation.

Robyn Van En is co-founder of one of the first CSA's in the U.S., located in South Egremont, Mass. She has kept records of people who have contacted her, and feels that in 1991 there were at least 100 CSA projects in Western Europe and Japan, with another 100 or more in North America. Her estimate for 1992 is 400 in North America. Robyn predicts that by 1993 there will be more than 1,000 CSA farms in the United States alone.

Currently, these farms are in nearly every state of the union and the number is increasing each year. They range in size from a few dozen members, up to several hundred. Examples of small CSA garden farms are the 32-member community supported garden at Dixon, Montana, and the 25-member Snow-Baker Farm in Marshfield, Vt. Larger CSA farms include the 150-household Intervale Community Farm in Burlington, Vt., the 500-member CSA near Zurich, Switzerland, and the 1000 member CSA in Japan that employees 14 farmers.

Robyn Van En is a national leader in the Community Supported Agriculture movement. Not only did she help start an early CSA in this country, but over the past several years she has given talks and lectures all over the country about the experience.

She has compiled a booklet describing the CSA idea, and has helped produce a video of the CSA at her Indian Line Farm. Her experience shows what can be done when a gardener and community members pool their resources in a cooperative farming enterprise.

When requesting Robyn's booklet remember to enclose $10 to cover cost of handling and mailing. If you like the CSA marketing system, ask about purchasing a copy of her video *It's More Than Just Vegetables*.

Another book that provides excellent philosophical and how-to information for CSA farming is *Farms of Tomorrow* by Trauger Groh and Steve McFadden. This book is available from Bio-Dynamic Farming and Gardening Association in Kimberton, Pa. The Bio-Dynamic group also publishes a very useful brochure about CSA farming. Be sure to ask for it when you order the CSA book.

Intervale Community Farm

Burlington, Vt.

We place great emphasis on human-scale agricultural systems that truly serve the needs of the farmer and the community. Our goal is to put the community back in farming, and the farmer back in the community.
-Andy Lee, 1990

The Intervale Community Farm began in 1989 as a backyard market garden with 12 families buying a share in the harvest. This garden was started by employees of Gardener's Supply Co., in Burlington, Vt. In October 1989, Gardener's Supply sponsored an all-day conference entitled: *"COMMUNITY SUPPORTED AGRICULTURE: Feeding Ourselves In the 21st Century"*. More than 100 food producers, distributors, and consumers attended. They were all interested in sharing knowledge and developing ideas to help create a new vision of Vermont's agricultural future.

The outcome of this conference was a plan to increase the size and scope of the Intervale Community Farm. The original 12 member families set about creating a new organic vegetable farm on land leased from the city of Burlington. The membership increased to 92 households in 1990, and to 150 households in 1992. Each share costs $295. Often, two households will share a share.

The result of this happy marriage of farmer and neighbors is that the farmer gets a guaranteed salary and the shareholding members get fresh, home-grown organic vegetables. The produce is ripe, full of flavor and nutritional value. The farmer benefits not only from the guaranteed market for everything grown, but also from becoming an integral part of the local community.

The initial members of the Intervale Community Farm CSA came from just two sources; the nearby Gardener's Supply Company and the congregation of the local Quaker Church. These members show concern for the environment and their quality of life. They have been willing to put in the time and effort necessary to expand the enrollment of the farm to a self-supporting level.

Intervale Community Farm's greatest success in recruiting, other than word-of-mouth, has been by using a 1-page flyer inserted in the *Vermont Times*, a local weekly newspaper. This paper has a circulation in Chittenden County of about 40,000. The farm core group decided to concentrate the flyers in the areas nearest the farm, a target audience of about 8,000 households.

The cost of printing and inserting the flyers came to $450 for 8,000 copies. We did three insertions over a 6-week period. Response was immediate, with nearly 50 new families joining the farm. These three insertions cost the farm $1350. The 50 families that joined paid $295 per share, for a total of $14,750. The flyer also makes an excellent poster for putting up on bulletin boards around town.

The Intervale Community Farm has a 7-member core group that helps the farmer manage the farm. Each core group member takes charge of a component of the farm management. The farmer handles operational management, scheduling and field management. The administrative committee handles hiring and paying the farmer and interns. The logistical committee handles the distribution of food, and the scheduling of farm chores that involve the members. The recruiting committee keeps expanding the membership. The communications committee handles the monthly newsletter. The financial committee keeps the books and makes out the checks that pay for supplies and payroll.

This core group meets once monthly to tend to the business of the farm. It sets policy and gives whatever assistance is necessary to the farmer. This model operates very much like a corporation board of directors, except that decisions are made by consensus. It serves as a representative of the shareholder group, and as a guide to the farmer. Its primary interest is to see the farm become financially and socially successful.

The CSA internship program is one of several learning opportunities connected with Intervale Community Farm. Community leaders, educators, landowners, and interested farmers have toured the site to gather ideas for similar projects planned in other locations.

One key element in the success of this new farm has been the Intervale Intern Program. We have joined hands with the University of Vermont's College of Agriculture to train interns and help them earn credits for a degree in Alternative Agriculture. Each student receives a salary and earns up to 15 credit hours per season.

Intern Tony Brunetti watering seedlings in the Intervale Community Farm's 12- by 30-foot Sun Tunnel greenhouse.

The direction of the Intervale Community Farm is to serve as a resource center and demonstration farm. We place great emphasis on human-scale agricultural systems that truly serve the local community. The CSA cooperatives are a great beginning in our newly emerging sustainable agriculture industry.

To quote Gardener's Supply president Will Raap:

> *America along with the rest of the world needs to move quickly to a more sustainable agriculture that doesn't abuse our soil and water resources, or our farm populations. We think Community Supported Agriculture is an ideal way to create this transition.*

Sample CSA Budgets

	Covelo, CA	Burlington, VT	Ann Arbor, MI	Kimberton, PA
INCOME				
Price/Share or total $ in shares	30 @ $325	105 @ $295	$30,192	$37,500
Sales from dairy	—	—	—	$1,000
Interest	—	—	—	$350
TOTAL INCOME	$9,750	$30,975	$30,192	$38,850
EXPENSES				
Farmer	$8000	$13,417	$15,171	$14,500
Apprentices	$500	$6720	$1200	$3900
FICA	—	$1529	$1,959	$1,250
Insurance (worker's compensation)	—	$1,480	$2,165	$1,780
Rent	—	$300	$4,000	$2,600
Utilities	—	—	—	$1,470
Office	$55	—	$360	$500
Organic certification	$75	$100	—	—
Seeds and/or plants	$200	$500	$500	$1,800
Potting Soil/Propagation Equip.	$400	$350	—	—
Well/Irrigation	—	—	$850	—
Irrigation equip. depreciation	$75	$500	—	—
Greenhouse	—	$900	—	—
Tools, maintenance, and repair	$75	$200	$900	$2,500
Tillage/maintenance for horses	$250	—	—	—
Fertilizers	—	$582	$485	$1,000
Season extenders	$95	$100	$210	—
Sprays	—	$200	—	—
Compost	$25	—	—	—
Equip. and/or equip. rental	—	$1,800	$1,700	$350
Fuel	—	$300	$435	$500
Capital payment	—	$1,397	—	$4,500
Communication & distribution	—	$600	$275	—
TOTAL EXPENSES	$9,750	$30,975	$30,210	$36,650

The Philosophy of Community Supported Agriculture

Community Supported Agriculture has a philosophy of socially and ecologically responsible agriculture. The farmers and the shareholders feel a need to treat the earth and ourselves in a user friendly fashion. We do not want to use chemicals or intensive tilling practices that will degenerate the soil. Instead, wherever possible, we want to use organic and biodynamic practices that will enrich the soil and, in turn, enrich our own lives.

In addition, we have a genuine desire to grow food for our fellow humankind. We want to know personally the people who are eating the produce we raise. The conventional marketplace does not have an established niche for this class of agricultural entrepreneur, so we look to the Community Supported Farm for a model of social sustainability.

In turn, the consumer shareholders have the opportunity to know the farmer who produces their food. They can share in the regeneration of the earth and their bodies through the raising and consumption of naturally grown produce. These members often come to feel that the farm is "theirs." They enjoy coming to the farm for field days and to help with intensive planting and harvesting chores. They look forward to coming together socially in a relaxed atmosphere, close to nature and their families and friends.

To understand Community Supported Agriculture we must first recognize that the conventional food industry doesn't give a hoot about the family farmer or the consumer. Conventional agriculture practices have absolutely driven small-scale farmers to a cash crop monoculture. To pay back borrowed capital, farmers have to use high performance practices, often at the expense of their land, health, and quality of life.

It is important for the potential community farmer to diversify all capitalization and crop risk over the numbers of a committed consumer group. In conventional models the farmer has always born the total risk. With membership gardening and CSA farming the consumers are accepting part of that risk.

The result of this cooperation of farmer and consumer in the CSA model is that everyone has the satisfaction of becoming part of the solution. They no longer have to remain part of the problem. It brings the community back to farming, and the farmer back to the community. The public needs to know where their food comes from and the amount of work, knowledge, and capital investment it takes to be a farmer today. The farmers need to know that someone cares, and is willing to support them.

Benefits of Community Support Agriculture

In most farming enterprises the farmer invests capital and work in the effort to earn a profit. In the CSA model, however, the farmer earns only a salary. In doing that, the CSA farmer does not have to bear all the risks of farming. Nor does he or she have the full responsibility of capitalizing and managing the business.

From the farmer's perspective, one of the major benefits of community supported farming is that customers pay in advance – before the growing season begins. This guarantees the grower a market for everything. Since the members have already paid for the food the farmer knows they will come to pick it up.

With the capital pool created by the advance payments, the farmer can purchase equipment and supplies as needed. The farmer gets a paycheck weekly throughout the season, instead of having to wait until after the harvest is complete. At some CSA farms the farmer also receives health and life insurance, vacation and sick days, and even retirement benefits.

In the CSA membership garden farms, the farmers give up the option of an increased income that might be possible due to a bumper crop. In exchange, they get a guaranteed market and a guaranteed salary even if the crop produced is less then expected. For example, the Intervale Community Farm manager receives from $12 to $15 per hour. This is on par with other skilled technicians in the community. He also receives health insurance and paid vacation.

Tim Laird gets insect monitoring advice from entomologist Colleen Armstrong.

If a few crops fail due to weather or pest infestation, the farmer will still get paid. The probability of a complete crop failure is remote. If the harvest exceeds expectations, there may be more than the members can eat. Based on the history of community supported agriculture, too much food is usually what happens.

Up-front payment guarantees shareholders that they will receive a share of fresh produce during the coming season. They can pick up the produce weekly, sometimes twice weekly. The price per share reflects a savings of 25 to 50 percent less than retail level for similar quality organic produce.

Consumers will want to join the community farm for several reasons. I thought the major goal for most customers would be the chance to save money on their food purchases and this is often true. Based on our experience, however, consumers care less about price than they do about freshness, nutritional content, freedom from chemical contamination and supporting their local grower. Recent national surveys confirm this opinion.

Community farm shareholders weigh and bag their own produce.   photo by Ken Burris

In 1988, a Harris Poll revealed that 50 percent of those surveyed would buy organic produce if it were regularly available. They would be willing to pay more for it than conventional produce. A similar survey conducted in 1989 by the Detroit Free Press found that 86 percent of their readers want to purchase organically grown food for their families. They seem willing to pay the higher prices commanded by organic growers.

In 1990, the University of Vermont's Center For Rural Studies did a survey of Vermont households. Two-thirds of the respondents said they are willing to pay up to 10 percent more for organically grown produce. Eighty-six percent said they will pay more for locally grown produce and dairy products to help support local agriculture.

Despite what these surveys show, however, it is not always easy to get consumers to invest money in a CSA farm. The idea is new and unique, and people are often slow to change.

It may help to recruit members if you offer a payment schedule. It creates more paperwork for the farmer or bookkeeper, but it helps the member families spread their expenditure over several weeks or months. The state of the present economy affects how eager people are to invest in a membership garden or farm. In a declining economy they may be reluctant to commit to what they may perceive as an added expense.

Most folks don't really give much thought to how much they spend annually for food. To overcome this hesitation, make up charts that show what the average family will spend weekly for vegetables and fruits. Often, this amount will surprise them. Compare that amount to what you are charging for your produce. If the buyers can readily see the savings, they will be more apt to join your farm.

Some potential members may be concerned that the crops will not be large enough to provide sufficient food for all the members. Usually, the first year experience will be not enough of some vegetables, and too many of others. For example, in the first year of the Intervale Community Farm we had way too many tomatoes and squash, but not enough sweet corn and snow peas. During the second year we adjusted the crop plan, and the amount of food distributed was more appropriate for what each family needed. Almost always it seems there is more food than the members can use. We give the extras to the local emergency food shelf.

CSA farm members are often just as active in setting up the format for the farm and recruiting new members as the farmer is. It is in their best interest to get as many members as the farmer and the land can support. This will spread the cost of production over a broader base, enabling the farmer to achieve better economies of scale. This reduces the individual cost of each share proportionately.

At some CSA farms, part of the share price is an agreement that members will work a certain number of hours each season. Intervale Community Farm began by asking members to volunteer eight hours per season to help with the farm. With 150 households each volunteering eight hours of labor, that equals 1,200 hours. This is the equivalent of having a full-time employee for the season. In some cases, shareholders can exchange work for food.

Extra hands are welcome as the Intervale Community Farm prepares strawberry beds for the winter.   photo by Ken Burris

Shareholder help will be particularly welcome for labor-intensive planting and harvesting, particularly berries, potatoes, beans and peas, squash and pumpkins. These chores can be turned into wonderful social events, allowing members of the community to come together frequently to visit with and entertain one another. There is a major joy in this communal sharing of the bounty of the Good Earth.

CSAs answer people's need to be more closely aligned with their food supply. These groups are well on their way to proving that these community supported farms work. They are a service to the community and to the environment. They are sustainable for the farmer and for the shareholders.

CSAs are clearly a great marketing system. There is a buyer before the plants even go in the ground. The farmer gets community support from the shareholders, expressed in plenty of willing hands, and a guaranteed salary. This is indeed a farm model for the future. I believe CSA farming is a very positive forward step in providing a model of sustainability for the farmer and for the community.

Feed 20 Families on Half An Acre

The average family is going to purchase about $400 to $500 (retail pricing) in fresh vegetables and local fruits seasonally. In many situations you may find your core group to be made up of vegetarians. They will spend greater amounts of their disposable income for vegetables.

If you live in a town having 2,000 families and you can only appeal to 1 percent of the population, you'll still get 20 families to buy shares in your membership garden. At $400 per family, that's $8,000 per year. Produce for these families can be grown on as little as half an acre, using intensive methods. This size garden will only need part-time management from the farmer and only limited help from the members.

I have included a budget in this section to help you figure out what your costs might be against this income. Since your customers will be picking up the produce at the garden it won't be necessary to have a delivery van. This budget assumes that you are working in your backyard, and not paying rent for land. After careful consideration of your new budget you may decide that $3,000 will cover all your starting costs for this half-acre mini-farm. Since your garden members will have already paid their fees, or at least a portion of them, you will have money on hand to begin gardening. Your net profit after expenses is about $5,000. This profit pays your salary, amounting to a part-time income of about $833 per month ($208 per week, or about $10 per hour) for doing what you enjoy.

Many of the items you are buying this first year will last for several years. During your second and ensuing years your production costs will decrease dramatically. The extra money will give you a raise in pay. You own all these tools and equipment you are buying. This allows you to build equity in your backyard market garden business.

If, instead of a half-acre, you have four or five acres to work with, you can sell $40,000 or more annually through a CSA club. If you are willing to work full time during the season, averaging 10 hours per day, six days per week, it's entirely possible that you could earn as much as $17 to $20 per hour.

Table 23 Budget – Half Acre Membership Garden

EXPENSES:

Equipment and buildings:

Tool Shed-wash stand	$200
Garden cart	150
Backpack sprayer	80
Walk behind tiller ($2000/5 years)	400
Greenhouse ($2000/5 years)	400
Trellis wire and posts	200
Seeder, one row	80

Consumed inputs:

Lime and fertilizers	200
Seeds	50
Sprays	100
Potting soil	100
Greenhouse heat and electric	500
Irrigation water (from town)	100
Organic certification (if applicable)	100
Part-time gardening help	800

Supplies:

Seeding trays	100
Electric varmint fence	200
Irrigation	200
Tools, hoes, rakes	200
Signs	100
Vegetable scales	150
Miscellaneous	100
Sub-total annual expenses	**$ 3,000**
Salary:	**$ 5,000**
Total annual expenses	**$ 8,000**

INCOME:

20 shares sold at $400 each	**$ 8,000**

In a 5-acre farm you will want to hire and train three or four apprentices. You can rely on occasional help from the farm members to fill your labor needs. Marketing through the CSA club will save you the labor and expense of running a retail operation. Keep your overhead low, and concentrate on growing the best crops you can.

To sell $40,000 annually in produce through a CSA arrangement you will need at least 100 members, each paying $400 for the annual share. To obtain that many members may require a minimum market area (5-mile radius) of 10,000 population, if you can get at least 5 percent of the area families to join. If you only get a 1 percent enrollment rate, then you will need a market area population of 50,000.

This 5-mile radius is just a suggestion. The CSA in Mt. Carmel, Ct., draws many of its members from New Haven, over 15 miles away. The Intervale Community Farm in Burlington, Vt., draws members from Shelburne and Jericho, both over 10 miles away.

Generally, I would advise you to concentrate a membership drive within your immediate area. These nearby people are your neighbors, and are more willing to invest in the future of your farm if they are close enough for frequent visits.

§

Pay Now, Buy Later

Codman Community Farm

Lincoln, Massachusetts

Your backyard farm enterprise may be too small to grow meat and poultry to complement the vegetables you are growing for your members. However, you can increase your income substantially by buying such products from nearby farmers and reselling them to your members.

This style of membership farming works very well at the Codman Community Farm in Lincoln, Massachusetts. They are currently raising hay and livestock on about 100 acres. Some of the hay sells to local horse owners. The farm also has community gardening plots and a self-serve farm stand at the main barn. The meats and hay tend to draw people who also buy vegetables. There is such a demand for free-range beef and lamb that Codman Farm has to buy livestock from other farmers. They then have the animals slaughtered and packaged, and sell the frozen cuts through the farm stand.

Codman Community Farm is not set up under the CSA format. It is a not-for-profit organization managing 100 acres of land owned by the Town of Lincoln. There are 250 members, each paying a $25 annual membership fee. The farm's major funding comes from hay and meat sales, along with an annual grant from the Codman Family Trust and from an annual auction of donated goods.

One subscription marketing service Codman Farm does provide, is a program called the "Food Tab." In this program anyone can pay an advance fee in $100 increments. Purchases of hay or meat are then deducted from their credit tab. For each $100 credit tab purchased the farm member receives $110 worth of produce.

This is a new program and about 40 families are taking advantage of the 10 percent savings. They like the convenience of not having to pay cash or write a check for each individual purchase. The advantages to Codman Farm, of course, are the advance fees to help with cash flow, and the guaranteed market.

Three things are important when considering meat and poultry sales. First, the amount of purchased livestock may have to be less than 50 percent of total farm sales. This way the operation does not become a commercial retail center in the eyes of state and town regulatory boards. Check this out with your local planning and zoning office.

Second, you will want to insure quality of the meat products by making sure that each contract grower is using sustainable growing techniques. Third, and probably most important, the slaughterhouse must be inspected by the U. S. Department of Agriculture to keep from running into Board of Health regulatory problems.

There is a real potential for the small farmer to use management and marketing skills to increase cash flow and profits, particularly during the off-season, by offering contract-grown fruits, storage crops, meats and poultry.

For starters, you might offer this service for beef only. First you will need to locate a grower in your area who has free-range beef animals for sale. Then, contact a local slaughter house for prices and schedules. After purchasing a steer, have it delivered directly to the slaughterhouse. Give directions on how the meat is to be cut and packaged.

With careful planning you can deliver the meat directly from the butcher to the consumer. This is less likely if most of your farm members don't own freezers. Without freezers it will be more common for members to buy a few pounds of meat each week when they stop by to pick up their vegetable share. You will need to purchase or borrow one or two chest-type freezers to hold the meat until it sells.

When arranging to have the beef butchered you can have the inferior cuts, such as flank steak and chuck roast, made up into hamburger. This will eliminate the problem of having too many low-value steaks and not enough hamburger. When you get the delivery time for the packaged and frozen meat you can send out a special flyer to your farm members. Let them know what is available, and at what price.

For example, the Codman Community Farm is selling one steer every two or three weeks during the season. They also market a dozen pigs and 30 to 50 lambs annually, most of which sell directly to their membership of nearly 250 families. Their marketing program is not more aggressive simply because they have a difficult time raising or buying enough livestock to satisfy the demand.

When searching for meat and poultry products for your garden members you may locate farms that are growing and processing the meats and packaging for resale. Simply buy the products at wholesale pricing and make them available to your membership. Remember to mark up the pricing to cover the added expenses and your time and effort.

Buying and reselling fruits and berries from other area growers is usually much simpler than handling meat or poultry. To be successful with fruits and berries you will need a reliable supplier and time to handle the logistics. Check around your area and find the growers who are selling wholesale and who use ecologically sensitive growing methods.

You may not find any fruit and berry growers who are strictly biodynamic or organic. There are multiple problems associated with the raising of fruits and berries organically that many growers have yet to overcome. It can be done, but most growers find that the fruits that aren't cosmetically perfect are not selling well and their enterprise isn't economically viable. However, many growers coast-to-coast have shifted to low-spray and integrated pest management growing practices. These are less harmful to the environment than conventional chemically oriented practices.

Starting a Community Supported Farm

In the membership gardening format you are trading retail marketing skills for recruiting skills. They are very similar, with one very distinct difference; you are selling your crops and being paid in full before you even plant them. In the CSA model you build your sales outlet by building your membership base. Fortunately, the recruiting can be done in the off-season when you have time away from the gardens. In undertaking the establishment of a CSA first examine the limiting factors.

- How much land is available?

- What is the population of the 5-mile marketing radius?

- How many families can you plan on joining and supporting the farm?

- How many families do you need to support the size garden business you hope to build?

- How much labor is available?

- How much of your time and capital can you spend?

- Is this the marketing scenario that interests you most?

If there is enough positive information in this preliminary study, then go to the next step. Try an informal market survey to see what the interest is within the community. Try talking to people; friends, business associates, church members, your family, and anyone else who will take the time to discuss it with you. If too many people say, "No way," then perhaps this isn't the marketing plan best suited to your area.

But, if everyone starts reaching for their checkbooks you may be on the right track. It's time to do a more formal market survey. No, you don't have to hire one of those highfalutin' and expensive market survey companies. Do your own survey. Type a brief but thorough description of what you intend to do, with a questionnaire for people to fill out and return to you. Working with a local church group or food buyers club is a natural place to start, since they already have a list of members with similar interests. They may even let you use their newsletter to distribute information about your CSA.

Selling Shares of Your Vegetable Harvest

The best way to sell memberships in your garden is through word of mouth advertising. As new families join, ask them to tell their friends and neighbors about your farm. If your members are doing a good job of supporting your farm they will help you grow the membership to the level you need to make it self-supporting.

Anything you can do to inform the public about your farm is worthwhile. Contact local news media and ask them to do a story about your farm. Don't be shy when asking for publicity. Local news people rely on the community for their stories. Yours will be a wholesome, feel-good project they will want to support.

Here at Intervale Community Farm we recruited Burlington's mayor, Peter Clavelle. Then we asked him to give a press conference announcing our farm. It worked great. We signed up several new members from this public appeal.

Always ask for input from potential members. Give people a list of vegetables that you feel confident that you can grow. Do this as a checklist so that they can mark which varieties they want. They can also give the approximate quantities they need by the week.

To help prospective members decide if your "share price" is a good deal, use market pricing information from your survey of grocery stores and farmers markets, or from the Cooperative Extension Service. You can give members an idea of what they will receive in value compared to the share price you are asking them to pay. Just be careful not to lock yourself in to last year's prices.

Questions you might ask in a survey are:

1. Number of family members, and ages. This will help determine annual consumption patterns.

2. Days they would like to pick up produce. Plan on two days or evenings each week, so you can keep produce picked regularly.

3. Vegetable and fruit varieties they are interested in, within the restrictions of your climate zone.

4. Do they have a friend or relative who would like a copy of the questionnaire?

5. Any other questions you feel appropriate.

Try to keep the survey on two sheets of paper. The first page is the descriptive information about you and your farm, and what your CSA plans are. This the reader can keep. The second page is the questionnaire they can fill out and return to you. Keep it brief, friendly, and informative. At first, all you are trying to determine is if there is enough community interest to support the size of CSA membership farm you envision.

If you are seeking only a few member families, hand-deliver these survey forms to a select group of friends or acquaintances. Concentrating on the residential areas near your farm will further enhance the potential for favorable response. Invite people to call you for more information. It's not a good idea to simply post the date of the meeting and hope folks will show up. We tried that here and got only a few responses. Now, we ask folks to call us for more information, then we explain the farm to them and invite them to attend an upcoming meeting.

People are busy, they forget these events but they don't want to be left out. So we use a post card or phone call a few days before the meeting to remind them. This is what doctors and dentists do, and it works well to keep people aware of the meeting date. With the post card reminder we expect about 50 people to show up for a potluck supper or an informational meeting. Without the post card we get only an attendance of about 20.

With any mailer you send to local residents, you might consider enclosing a stamped, self-addressed envelope. This will double the cost of postage but you want to make it easy for them to respond, and this will increase their response rate. Keep in mind that less than 20 percent of the recipients of your survey will take the time to fill it out and return it. At least this is the response rate we see here at the Intervale Community Farm, even among our established members.

You may find that the response is negative, or only lukewarm. If that is the case, consider yourself fortunate to have only lost a small amount of money in your market survey effort.

On the other hand, you may be pleasantly surprised to receive 20 or 30 positive replies showing sincere interest in joining your community supported membership garden or farm.

At the Intervale Community Farm we find that people who really like the idea will call back within one or two days after receiving the survey. After hearing about our farm plans they usually join immediately. For those who want to get more information we invite them to our next monthly meeting.

Once you have enough families interested in learning more about your proposed community membership farm, your next step is to schedule one or several informational meetings. These can be either at your farm, or somewhere convenient within the community. We have used both methods, though, and find that having the meetings at the farm is more productive than meeting at the local library, for example.

Invite not only the families on your prospect list, but also get some free press coverage from local weekly or daily newspapers. Put up some posters and send out some flyers announcing the meeting. Be sure to give a phone number for folks to call for additional information. Ask your core group families to bring along a friend or neighbor.

You might consider serving coffee and donuts, or punch and cookies, or even a potluck supper or afternoon tea. Show a slide presentation or video of your farm, or similar agriculture-related scenes. This will get your guests into the proper frame of mind to be receptive to your proposal.

Your presentation will be more complete if you give a talk about the history of community supported farming. In your talk, list the benefits the members can expect to receive. This is what they are buying. Some of the benefits are nutritional value of fresh produce, taste sensations, and price savings. Be sure to discuss the issue of preserving rural farmland and the potential for keeping the community's food buying dollars in the local economy. These are good reasons why the community should help to support local farmers who are using environmentally friendly farming techniques.

It will help if you have one or two community leaders help with the presentation. Ask the mayor or other well-known residents of the community to help you out. Agents from the local office of the Cooperative Extension Service or the vegetable growers association are people you can ask for help. Extra voices lend credence to any offer that might otherwise be construed as a private business venture that will benefit the farmer only.

What you are offering is a service to consumers and the community. This should be understood and appreciated by the interested families. When discussing budgets and management it's OK to talk about your salary and capital costs; people will expect that. After all, they work for a living, too, so they can understand that you aren't doing this for free.

After your presentations are over, and you count the results, you may find that you have gathered enough families to support the size membership garden you have in mind. Or, you may have only a few of the members you need to make this a profitable venture. This may cause you to decide to discontinue the effort and look elsewhere for a market. The response to your first presentation may be strong enough, however, that you will decide to hold more meetings to continue recruiting the number of families you need.

If your recruiting efforts have been less successful than you had hoped, then consider down-sizing the venture to fit your new group size. As an example, Intervale Community Farm only had 12 members in 1989. Our goal for 1990 was 120 members. By the first of May we had enlisted only 92 member families, so we simply scaled down our cropping plans to fit the new membership level.

Naturally, all this recruiting and preliminary work should take place during the off-season. You may even start recruiting the year before you start your membership garden. You want to know at least a month before you start seeds in the greenhouse what and how much to grow.

During this planning phase your shareholders might ask that you grow things besides vegetables. You might consider growing fruits and berries, flowers, and perhaps even poultry and meats.

*A booth at the local fair is an excellent way to recruit new
members for the Intervale Community Farm.*

What all you can produce depends on the amount of land you
have, and the time you can spend on the project. However,
since you already have the buyers in your CSA group, you can
contract with other farmers to provide your farm members
with meats, poultry or berries.

The Intervale Community Farm is considering offering this
type of compatible service program in the future. We can help
our members gain access to locally grown meats and fruits at
a reduced price. This will create new markets for our friends
on other Vermont farms. Eventually, the Intervale
Community Farm hopes to expand and grow all the meat and
poultry needs of our membership.

§

Home Delivery Membership Garden

Selling Convenience

I've given this home delivery membership garden a separate section because of the differences that occur once you start making home deliveries. The first and biggest difference is that the customers who buy shares in a home delivery service are the ones who want convenience. They are willing to pay the extra charges for weekly delivery.

There are two types of home delivery membership gardens. The first is similar to the CSA format. Members buy a share in the farm, and get a weekly delivery of the harvest. The annual membership fee is usually several hundred dollars.

The second type home delivery is for families who pay a membership fee of $25 or $50 and agree to place an order each week for vegetables and fruits. In this case, the gardener retains autonomy and can sell food to others as well as to members.

Recruiting will be much the same as we have already talked about, except that you really want to keep all your members in the same neighborhood if possible. This will make deliveries easier and quicker.

Conceptually, it seems fairly easy to get customers for your agricultural home delivery service. All you need is to convince buyers to buy from you. In practice it may not be that easy. It may require you to wear out a pair of shoes walking door to door and talking to people. Show them color pictures from a seed catalog or a brochure, or a picture scrapbook of your farm.

Ideally, of course, you would want to get all your customers in a fairly centralized area, and all the same type customer. "Nine to Five" working couples, for example, would all be home pretty much the same time each evening, or Saturday mornings. In communities with school age children you can schedule deliveries in the afternoon when the kids are home. They can put things in the refrigerator, and pay you.

I know it sounds difficult to get a list of customers who will be available when you can make deliveries. Keep in mind, though, you only need a few families to support your market garden. Just keep asking and you will find them. You can also work out a plan to leave the grocery delivery in a box on the porch, in the garage or just inside the kitchen door. Since the produce is fresh, and delivered quickly, it will resist wilting for several hours, as long as it is in the shade.

Naturally you will charge more for this home delivery service. It's more work than if the customers were coming to your garden and picking up their weekly share. There will be extra trouble and expense in making multiple deliveries. You want to be paid extra, at least enough to cover the extra costs. You may be able to get the members to volunteer to do the deliveries, or trade a share to someone who will do it for you. In a really small membership garden you can probably make the deliveries yourself while you are running your other errands.

Impress on your customers the importance of having several shareholders in a particular section of your town. Your delivery expenses will be lessened, and you can pass the savings on to them via lower per unit food pricing. This will help bring in new members through neighbors and friends of your core group.

Along with the supply of vegetables you can also include free recipes or offer a cookbook. These will encourage your customers to use their produce supply quickly. If you teach them how to prepare and cook vegetables properly, they will get more enjoyment and nutritional value from your service. They will be more willing to recommend it to other members of their family, and to friends and neighbors.

Can you do this as a part-time business? Yes, of course. That is the best way to get started. Will you need a special delivery van? Not yet. You can get by with the family car and a small trailer. Just be sure to cover the vegetables in transit so they don't get wind-blown, wilted in the sun or rained on.

We are starting one of these home delivery services here at the Intervale Community Farm. For the first year we plan to hire a retired fellow with a pickup truck to make the individual deliveries. Another idea we may try is to group the deliveries to key locations in the city. The members can stop on their way home to retrieve their bag of groceries.

Because each family will have paid their share in advance we will not have to worry about individual payments for each delivery. Also, since they have already chosen the veggies they want us to grow we will not have to worry about what to deliver to them. And, we won't have to bother taking individual orders each week. They simply get a full share of whatever we harvest each week.

If they don't use all the produce they can give it to friends or neighbors. This will be an excellent way to solicit new members for the membership garden for the following year.

If you are making weekly deliveries you can sometimes earn extra money by offering additional items from the wholesale produce center. Bananas, oranges, grapefruit are excellent additions to your produce line. This will expand the benefit of the service to your customers. I'm particularly interested in collaborating with small-scale growers in other regions of the country who can send these exotics to me for distribution. This could be termed a "long distance" CSA.

To start selling compatible produce to your garden members make a deal with local farmers. Ask them to provide eggs, meat, poultry, honey, apples and other fruits, apple cider, and maple syrup. Consider everything that grows in your area. Keep in mind the limited space in your delivery vehicle. Don't take on more than you can handle. You may not want to operate a full scale home shopping and delivery service, but in certain neighborhoods this business can be very profitable.

To set up a home delivery service you first want to know what to grow, and in what quantities. The way to find out is ask your customers. Start walking and knocking on doors. Up one street and down the other. Don't go jumping around all over town unless you want to wind up with a widely scattered distribution system. You may get higher prices by selling in that fancy new subdivision across town, but the travel time cuts into your profits. You will be happier in your own neighborhood at lower prices. Don't drive by your market to get to a market.

When searching for customers in the summer you can bring along a nice basket of fresh produce from your home garden. This visual sales aid will allow you to give out free samples.

When a family shows interest, sign them up. Put them on your newsletter mailing list and stay in touch with them.

If you are planning on growing vegetables on only a few thousand square feet you may already have enough customers in your family, friends, neighbors and business associates. This will simplify marketing tremendously. With each family using $500 worth of fresh produce per season, you can supply 10 to 20 families from less than half an acre. This size garden will allow you to build a part-time business almost instantly.

Maybe you can get all the customers you need right at one company or office building. Just deliver all the bags of groceries to the same place and the shareholders can pick them up at the front desk on their way home.

This is a marketing option chosen by Ward Sinclair and Cass Peterson in Dott, Pa. They are former writers for *The Washington Post*. When they started their market garden in 1984 they sold a few bags of groceries to friends at *The Post*. The next year their loyal customers grew to 35, and by 1990 their membership had grown to about 125. Their payment schedule varies by the size of the bag of groceries delivered each week. Total payments for the year, from one office building, adds up to more than $20,000.

As your land base grows through purchasing or renting nearby land you can add customers as needed. Even if your land base doesn't increase, your productivity will. As you gain experience and bring the fertility and productive capacity of your soil up to the optimum levels you will get greater yields.

If you want to grow beyond this neighborhood group you can grow your garden to five acres, or even 25 acres. As for maximum size of a home delivery service, I'd say that depends on your other limiting factors, such as land, nearby population and labor resources. I'm convinced that the market will never be saturated in most towns and cities in America. As you keep adding land, and helpers in the gardens, you can keep adding to your membership. At some point, however, you will reach the upper limit of delivery scheduling.

You can then use your home delivery subscribers as a core group to set up a pick-your-own farm or a community supported farm. This Home Delivery Membership Garden idea is indeed a vision of our garden farming future. You can feed 20 families from your backyard and make a decent summer income. Or, you can expand to 60 or 100 shares and make it a full-time job. It's all up to you. You're your own boss, which is one of the best benefits of being a backyard market gardener.

§
Clientele Membership Club

(CMC), A 'Guaranteed Market'

You may be thrilled with the potential of the membership garden or Community Supported Agriculture as a way to market your crops. These methods have a multitude of advantages. The two most important are the guaranteed market and guaranteed salary for the grower. The big advantage for the shareholders is the season long supply of fresh, organically grown vegetables, below market pricing. Both sides benefit, making this a win – win marketing plan.

On the other hand, you may not want to take on one or more co-partners. You might not want to divulge information about your financial position in your farm. You may want to retain autonomous control of your operation. Also, you might not want to ask families in your community to invest $400 per share.

Then consider the CSA's cousin, the Clientele Membership Club (CMC). The CMC operates on many of the same principles as the CSA. You get a committed group of consumers to buy your produce, you get money up front and you get closer association with the folks who eat your food. There are three major differences in the CMC: (1.) Membership fees are lower, (2.) you retain autonomous control of your garden and (3.) the distribution system is more flexible.

The Clientele Membership Club marketing concept has been under development since 1974. The originator of the idea, Dr. Booker T. Whatley, is a former professor, horticulturist and small-scale farm authority at Tuskegee Institute in Montgomery, Alabama. Dr. Whatley co-authored the book *How to Make $100,000 Farming 25 Acres* with the editors of *NEW FARM* magazine.

Dr. Whatley has designed his plan for the small farmer having from 25 to 200 acres. Your garden farm may be quite a bit smaller than that, but there is a tremendous amount of good ideas and sound advice in Whatley's handbook.

Table 4. Booker T. Whatley's 10 Commandments for Successful Small Farming.

Thy Small Farm Shalt:
I. Provide year-round, daily cash flow.
II. Be a pick-your-own operation.
III. Have a guaranteed market with a clientele membership club.
IV. Provide year-round, full-time employment.
V. Be located on a hard-surfaced road within a radius of 40 miles of a population center of at least 50,000, with well-drained soil and an excellent source of water.
VI. Produce only what thy clients demand and nothing else!
VII. Shun middlepeople like the plague, for they are a curse unto thee.
VIII. Consist of compatible, complementary crop components that earn a minimum of $3,000 per acre annually.
IX. Be 'weatherproof,' at least as far as is possible, with both drip and sprinkler irrigation.
X. Be covered by a minimum of $250,000 worth ($1 million is better) of liability insurance.

The heart of the Whatley Small Farm Plan is the guaranteed market. This is done by recruiting a group of member families to buy the produce from your farm, whether it's vegetables, meat, poultry, berries or whatever. This is very similar to the previously discussed community supported farm. But, Whatley is suggesting that you charge an annual membership fee of $25 to $50 for families wishing to join the club.

This simply gives the customer the right to come to your farm and pick their own. Club members buy produce on a first come-first served basis for 40 percent less than retail, and they pick it themselves. This differs significantly from the

CSA marketing plan in which each family receives an equal weekly share of the harvest.

Another important element of the Whatley Plan is that the farmer should earn a minimum of $3,000 per acre per year. Obviously this excludes such enterprises as hay crops, conventional livestock and all field and cash grain crops. To maintain the $3,000 per acre income level the farmer will need to concentrate on higher value crops and livestock.

Whatley's plan also stipulates that you should have as many as 10 individual crop "profit centers." Then, if for whatever reason, one of your crops does fail, you'll still be operating at a 90 percent efficiency level. That still leaves the grower with lots of possibilities, such as vegetables, berries, fruits, poultry, feeder pigs, exotic livestock, feeder lambs, flowers, herbs and many value-added products such as jams, syrups and sauces. You can add fee-fishing if a pond or lake is available, and even sell cut-your-own Christmas trees.

Whatley has set up this plan to enable the farmer to realize daily income for the entire year. Income begins in January when the membership dues start coming in, then progresses through the seasons. First crops in the year-round rotation can be potted plants and bedding plants, spring greens, Easter lamb or turkey. Summer crops give way to fall crops such as Halloween pumpkins and Thanksgiving turkeys. The farm then finishes out the year with Christmas trees and turkeys for Christmas dinner.

Obviously, this plan will enable you to work at the farm on a full-time, year-round basis. Your member families do a good deal of the harvesting, so you won't have to rely on hired help as much as you would in a conventional farming situation. With a preselected group of customers you don't have any middle-person. There aren't any brokers, wholesale produce houses, producer's cooperatives or direct wholesaling to supermarkets. All the money you make after expenses is yours to keep. You also take all the risks of crop failure or other naturally caused catastrophe. Your members don't share this risk with you.

Dr. Whatley feels that this type of farm should be located within a 40-mile radius of a metropolitan statistical area having a population of more than 50,000. From this market population the farmer can get a club membership of close to 100 families. This is based on a membership group of less than 1 percent of the households in the area. This number of customers can generate as much as $100,000 annually in sales. That's $1,000 per family, but it includes such things as freezer meats, fruits and berries or fee-fishing.

I agree that a 1 percent recruitment factor is more than realistic. With creative and persuasive marketing and quality produce the farmer could even expect 5 percent. Some growers may find it possible to organize a buyer's club of upwards of 500 families, capable of generating $500,000 in business annually.

However, the 40-mile radius may not be appropriate for all areas of the country. Here in the northeast, a 40 mile drive probably would encompass more than one major population area. In the less populated areas of the country, driving such a distance to buy food may be commonplace. You should give some serious thought to the site-specific marketing possibilities in your area, and what your potential customers are used to. To me, a 5-mile radius seems more realistic if you expect your customers to visit your gardens on a regular basis.

I agree wholeheartedly with Whatley that you should not grow anything your customers don't want. If you feel a particular crop is worth trying, for Heaven's sake try it on a small scale first. Grow what your customers want, charge what they are willing to pay and stay out of the commodity markets.

There are many components in Dr. Whatley's plan. It is has complex ideas, and is beyond the scope of most backyard market gardens. But, I recommend you buy his book and study it carefully. You can tailor parts of his plan to fit your circumstances.

I'm not sure anyone can follow Whatley's plan exactly. But, I do know that many growers, myself included, are following one or more of his suggestions. The Clientele Membership Club is the beginning of a whole new way of thinking about agricultural marketing in this country. Do what I did, adapt some of his ideas and start increasing your profits.

Subscription Marketing Summary

The one common denominator for these subscription marketing methods is that your crop sells before you even plant it. That eliminates at least half your worries and concerns before you even get into the planting season. You know what and how much to plant and you have plenty of folks lined up to buy your harvest.

Secondly, for community supported farms, you will be getting advance membership fees from your customers. This will help to eliminate concerns about your start up costs. For a dozen or so families subscribing to a membership garden, their deposits might only add up to a few thousand dollars. With a hundred CSA members each paying $400 per share, you will be getting start-up capital of $10,000 to $40,000, depending on the membership payment schedule you choose to use.

In other types of direct marketing such as farmers markets or roadside stands, you can't sell the crop until you've grown it. Anything that matures early, before the markets open for the season, will be of little value to you. Anything you can't eat or sell will have to be used as a charitable donation or as compost material.

Another advantage of membership gardening is your ability to expand your enrollment almost effortlessly. Your core group becomes your ad hoc sales committee. If you need more members to handle your increased productivity, just spread the word. Your core group will go to work for you, bringing in relatives, someone from the car pool or another neighbor.

A requirement of starting and maintaining a CSA or membership garden is to keep the membership involved in the farm. Always keep an eye out for opportunities to encourage members to invest themselves personally in the growth of your farming project.

One really great way to do that is with the farm compost heap. Encourage your members to join in your recycling efforts. Ask them to bring their leaves, grass clippings and kitchen waste out to the farm regularly and add it to the compost pile. They will feel like they are part of the effort to regenerate the soil. This will give them an immense amount of satisfaction in seeing part of their household waste stream directed away from the local landfill and into a worthwhile use. Always ask your farm members to bring their own bags and boxes. This will give them an even greater opportunity to participate in recycling. It will cut down on your costs of providing these things, too.

Setting up and maintaining a membership garden or farm requires that you have a newsletter. Even if it's only one or two pages each month or every other month. It can be as simple as a post card or a mimeographed sheet. If you have only a few members you can telephone them directly, or set up a monthly phone tree with news and events. This will keep your members informed as the crops change during the season, and it will keep their interest up during the off-season.

There will be some naturally occurring attrition as people drop your service. Some of them will move away or family size will decrease. Others may become unhappy with your service or produce. You need to be on top of things. Keep your farm and your newsletter interesting and vital. Then you can go into each new season with increased membership and bright prospects for the coming year.

Use your newsletter for crop information and pick-up scheduling. Keep the newsletter interesting by including little news items, like farm members who have births in the family, weddings or even vacation trips to interesting places. Use the newsletter to schedule fun type functions at the farm, such as veggie cookouts with fresh vegetables on the grill and each member bringing a side dish, Easter egg hunts for the kiddies, pumpkin carving contests, scarecrow contests, and so on.

These functions serve a dual purpose of keeping your membership involved personally in your farm, and keeping you in contact with your customers. To me, these little celebrations are a fun part of being a community-centered farmer.

There is a groundswell of interest in membership gardening and Community Supported Farming. I predict the number of farms doing this will double or even triple nationwide each year into the future. I feel that there is an outstanding future, both aesthetically and economically, for any grower contemplating a shift to CSA farming and membership gardening.

Card Table in Your Front Yard

Tailgating at a wide spot in the road may be the simplest and least expensive way to sell extra produce from your backyard market garden. Just put everything in the trunk of your car, go find a convenient location on a nearby busy street and set up for business. Many towns have one or more of these roadside entrepreneurs. Maybe they only make a few hundred dollars each season, but they often don't have to work very hard to do it.

Tailgating relies on a convenient site along a well travelled road. In some areas a permit from the local zoning office is necessary for street vending.

Another way to describe this marketing option is *mobile marketing.* Vegetable growers like Jim Crawford in Hustontown, Pa., have found this to be a profitable way to sell food directly to consumers. Crawford started out with an 8,000 square foot backyard market garden two decades ago. He now grows crops on nearly 20 acres. He markets this produce

145

at different neighborhoods in metropolitan Washington, D.C., five days each week.

Maybe you could start out the same way Crawford did. Put the veggies in the car and go find a friendly neighborhood in which to start your private farmers market. Or, you could simply set up a small market with a card table in your front yard. That eliminates traveling altogether. You can even make it "self-serve" so you don't have to stand there waiting for customers. Spend your time working nearby in the garden and let the customers wait on themselves. You only need a card table, a shady spot on the front lawn, a cigar box for making change and some good looking vegetables to sell. Depending on the type of neighborhood you live in, this front yard marketing system can net you a few hundred to a few thousand dollars each year. Maybe more if you have a big garden and a really top notch location.

Selling produce from a card table in your front yard is a low cost and easy way to start your part-time backyard business.

Advertise your front yard market by placing signs at the nearby major intersections and along your street a few hundred feet on each side of your house. Same thing applies to tailgating alongside a nearby busy street or highway. Put up plenty of signs. Don't make the customers guess where you are and what you have for sale. They won't.

When figuring out the sizes of signs you need, allow one inch of letter size for each 10 miles per hour of the speed of traffic passing your site. If traffic goes 40 mph use 4-inch letters. Use a white background with black, dark green or red lettering. These are the colors that are easiest to see in most light conditions. Try to put a logo or vegetable caricature on the sign. Give some supporting information such as "fresh," "organic," "homegrown," "NOW." Look for action words that will stimulate interest and activity from passersby.

Signs need to be big, colorful, easy to read and grab attention.
photo by George DeVault

Put the signs on each side of your stand, at least 100 feet away for each 10 miles per hour of traffic speed. If cars are passing your stand at 40 mph, put your signs 400 feet on each side of your stand. This will give your customers enough time to see you and slow down to stop and shop.

Check on zoning permits for signs and structures. If a permanent sign isn't allowed, use moveable structures and A-frame or sandwich board signs. A good place to advertise is on your car or truck, either door signs or roof signs. This can overcome zoning regulations and sign by-laws altogether, and still get your message out to the public.

Use your truck or car as a billboard, especially in zoning areas where you can't get a permit to put up signs.

Keep a notebook with you and list the number of customer during each hour. Write down the total amount purchased and any comments. Do this for a few days, even a few weeks and look for a pattern. You may find that the bulk of your customers come to your booth or stand during the lunch hour, or maybe from 10 am to noon. Maybe it will happen from 3 pm to 6 pm. It may not profitable to keep the stand open longer hours, unless you are in an area where there is daily traffic that will stop.

Wesley Court lives in Burlington, Vt., and relies on his neighbors for the produce he sells at his card table stand. His best seller is free-range eggs from his next door neighbor's flock. Wesley doesn't have a lot to choose from at his stand, and he doesn't make a lot of money. That's OK though, he's only 7 years old. Second graders just don't seem to need a big income to be happy.

An upside down crate, beach umbrella, rocking chair and veggies from his neighbor's gardens puts 7-year old Wesley Court in business.

Ed Rand uses his front yard on a busy street to sell produce for other market gardeners. He doesn't have his own garden – yet.

My friend Ed Rand has a small stand on North Avenue in Burlington, Vt. He doesn't have a garden. He drives around each morning in his pickup truck and buys produce from the market gardeners in the area. He opens the season with strawberries, asparagus, peas and spinach, and ends the season with apples, pumpkins, winter squash and potatoes. He isn't open on rainy days, and his stand is mostly self-serve. Still, Ed manages to clear nearly $3,000 each year from a table in his front yard. He considers this the perfect retirement business. It gives him the opportunity to drive around in the morning and visit with his farmer friends, then he sits in the shade in the afternoon and swaps yarns with his neighbors and customers.

Diana Doll uses her push cart to sell her flowers and vegetables in Burlington's downtown pedestrian mall. She raises most of her produce in a half-acre market garden in the Intervale.

However, there are a few problems with some front yard marketing systems. The variety and quantity is sometimes too small to cause people to stop frequently to shop. Sometimes, the quality of the produce is unappealing. This is particularly noticeable toward the end of the day when the only things left on the table are two or three tomatoes and a couple of tired looking cucumbers. Ed Rand overcomes this problem by buying fresh daily from several area growers.

Try to plan your harvest throughout the day. If you do it all in the morning things will wilt by the day's end. Of course, if you aren't home all day you can't pick produce for the stand as often as you would like. You just have to sell what you can, and compost the rest.

Only certain vegetables lend themselves well to this self-serve stand technique. Pumpkins, winter squash, decorative gourds, Indian corn, potatoes, carrots, and tomatoes are a few. These varieties don't mind sitting around waiting for a buyer. Their quality is not harmed by being out in the open air, but they <u>must</u> be in the shade.

151

Pay closer attention to the items that need refrigeration. Such vegetables as lettuce, peas, broccoli and salad greens wilt quickly. Don't display them for long periods unless you can keep them chilled with crushed ice. Even wet newspaper laid over them will help a little bit, but it does block the view of the veggies.

An even better idea is to keep fragile produce in an old refrigerator. For power, simply run an extension cord from the house to your stand. If you're really lucky, you may find an old reach-in soda cooler, which is much larger than a home refrigerator. Keep a sharp eye out for used coolers at convenience stores, bars, groceries or even restaurants that are being remodeled or going out of business.

Granted, you'll have to sell extra produce to pay off this added expense. But, your customers will appreciate the added freshness, and you won't be composting so many leftovers. You'll also get better prices for your well-cooled produce, and you can keep it for longer periods. Chances are these savings will allow you to recover the cost of a used refrigerator in only a month or two.

Even with refrigeration you will want to put your display table in the dense shade of a building or large tree. If that's not possible, build a canopy. A beach umbrella can work sometimes if you can be there to redirect it as the sun moves during the day. Otherwise, it won't do a very good job of shading your vegetables for the entire day.

You may find you can sell more than you can grow in your small market garden. That's fantastic. Go see other gardeners in your area who have extra produce, but no sales outlet. You can start selling their produce on consignment.

If you are selling produce for other growers on consignment you don't have to pay for it until you sell it. This is not unusual in the produce business. Larger growers sometimes send their produce to a broker and hope the broker can find a buyer for it. Trust, integrity and a good personal relationship are essential for successful consignment sales. You will need to establish some ground rules for quantity, quality, price, availability, accounting and even returning unsold produce.

To find other growers who would be interested in supplying your stand, try contacting members of your local garden club. You may try putting up some posters or run an advertisement in the local weekly newspaper. Let people know that you are looking for other part-time growers to grow produce for your stand. Sometimes, commercial growers in your vicinity will be happy to sell to you also. I think you will be pleasantly surprised at the amount of response you will get.

When Your Card Table Grows into a Farm Stand

An inexpensive stand may be made as genuinely attractive as an expensive structure. The operator's personality will be his most valuable asset. – Gilbert S. Watts, Roadside Marketing

From a viewpoint of maximum profitability, my first choice in marketing systems would be a market garden with its own farm stand. By its very nature the farm stand is more expensive to set up than any of the other methods. Opening a farm stand often means that you need more cash for a building, refrigeration, a part-time or full-time attendant, advertising and dozens of other expenses. It also requires more sophisticated management than many backyard market gardeners may want to provide. But, in the long term, it can be far more lucrative than many other methods of selling food.

Many first-time market growers may not consider the farm stand as a viable option. From your point of view there may be severe limiting factors. One is the need for an excellent location on a busy street. You need to be between the major shopping districts and nearby residential areas. It's always best if you can be on the right hand side for evening "going home" traffic. Then, it's easier for your customers to stop and buy from you.

The market gardening business is no different from any other business in this respect. Location is everything. If you are going to sell retail from your garden farm you must be close to the customers. It is even better if you can be between the customers and the major shopping districts. People have to pass by your door to get anywhere. This is especially advantageous if your long range plan is to build up your stand into a profitable business and then sell it.

With careful planning, you can open a nice little farm stand for very little money. One thing you must have, though, is a decent looking place. Don't get carried away with scavenging and bartering. You may wind up with a hillbilly ranch conglomeration of used sheet roofing for siding, used boards from the old pig pen for benches and somebody's discarded table umbrella as a canopy. This can look unappealing and uninviting.

You can certainly save some money by using some of these free materials. But do it so your customers can't see it. You want nice people to stop here, so make them feel welcome. They need to feel confident that your produce and your service are top quality.

No, you don't have to spend a lot of money for new walls, shelving, doors and display benches. It's OK to recycle certain materials that fit and look decent. Choose those materials that can be painted or washed and made to look clean. Concentrate on sprucing up the areas that the customers can see and shielding unsightly areas that you don't want them to see. Strive to create a visually exciting and pleasing aura around your stand that will attract customers and make them feel comfortable.

For example, Shepherd and Ellen Ogden, owners of The Cook's Garden in Londonderry, Vt., built a pole structure about the size of a one car garage for their market garden farmstand. They made the building attractive by adding a canopy and well-designed sign to the front. Perennial flower beds along the sides covered up ugly features in the landscape.

They did the work themselves using recycled materials and the results have been outstanding. Many people familiar with the original appearance of the site are amazed that the Ogden's have done so much with so little. New customers think this is the way it has always looked and are pleased to stop in and look at the wonderful array of fresh goodies.

Shep and Ellen have since closed their retail farmstand to devote full time to enlarging their seed business. The market garden itself is now a display garden for dozens of varieties of lettuces, tomatoes, exotic salad greens and beans. These are all special varieties that they carry in their seed catalog.

Shep Ogden leading a workshop at the Cook's Garden seed house. The building was formerly a road side stand.

To fill local demand for fresh produce in their local area, Kate Wright and her husband John have opened Working Hands Farmstand on a converted hay wagon in front of their house on Rt. 11 in Londonderry, Vt., population 1,500. John is a full-time dairy farmer and built the roof on the hay wagon. It has sides that fold up to form a canopy, and it can be towed into the barn at night.

Kate bakes pies and grows some of the vegetables she sells at the stand. Other gardeners in the area grow most of the produce for her. Sometimes, she relies on the local food distributor for produce to keep her shelves stocked. Kate would like to see gardeners in her area form a producers cooperative. That way they can grow all of the food she can sell without competing unnecessarily with each other.

he stand is open Friday, Saturday and Sunday during the season. Sales average $700 to $800 per weekend. The stand sells about 100 pounds of tomatoes each weekend, and 10 to 12 bushels of corn. There are 7 dozen ears in a bushel. Kate buys each dozen for $1 and sells it for $2. A local grower produces the corn, but sometimes Kate helps pick it. She bases her prices on grocery store prices, trying to stay on the high side for the better looking varieties. She also sells cheese, which she buys wholesale. Her favorite way to get to know customers is to swap recipes with them.

Kate and JohnWright remodeled a farm wagon for their farm stand on Rte. 11 in Londonderry, Vt. The farmstand can be towed into the barn for night storage.

TThe Codman Community Farm in Lincoln, Mass., also had good results in opening a farm stand on a remodeled hay wagon. They painted the old wagon and added a new deck and canopy. This canopy keeps the produce protected from the rain and sun. They have created a very attractive and useful structure that can be moved under the shade tree by the barn during the day, then stored in the barn at night.

Because the unit is on wheels it is exempt from restrictive zoning and historic district zoning ordinances. These ordinances preclude the building of new structures in their area. Pulling the farm stand in the local Fourth of July parade also brings the farm recognition and new customers.

Farmers Markets

It may not be unreasonable to envisage a renaissance of direct marketing: produce from neighbouring farms being brought in for direct sale in towns, and townspeople going out into the country to buy their food. The extent to which such changes could develop is unlimited. – Lord Northbourne, Look To The Land, 1940

Selling your produce at your home, or at least in your hometown, is usually the simplest and least expensive way to get your produce to market. It can also be the most profitable. But, there may be some compelling reasons why you can't or don't want to do that.

Perhaps your farm is just so far from neighbors that you can't drum up a decent bunch of shareholders for a membership garden. You may be so far out in the boonies that a card table in the front yard won't work. Other growers may have snapped up all the retail opportunities in your locale. In that case, your next best marketing system might be to put the produce in the car and drive it to the nearest farmers market.

Getting involved in selling at farmers markets is usually very easy. Call your state department of agriculture and ask for a list of markets in your area. Ask them which ones they would recommend you attend.

Across the country the past few years have seen many new farmers markets opening, and older markets are expanding dramatically. There has been a tremendous groundswell of interest in these new farmers markets, particularly in the inner cities. In Texas, for example, nearly 100 farmers markets have been added in 4 years, accounting for nearly $36 million in sales annually.

Part of this resurgence of interest in farmer's markets is due to the new lite-diet mindset of American consumers and to a reawakening interest in gourmet cooking. Also, part of the renewed interest in locally grown organic food has to do with recent pesticide scares. There have been frequent newspaper stories about carcinogens in fruits and vegetables imported from major growing regions in the West and Mexico. Many consumers now have a perception that almost anything they buy in the supermarket is contaminated and might be bad for them.

Another reason farmers markets have become so popular recently is the old fashioned flavor and homegrown goodness of locally grown food. People are just plain fed up, literally, with the bland, blister-packed, trucked-in, chemically contaminated vegetables and fruits available today at most supermarkets. Flavor and freshness are why people shop at farmers markets more than any other reason.

There are still many among us who crave the sweet delicious flavor of real tomatoes. We yearn for carrots that are juicy, and apples that are good for us. We, and consumers like us, are the ones who participate in agricultural solutions, by buying goods from local market gardeners at community farmers markets. We appreciate the full flavor that is only available from fresh produce harvested at the peak of ripeness. "Fresh" means picked within the last few hours, not days or even weeks as is the case with most supermarket produce, which is trucked across the country from Florida, California or Mexico.

Those of us who demand the real taste of fresh produce will gladly visit the local farmers markets regularly. We'll buy all we can use until next market day. My friend Helen Oshima, owner of Fern Hill Herb Farm, in Pembroke, Mass., says, *"People are literally starving for good tasting vegetables!"* She is absolutely right, and what's more, people are willing to pay the price to get the freshness and nutritive value they deserve. That's why farmers markets are making a comeback all across America.

Follow the Farm-to-Market Roads

Selling your produce at a farmer's market will be a challenging, invigorating and rewarding experience. You only have a few hours once or twice each week to sell everything you have harvested. If this is your only chance to sell your produce and you don't, then you'll have to carry it home for composting. That's not a good way to be economically sustained.

Marketing fresh food at a busy farmers market is a great way to get new customers, sometimes *lots* of them. Some growers may feel overwhelmed by having all those customers all at once. They often line up in front of the booths, asking questions and buying produce for several hours straight. In the busier markets the customers per day number in the thousands.

I must admit that I've had a couple of times when my brain couldn't keep up during a busy sales rush. I've had to stop the momentum, just briefly, to gather my composure. I remember one remarkable day at the Boston City Hall Plaza Market when I had a continual sea of faces in front of me for four straight hours. I sold everything I had in the van, even the lettuce and sweet corn I wanted to take home for supper. That day I grossed more than $1,000 in sales, so I didn't feel a bit bad when I had to go back to the garden for salad fixings for supper.

To some farmers this is a drawback to marketing at farmers markets. They don't do well meeting the public in a sometimes frenetic atmosphere. But, to me it's a blessing. I spend most of my week as a grower, raising the finest vegetables I can, with only three or four days each week dedicated to marketing.

I don't have to worry about promotion, advertising or even location. The state department of food and agriculture does it all for me. All I have to worry about is getting the fruits and vegetables grown, harvested, on the truck, and into the market. Then I let the customers take them off my hands. No middle people, no overhead to speak of, full retail prices and a substantial amount of money in my change-apron at the close of each market day.

A major difference between farmers markets and a farm stand is the amount of display space that is available. At home I can put everything on a picnic table or build display benches clear across the front yard and load them up. It just depends on how many vegetables I have, how many customers I think I can attract and how much space I need to display everything. At the markets, however, there will be a strict limit on space at the booths or stalls.

At the Boston City Hall Plaza Market, for example, each grower gets a width of 12 feet for their display. At another market in Jamaica Plain, just outside Boston, spaces are 15 feet wide. In the Boston suburb of Brighton Center, there are only two growers selling in a large parking lot next to the bank. They can use all the space they please.

At some farmers markets you can get up to 30 feet of display space.

Even if the markets in your area don't limit your booth size you still have to think about how much you can carry in your car or truck. With these small spaces for transport and display it becomes even more important for you to choose as many high-value crops as you can.

Successful selling at farmer's markets should begin early in the spring or even the year before you bring produce in. Start by calling your state department of agriculture. Ask for a copy of the market list showing the locations, dates and times of every farmers market in your general area. As an example, there are 15 different markets to choose from within a 40-mile radius of Boston. This is probably not true of every city in America, but you will likely have your choice of several farmers markets within range of your backyard market garden.

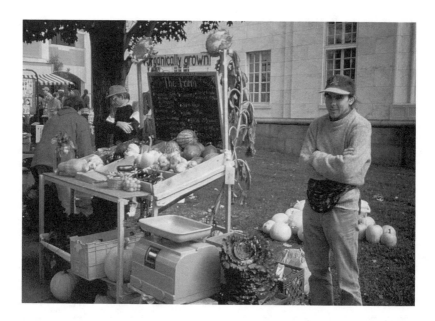

Some market gardeners only grow enough produce for a small space.

Visit the ones that interest you two or three times over the course of a season and see how they work. Pay close attention to the general crowd that attends each market. Keep lists of what vegetables the growers are displaying and the prices.

If you hang around long enough at each market you can tell which growers are doing the most business, and why. These are the growers you want to study and learn from. Whatever they are doing right will work for you, too.

All salespersons are not born equal, that's for sure. At one market I was averaging $800 per day in sales, while the fellow next to me was only able to get a $200 day occasionally. Looking over his disorganized and poorly presented display and his *"to heck with you"* attitude offers several clues about why he isn't more successful. But, I only knew how to do it right because I watched and studied the successful growers at several different markets.

When attending markets in larger cities that have a large and diverse ethnic population keep an eye out for particular groups that are not being catered to. Look for opportunities to grow specialty crops for these groups. This will give you a leg up next year when you do your planting charts.

Keep a watchful eye out for "yuppies," too. They like to buy basil in large quantities for making pesto, and they absolutely love fresh cut flowers and gourmet sweet corn such as Burgundy Delight. Fancy, unusual or trendy varieties appeal greatly to this group of buyers.

The following chart will give you an idea of which are the most popular varieties of vegetables nationwide. This chart is from National Gardening Association, Burlington, Vt.

Naturally, you may want to make some adjustments based on your specific region. For example, in New England sweet corn is more popular than onions, and potatoes sell faster than cabbages.

Table 5. Popularity of Vegetables

Variety	Demand	Variety	Demand
1. Tomato	85.4%	21. Squash	11%
2. Peppers	57.7	22. Turnips	10.7
3. Onions	50.3	23. Pumpkins	10.2
4.Cucumber	43.4	24. Spinach	10.2
5. Beans	43.4	25. Herbs	9.8
6. Lettuce	41.7	26. Dry Beans	8.9
7. Carrots	34.9	27. Asparagus	8.2
8. Sw. Corn	34.4	28. Sunflower	8.2
9. Radishes	30.7	29.Sw.Potatoe	5.7
10. Cabbage	29.6	30.Brus.Sprt.	5.7
11. Peas	29.0	31. Celery	5.4
12.Squash	25.7	32. Chard	3.5
13. Potatoe	25.5	33. Kale	3.1
14. Melons	21.9	34. Kohlrabi	3.0
15. Beets	20.6	35. Dried Peas	2.5
16. Broccoli	19.6	36. Parsnips	2.2
17.Caulif.	14.0	37. OrienttVeg.	
18. Okra	13.6	38. Peanuts	1.9
19.Eggplant	13.0	39. Leeks	1.2
20.Rhubarb	12.2	40. Artichokes	8

One thing to look for when visiting potential markets are signs of active promotion. This needs to come from the market master and the community. Look to see if they have posted big signs and banners. Have they generated plenty of publicity and sent out flyers or placed them on windshields and in store windows? If you see these promotional activities you know the community's leaders want this market to be successful. They want to help it stay in business and grow as a vital contribution to their community and the local economy.

Annilee Johnson (right) relys on signs like these to attract customers to the dozens of farmers markets she has helped open in Massachusetts. Photo courtesy Mass. Department of Food and Agriculture

Some markets do not receive proper promotion. I sold vegetables at an unprofitable market for a few weeks. It is in a small city southwest of Boston. It has no market master, no signs, no press coverage, no support from community leaders and damn little business. If you find yourself selling at one of these languishing markets, get out. Cut your losses and move to a better area.

It makes no sense to bring in a van load of fresh veggies, then sit and twiddle your thumbs for hours. Nobody knows you're there. If you have to take more than 10 percent of your load back home then you're at the wrong market.

There are, of course, ways to upgrade a slow market and make it profitable for the garden farmers who sell there, but turning a troubled market around is a tough job. Find out who has the ultimate responsibility for the success of the market. It may be the county extension service, the state department of agriculture or a local governmental office. Ask the proper agency for funds to upgrade the market. Have signs and banners made up and displayed at major intersections in town. Use flyers for store and car windows. Ask for free newspaper ads and radio spots to publicize the market. Ask the mayor to come down on opening day and again later in the season to help with promotion. Be sure to get your picture taken with the mayor and get it in the local paper. That really helps your business.

Most radio and television stations and local newspapers will be happy to publicize a new or expanding farmers market. Community leaders will be, too. These markets are wholesome and fun, so almost everybody will be willing to do something to help them be successful.

Like any other business endeavor, the proper location within the community is at least half the battle for decent sales and profits. The Boston City Hall Plaza market, for example, is a sure winner in this respect. It's right in the middle of 1 million people. Just one high-rise building can have as many as 4,000 office workers in it. There are a dozen of these buildings within walking distance of the City Hall Plaza market.

Conversely, the Hingham Farmers Market, about 20 miles south of Boston, is a slow market. It is at the rear of an off-street parking lot, removed from central traffic areas, with little visibility. There aren't any banners or periphery signs, other than the one directly at the market. It gets very little advance publicity from year to year. Since it is in a well-educated and affluent market population of nearly 20,000 it does not have to be such a slow market. With some publicity and a more visible location within the community this market could easily become one of the better markets in the area south of Boston.

One way to judge a particular market is to talk to other growers who are selling there, and to growers who have stopped attending that market. Find out why some vendors stay while others leave. Be careful of answers you get from potential competitors, though, as their natural instinct to limit competition might cause them to be somewhat less than truthful. Growers who don't sell at a particular market will likely be more candid about the reasons why.

Sometimes growers leave a market because they are throwing away too much produce after the market day. They are either losing money, or not earning enough to make the effort worthwhile. They may shift to a different market to get closer to home, or into a newly opened market in the city. Or, they may have been waiting for their number to come up on a waiting list at a well-established city market.

Growers who stay at a poorer market do so for one of several reasons. It may be close to their home so they don't have to travel far. There may not be a better market on that particular day within their area. They may not have enough quantity, quality or varieties to compete successfully in a bigger market. Sometimes, they stay at a slow market simply because they may feel inadequate and threatened by the bigger markets. Often, these larger markets have larger crowds, with more aggressive vendors and customers.

Probably the biggest reason growers stay year after year in a lukewarm market is because they feel comfortable there. They may lack marketing and promotional ambitions necessary to compete in the bigger markets. Don't be afraid of these bigger markets; cautious yes, but try them anyway.

Be attentive when talking with your state department of agriculture. You may be encouraged to go to a market that has only one or two growers. The department may tell you how nice the area is and that customers are begging for more vendors and more varieties. This may be true, and often-times it is. But, it can also be true that a particular market needs growers because its lack of business keeps the experienced growers away.

I think you will find the biggest problem facing agriculture departments in most states is finding enough growers to satisfy the demand. This is especially true near metropolitan areas. If you are on the fringe of a city then you have a ready-made market.

The only time I've been personally disappointed by the state department of agriculture recommendations was the story I mentioned earlier about the small city southwest of Boston. The business was just not there, yet the state agriculture department kept sending growers, hoping that things might improve.

My experience in two other situations was much better. The department was correct in assessing the potential for profitable sales at these two markets. I'm glad they encouraged me to go to them. One in particular turned out to be the most profitable of the three markets that I attended each week.

Figure out which markets you want to sell at. Base your judgment on your visits to these markets and your conversations with other growers, the market masters, and your department of agriculture people. Don't forget to interview customers who are attending the various markets you are looking at. I've yet to meet a customer who doesn't have an opinion, one way or the other, about their local farmers market.

Finally, never get so locked in to a particular market that you can't make a change later in the season if conditions just aren't profitable for you. It's OK to be loyal to a market master who is trying to improve a slow market, but don't be foolish and stay with a market that is not profitable.

It's fun to sell at farmers markets. A farm stand can be more profitable, but can also become a grind after a too-long season of six or seven market days each week. Farmers markets give you two or three chances each week to get out of the fields and into town. You can dust off your smile and visit with folks, share stories and jokes and just generally have a good time.

Any direct marketer has to love people to be fully satisfied and successful with this type of marketing. In my case I really do enjoy meeting people and sharing some of my life with them. But, I like to do it in smaller doses. Three days in town is just about all the fun I can stand in any given week.

After you have decided which markets interest you, approach the market master and ask to join the market. You may be accepted right away, you may be turned down, or you may get your name on a waiting list.

Some markets will not have room for another mixed vegetable grower without diluting the market unnecessarily. They may be looking for more specialty crops such as flowers, herbs or fruits. If you don't fit or can't get in, don't feel badly toward the market master. Most market masters would love to have new growers join the market, but they are often severely limited by parking or traffic problems.

Whichever market you chose, you should approach it with the same amount of planning and preparation that you would if you were opening any other kind of business. Prepare a business plan, complete with growing and marketing plans, budgets, and well-defined goals.

If you decide to grow organically, then you will need certification from your local or state organic growers network. If one isn't available, or they don't have a certification program, then you might consider helping to organize it. In most states this certification is necessary before growers can advertise products as organic at the state-sponsored farmers markets.

When you are in a farmers market with a dozen or so other aggressive vendors the word "Organic" on your sign will attract attention to your booth. Being "certified" doesn't usually make much difference to customers, but it does give you the right to use "Organic" in your sales promotions. The organic certification is definitely worth the effort and the cost. However, if you are not an organic grower don't try to fake it by saying you are. The other growers and customers will jump on that quicker than a goose on a June bug and report you to the market master.

How Much Land is Needed to Grow Farm Stand Crops?

How much land will you need and how many market days each week will it take to have a profitable season? That depends on which limiting factors you have identified in your business plan. What are your goals? What do you hope to do? How much do you want to earn?

You may have a full-time job off the farm. You may only want to grow a quarter or a half-acre of produce. Do you want to do all the work of growing and marketing yourself? How many days each week can you go to farmers markets? Saturdays may be the only day you have available to go to market. You may want to hire workers to do the garden chores while you spend more time at several different markets.

If you want to make a few thousand dollars each year from your backyard, in your spare time, then the Saturday Farmers Market may be an excellent way to do it. A table set up measuring 4 by 12 feet will give you 48 square feet of display space. You can add additional display space on the truck or station wagon tailgate. In total you can figure on less than 75 square feet of display space. Each square foot of space is worth about $8 to $12 in sales per day, if you have a good selection, a good market and are a good vendor.

I've usually averaged about $9 per square foot per day in gross sales. Many part-time growers I've talked with try for gross sales of $300 to $500 per day. Personally, I'd shoot for $1,000 each day and settle for $750. If your goal is $300 then you might find yourself willing to settle for $200.

In New England, the farmers market season starts in June and ends in mid October. This gives growers about 15 weeks of active sales. If you are attending one market day each week and averaging $500 per day, your annual gross will work out to about $7,500.

If you spend three hours each evening working in the gardens and eight hours each Saturday harvesting, traveling and selling, you will average about 450 hours annually in the enterprise. This works out to a very respectable $16 per hour gross income for a part-time business doing what you love most to do. If you net about 60 percent after expenses (remember, low overhead) you can look forward to pocketing about $4,500 net income for the summer. That's roughly $10 per hour. Don't forget, all of your business expenses are tax deductible and can often be used to off-set taxable income from your full-time job.

How much land would you need to support this one market day per week? Again, that depends a lot on your crop mix and the fertility and health of your soil. According to the Gallup survey commissioned by National Gardening Association, the average home gardener manages to grow an average of 80 cents per square foot, using retail prices at the supermarket as a comparison.

Concentrate on high-value crops and intensive cropping techniques. This way you can grow $7,500 worth of vegetables on about 10,000 square feet of land. This quarter-acre plot includes driveways, paths, and work areas.

The Ecology Action staff, working with John Jeavons in California, says it's possible to produce $5,000 to $20,000 on one-eighth to one-half acre of good soil. Their figures are for raising a mix of low-value and high-value crops. A market grower concentrating on high-value crops can do much better than that.

Sweet Corn Sure Is Popular, But It's Not Very Profitable

A good variety of sweet corn pulls people to your stand like nothing else you can imagine. Each market day will require about 50 dozen ears. One market day each week for a 15-week market season might require a total of about 9,000 ears.

To grow really good sweet corn requires that you have really good growing conditions. The soil must be healthy, you will need irrigation and you must pay strict attention to pest control, cultivation and fertilizer side dressing. Select a variety that will produce two ears per stalk and plant successive crops so you will have a continuous supply throughout the season. To produce 9,000 ears of good sweet corn might require as much as 12,000 square feet of land.

This size planting allows for a 20 percent to 30 percent loss factor. That's easy enough to do with sweet corn, particularly if you are using organic growing methods. Unfortunately, it's hard to get a high-yielding crop of market quality sweet corn each year without using chemicals. I know it can be grown organically, but too many customers turn up their noses at the worms. If you want organic certification you can't use any of these chemical pesticides, and will have to rely on less-effective organic controls.

Sweet corn usually sells for about $3.60 per dozen ears, or 35 cents per single ear. (East Coast prices, 1991). If you average only one ear per square foot, then the gross value of the crop is only 30 cents to 35 cents per square foot. This is why I call sweet corn a low-value crop. Compared to tomatoes or carrots worth as much as $2 per square foot, sweet corn isn't very profitable.

169

Other problems with growing sweet corn are the raccoons and deer. It's almost a necessity to invest in electric varmint fencing. We didn't use any fencing one year and lost our entire corn crop. Deer ate the corn silks and raccoons ate the ears. The deer ate our snow peas, too, and a good bit of our early lettuce crop.

Dylan Zietlan adjusting electric fence strands to keep out raccoons and deer.

The following year we installed solar powered electric fencing around a full acre of sweet corn at a cost of about $600. The fencing is easily portable and will last for several years, so the expense isn't too bad, especially considering the greatly increased number of sales that will result by having the corn available.

If you don't have enough space to grow sweet corn, then look for more land. Ask your neighbors, or look for nearby private or public land that you can rent or borrow. If you just can't find any good land to use, then contract with another grower to grow sweet corn for you.

Getting Ready for Your First Farmers Market Day

Be prepared. To get ready for your first market day will be easy if you have given careful thought to the critical path. Tasks include harvesting, washing, grading, packing, transporting, setting up your booth and making sales.

The day before the market begins should be spent organizing all your equipment and supplies. Store them in the truck or car, or have them standing by in a neat pile ready to load with the vegetables. When you arrive at the market you can set up your stand quickly and easily.

Get the truck or station wagon ready. Have your canopy made up and rolled or folded neatly, and display table and signs all prepared. Have the harvesting and display bins handy, the washstand all set up and ready to start picking. Be sure to have your clothes, change apron and money for making change all set to go. With these items all laid out you will have a much easier time getting set up for your first market day with the least amount of fuss and bother.

To help organize the task, take a little time and think your way through the steps required to get your stand set up. Look for any bottlenecks or delays that can slow down your setup time. Then you are ready to start selling groceries. After you have been through it a few times it will be easy and almost effortless to unload and set up your display. My worst time for setting up my booth was nearly one hour. My best time was less than 15 minutes.

For those of you who have a van, pickup truck or suburban, there is a neat kit you can buy that will help reduce your set up time. It is a sliding floor that fits inside the truck bed. When you pull it out at the market your display is almost instantly set up. It comes in real handy, too, for eliminating all that crawling around on your hands and knees inside a pickup cap to pull out boxes of veggies. The frame costs less than $300. All you add is plywood. It's available from Deck Slider, Box 508, Emmaus, PA., 18049.

You need a canopy to keep your fresh produce looking good all day in the hot sun or in the rain. Pop-up tent canopies are very good for this. They are easy to set up and give your customers a chance to get in out of the weather, too.

171

On the morning of the market or even the night before, prepare a list of things "to do" so that you don't leave something important at home. Make sure you have your water jug, because your mouth gets dry talking to so many people. Also, a watering can with fresh water to sprinkle your display throughout the day to keep it fresh looking.

Without my "to do" list I'd be continually leaving something at home, like my change or hat. Once I left three boxes of tomatoes sitting on the back porch. Another time I forgot the sawhorses and plywood sheets for my display table. I had to buy a newspaper and spread the sheets on the pavement so I could display my produce. With all that stooping and bending while waiting on customers I had a terrific backache by the end of the day. Yes, I kept a watchful eye out for visiting dogs, too.

After getting your vehicle organized you can turn your attention to which crops are to be harvested for the day. Follow your shopping list so that you have enough of each variety, without picking more than you will need. If you are a new hand at selling at farmers markets it will take some practice to learn just how much of any given variety you will need each day. This is certainly not an exact science, but after a few weeks you'll see some patterns begin to emerge.

In the beginning I simply picked all of everything that was ready and took it to town with me. If it didn't sell at the farmers market I would stop at some restaurants on the way home and try to unload the leftovers. One of my favorite going-home stops was a beer and wine store where the owner would buy all the homegrown lettuce, tomatoes, peppers, sweet corn and cucumbers I could give him. He sold them at a premium to the going-home crowd who frequented his shop.

Plan to pick slow-to-wilt crops like green beans, tomatoes, peppers, eggplant, and squash the evening before, and store them overnight in a cool basement, refrigerator or walk-in cooler. Pick the fragile crops like lettuce and sweet corn just before you leave for the market.

Don't buy expensive harvesting containers. Look for used crates and baskets from your local supermarket. Used grape lugs (flats) are handy, too. The crates and baskets keep individual crops from getting crushed in the truck. Use the grape lugs to display produce at the stand. Organic certification rules forbid using crates and boxes with chemical fungicide residues from commercial packers. Select crates and flats carefully and wash them thoroughly before using.

With a well planned garden you can use a wheelbarrow, garden cart or crate to pick each crop. Use the washstand to clean each item and check for bugs and defects. Then pack directly to a crate or box and set them in the shade or in the walk-in cooler until it's time to leave for the market. Washing produce is critical. It has to look fresh, clean and appealing, otherwise you can't sell it easily. For tomatoes, eggplants, peppers and cucumbers you can use a damp cloth to wipe off dirt and bring out the natural sheen. This makes the vegetables really glow as they sit on your display waiting for a buyer.

Don't put any produce in the truck until you have all your crops picked and boxed. This will help eliminate over-heating in the truck. Also, you can set things in the truck in the order in which they will be taken out at the market for display. This careful packing is an important key to quick set-up times at the market.

Many vegetables such as beans, squash, zucchini, cucumbers and sweet corn will decline in quality or future yield without regular picking. It's best if you can pick everything that is ready. If you have extra produce then go ahead and take it with you and push it a little bit during the day. Some gentle encouragement or a good recipe can move a lot of any given item for you. Even if you give it away as free samples or to the soup kitchen you will feel better knowing that it didn't go to waste.

You Should Look As Good As Your Veggies

Your personal appearance is just as important as the appearance of your vegetable display. Harvesting, packing and loading vegetables is hard work that often leaves you dirty, sweaty and smelly. Always allow extra time to run in and shower and put on clean clothes before you leave for the market. You must look as fresh and clean as your produce does when you arrive at the market.

Eat a good breakfast and take a few minutes to relax over a cup of coffee or tea before you leave for the market. Also, be sure to pack a lunch, unless you are fortunate enough to have a

173

friendly market master who will fetch a sandwich for you from the local deli at lunch time. Arriving with pent-up anger at the rain or lack of it, or the traffic or whatever, will reflect in your conversation and will turn customers off.

I always try to leave my troubles at home and concentrate on being friendly, helpful, courteous and pleasant with customers. I've gotten in the habit of meditating briefly before starting to meet customers. I simply sit in the truck, close my eyes, breath deeply and think about absolutely nothing. This 5-minute relaxation technique can be as good as a nap for rejuvenation and rest. It clears my thoughts and opens my mind to the adventure and opportunities of a new market day.

At a busy market you might meet a hundred or more customers during the day. It's possible one will get under your skin. Just ignore it and go on to the next person in line. Most customers will go out of their way to be pleasant and accommodating. But if you have a surly attitude you can bet the customers will sense it and make a comment. Or worse, they will leave you to your attitude and go buy from your competitor.

If you find unpleasantness, yours or the customers, to be a continuing problem, invest in a good sales training class. At least buy a copy of Dale Carnegie's book *How to Win Friends and Influence People*. Maybe the customers are reacting to your frustration and disagreeable attitude.

If you do lose your patience, and this may happen occasionally, just be quick to excuse yourself. Apologize to the customer, give him or her a free sample of something, then go on to the next customer.

You may encounter a market that has an unusually high number of unfriendly or rude customers. This happened to me once. The only way I could overcome the animosity was by being patient and friendly, yet firm. After a couple of weeks I really noticed a shift to positive customer feedback, proving again that using the Golden Rule really works.

Try to arrive at the market at least half an hour early. This gives you a chance to get set up as quickly as possible, without feeling rushed and flustered. Then you can take a few minutes to relax and gather your wits before the first onslaught of customers begins. If you are late, people may be already lined up and impatient. Then, you are apt to get rattled and make the wrong change or hurry and not get their full order. Being late is annoying, both for you and the customers.

I've found another good practice is to visit briefly with the other vendors before the market master starts the market day. This gives me a chance to check out the pricing and varieties that they have on display. More importantly, it gives me opportunities to spread some of my cheery attitude and get my fellow growers into a good frame of mind, too.

Believe me, a happy market is a wonderful place to work. If there is in-fighting and grouching amongst the vendors it will spill over to the customers and cost everybody some slow or lost sales.

Pricing Plays a Key Role in Profitability

A blackboard and several colors of chalk will work as a price list. Don't try to get by without displaying your prices. The customers will drive you nuts asking for them all day. Have the price board all made up before you leave for the market so you can concentrate on getting set up as quickly as possible. However, unless you know the market and the other vendors well, wait till the last possible moment to insert individual prices. This way you can check out your competitor's pricing before committing yourself.

Just before kickoff time I like to take a quick walk around the other booths and eyeball their displays and price lists. If my produce looks as good as theirs, and usually it looks better, I will put my prices about 10 percent higher than everybody else, especially since I am the only organic grower in most of these markets. If there is a grower with outrageous prices I try to be well under that level, yet still higher than the other vendors.

Occasionally, I've been criticized for placing my prices on the higher side. My game plan is to make more by selling less. Sure, I've discouraged a few customers with my higher prices. But, once they get a taste of my delicious, homegrown goodies they usually don't mind the pricing one bit. Maybe there is a little grumbling from time to time, but that is usually followed with a compliment or comment about how good everything looks and tastes. Market gardening is serious business to me, and I want to make a profit, so I can *stay* in business. My livelihood depends on it. Customers often tell me it feels good to stop by once each week for this wonderful food. *I need to stay in business so they can keep saying that.*

It's not a sin to charge money for food. It's important that we charge a fair price to earn enough to keep our farms financially sustained, and ourselves and our families fed, clothed and housed. It's not the farmer's responsibility to provide cheap food in this country, particularly when Americans spend roughly 11 percent of their income for food, and 12 percent for "entertainment," which includes smoking and alcoholic beverages.

Often, I hear would-be business owners saying they want to bring a better product with a lower price to the public. Usually, that is not possible. If it were, the existing businesses would already be doing it. Your goal should be to bring a better product to the marketplace and charge what it is worth. If customers feel they are getting fair value they will buy from you.

The table below shows that a modest increase in pricing can have a very positive impact on your net profits. A 10 percent increase means you can make the same profit by selling 28 percent less food. Don't put your prices too high, though.

Customer complaints should be handled quickly and positively. If a customer doesn't like something, give the money back without fuss. Believe me, you'll make friends by having this firm policy. With thousands of customers over the years, I can only remember one time that I've been asked for a refund or an exchange. That happened when I let a few wormy ears of sweet corn get by me.

Always have a conversation ready for the occasional complainer who feels your prices are a "rip-off." Be polite but firm and explain that your costs are higher than the supermarket because you do all the work yourself. You don't rely on machines or migrant workers to do your planting and harvesting.

Table 6: What Happens When You Raise Or Lower Your Prices?

According to Walter J. G. Carpenter, Extension agent for Rensselaer County, NY: *"A 20 percent price cut means that a 400 percent increase in sales volume is necessary to realize the same profit obtained before the price was lowered. A 3 percent price cut means you must sell 13.6 percent more volume. A 3 percent increase in price however, means the vendor will obtain the same profit on 10 percent fewer sales."*

A 3% price cut means you must sell	13.6% more volume
5%	25.0%
10%	67.0%
5%	150.0%
20%	400.0%

A 3% increase = same profit on	90.0% of the same volume
5%	83.5%
10%	71.5%
15%	62.5%
20%	55.5%

Tell them about your latest increase in real estate taxes. The price of gasoline just went up. Cost of insurance is out of sight. There are many other reasons that are honest and make sense. It costs money to grow good food, and you have the right to recover your costs and to earn a fair wage for your labor.

You try very hard to bring only the finest and best tasting vegetables to the market, and there are certain problems in doing that. Share this information with your customers so they can empathize with your problems. This helps them rationalize why your prices are higher than others. What you are selling has value. Help your customers recognize and appreciate that value.

Tell your customers the valid reasons why you have to charge higher prices. But, never speak negatively about your competitors. Just say you are glad those other vendors can afford to sell their produce that cheaply and let it go at that.

If you get into a verbal contest with a customer in front of a group of shoppers you will wind up losing more than one sale. Worse, if your competitors hear rumors of the bad things you might have said about their produce, you are apt to start a first class squabble, with no winners.

Ways to increase sales and have more fun

Wear a name tag and have your farm name where the customers can see it. Let them know where you are from. They might have relatives or friends living right near you, and that usually helps you get a new customer. They like to appear loyal to their hometown farmer.

People like to be on a first name basis with their farmer. If they give you their name, write it down so you won't forget. People love to be recognized. Once they feel that you care about them they will be more inclined to walk by your competition on the way to your booth.

You can increase sales by knowing your customer's name. It really helps you and them enjoy the market more, and they won't hesitate to recommend you to their friends and neighbors. Everybody likes to be somebody, so make your customers feel like they are SOMEBODY! Just do it without fawning or appearing insincere.

Remember, the best education in marketing you can ever get is from being a street vendor. In one sense that is exactly what you are when you join a farmers market. Just don't act like some of the more aggressive street vendors that you see at county fairs and ballparks. Don't hawk your wares, and don't snarl if the customers don't buy from you.

As people approach your booth greet them with eye contact, a smile and a positive, pleasant voice. Spend as much time as possible conversing with each customer. If they don't buy something during their visit with you then simply wish them a pleasant day and go on to the next customer. This positive attitude will pay huge dividends in the weeks and years ahead. People will remember your courtesy and stop by again. Next time they will buy something, you can bet on it.

If you have helpers it is important that you spend every spare moment you can in training them. They are an extension of you. Your customers will judge your farm by how your employees look and act. Nobody knows as much about your farm and your produce as you do. Try to convey some of that specialized knowledge and understanding to your helpers, so they can pass it on to your customers, too.

Always be sure to listen to your helpers if they have suggestions. Just because you are the owner doesn't mean you see all the problems or have all the answers. Someone else coming to your booth for the first time might spot shortcomings that you may have completely overlooked.

Involve your helpers in as many functions of your farm as you can. Encourage them to visit other growers in the area to see how different farms operate. Help your workers learn and understand the enormous amount of work, energy and pride that goes into your crop. This will help them convey that information to your customers in a meaningful way.

"What Else Can I Get for You?"

Just before completing a sale the best thing you or your helpers can ask any customer is, *What else can I get for you?* This simple question is loaded with the promise of more sales.

If you merely ask, *Will that be all?* the customer can very easily say, *Yes, thank you.* But, when you ask them *"what else can I get for you?* they will be inclined to look back at your display to see what else they can use. They are glad you are willing to take the time to let them decide. Chances are that two out of every three customers will ask for something else. Try it, you'll like the positive response you will get.

Gently inform your customers if you have special quality or special pricing on any particular items. This is especially useful if you have an abundance of certain vegetables you need to sell. Offer a recipe, or two-for-one pricing. Be sincere, courteous and helpful, and your sales will increase.

Recently, I shopped at a whole foods store in my neighborhood and bought hamburger. As the butcher was wrapping the order he considerately asked me if I'd noticed his special price on chicken wings.

I didn't intend to buy chicken, but his manner was so sincere and helpful that I bought 2 dozen wings. I appreciated his thoughtfulness, and the chicken wings were delicious. Now when I shop for naturally grown meats I make it a point to stop by his store.

Knowingly or not, this grocer made me feel wanted and appreciated. I tried something new and was pleased with it. I won't hesitate to return to his shop in the future, nor will I hesitate to follow up on any suggestions he has for new meal ideas. Plus, I always recommend his store to my friends.

This is the same type of word of mouth advertising that you want to have happening for your market garden business. Work to create that aura of wholesomeness that people are looking for. If they find it at your booth, you will not only increase sales but have a lot more fun as well.

More Ways to Attract Attention and Increase Your Sales

The best way to attract customers to your farmers market booth besides outstanding quality and pleasant service is with visual excitement. Pay close attention to mixing the greens, reds, yellows and whites to have a colorful and visually appealing display. Get in the habit of looking over other people's displays. Check out the other growers at farmers markets, roadside stands, even supermarkets. See if you can pick out the sections that are attractive and catch your eye.

Learn to look for areas where improvements can be made. Visual excitement is a powerful marketing tool and will prompt people to stop at your booth. You want your customers to see your stand first, not your competitor's just a few feet away.

Every grower in the market will have the standard varieties such as sweet corn, tomatoes, and lettuce. Always include a few new varieties in your display. If you can display something unusual and curious looking, people will stop at your stand to admire them and ask questions. Examples are Daikon radishes and Chinese cucumbers.

You may not sell many of these oddities, but when customers stop to chat, you will get a chance to show off your knowledge and expertise, and your other produce. Hopefully, they will then buy the standards from you, and not go away empty-handed.

When your customers get off the bus or out of their car, you want them to see what you have for sale. When the boxes lie flat, your customers can't see the produce from a distance. Prop up the boxes on shelves and slant them toward the customer.

Walk away from your stall 100 feet or so and look back at your display. Everything should be clearly visible, alive and enticing. If it doesn't command attention, then you aren't setting it up right. Start over, and keep trying till you feel confident that it looks great. Then ask your customers what they think of it. They may have some good suggestions on how you can improve it. Even if they don't, it's a great conversation starter, especially if you are shy with customers.

Once you have designed a successful display stocking pattern, keep it up. Try sticking to the layout as best you can throughout the season. Your customers will become familiar with the display and feel comfortable with it, and you.

Another way you can attract attention is to wear something suitable yet distinctive. In my case, I have a woven straw cowboy hat that I bought several years ago while vacationing in Montana. I wore this hat three years in a row at the markets I attended. I've overheard customers asking for "the guy with the hat" when they didn't know my name.

I also play my truck radio, just loud enough for the customers to hear it maybe 25 feet or so from my booth. It doesn't matter which station. I happen to like classical and bluegrass music and haven't noticed much of a difference in customer appeal, but I do know it works. It's like a subtle magnet drawing people to my booth.

I got the idea for the music from an elderly garden farmer in Brockton, Mass., who always plays old Gene Autry tapes on a cassette player. What a fantastic marketing idea this old gentleman has. Everybody likes Gene Autry, and the rhythm and beat of the music is pleasing to the ear.

Sell Yourself, Nobody Else Will

Earlier, I said that I didn't worry as much about promotional marketing at farmers markets, compared to at-home or roadside sales. Most of the time this is true. But, you can always stir up more business for yourself and the other vendors at the market if you do some pre-market self-promoting.

Maybe you're trying to entice the customers you meet at the farmers markets to drive out to your farm on a weekend to shop. More likely, you just want to get more customers to shop at your booth. Self-promotion will work in either case.

Put up banners and colorful canopies to attract customers to your farmers market booth.

Make some flyers describing your farm and produce. Put them on windshields and in store windows a day or so before the market opens. If you don't have time to distribute handouts, hire a kid on a bicycle to do it. This will start spreading your name around and encourage customers to walk by your competition to ask specifically for you.

When your customers stop to visit be sure to give each of them your business card. It's professional, economical advertising and will help to keep your farm name in their minds. Also, consider weekly flyers to put in each bag of groceries. This will help the customer anticipate new varieties as the season progresses. A weekly recipe sheet with your farm name and logo is also a good way to continue expanding your circle of friendly customers and spreading your message. Encourage your customers to keep these recipes in a binder for ready reference. Naturally, your farm name is on each sheet so that as they use the recipe file they will be continually reminded of your farm.

For several years I have noticed a true phenomena, one that cannot be justifiably explained. The more customers you have in front of your booth, the more that will show up and join in the activity. I've heard this compared to a "feeding frenzy," reminiscent of sharks gathering around a fresh kill. It usually takes place within the first hour as the market opens. There are a lot of theories as to why this is true. I've stopped trying to rationalize it, I just enjoy it and work faster.

Many customers arrive at the market with pent-up anticipation. Some arrive early and stand in line in front of your booth while you are setting up. Some of them are anxious to get first pick of the fresh vegetables. Others simply want to get the shopping done and go home.

Do whatever it takes to get that crowd of people in front of your booth and keep them there. At one point I tried to hire a local bluegrass fiddle player to stand beside my booth and play a medley of snappy, country sounding tunes. Unfortunately, the market master was a bit concerned about the idea, so I never did it.

If you have a chance to do something similar, though, don't hesitate. Decent street fiddlers can be hired for $30 for an afternoon. The crowd they will generate and the increased sales that will result should more than pay that cost. This is especially helpful if you are a new vendor in the market and get stuck at the end of the line of booths. Use creative promotions like these to pull the customers to you rather than settle for the overflow from the other booths.

Look for customer needs when planning your marketing program. One big aspect of successful selling is to learn to appeal to the customer's senses to increase sales. We all have five physical senses that we rely on to get what we want out of life: *touch, smell, sight, taste,* and *sound.*

Let your customers touch the produce. Don't worry about a little bit of spoilage caused by aggressive handling. Let the customers feel the weight and firmness of your vegetables.

They will know that these veggies are full of nutritional value and were harvested within the past few hours.

You will be conveying your confidence in the produce by allowing customers to touch and feel. If the produce isn't fresh you wouldn't want the customers to know. By letting them touch and feel you are assuring them that your produce is fresh-picked and ready to eat. You are conveying your trust in the customer by letting them fondle the goodies. You are *proud* of your produce, let your customers know that.

Smell is a wonderfully powerful sales tool that will help you increase sales. Imagine yourself walking up to a colorful and enticing display of vegetables, flowers and herbs. Let your sense of smell appreciate the wonderful aromas. Who can resist the smell of fresh onions, ripe tomatoes, the aromatic herbs such as basil and dill, and especially the cut flowers?

At the beginning of each market day I crush fresh basil and drop it in my shirt pocket so I'll smell like a farmer. I know it sounds silly, but try it sometime. I got this tip from a retired market gardener in Concord, Mass. I'm convinced I sell more basil and tomatoes because of it. Besides, I like the smell. It helps to cover body odors after a few hours in the sun, it makes me feel good about myself and it's a soothing remedy to the hectic pace of the market day.

Your *visual* impact and that of your helpers, stand and display of vegetables, herbs, and flowers cannot be underestimated. First, you want your display to be neat and well organized. Mix the greens and reds and whites and yellows to create an exciting array of vitality and colorfulness.

Second, keep yourself and your helpers well dressed and neat looking. When customers look in your direction you want them to see something nice and appealing. Always be sure to pick up any trash on the ground, and keep your booth clean. And never smoke in front of the customers, because it often turns them right off. Even the smell of tobacco smoke on your clothing can discourage some shoppers.

The best way to get your customers to *taste* your produce is to offer free samples. Have a clean, covered casserole dish handy, with a napkin holder and tooth pick holder and encourage them to try something. For samples you can slice a cucumber or a melon, or give them fresh berries. Cut tomatoes have always worked best for me. Keep a trash can handy for the dirty napkins. You don't want to create litter around your booth.

When you offer free samples you will find that many customers who may have planned to walk right by your stand will stop and take a taste of something. This gives you a chance to engage them in conversation and that leads to sales.

Conversation with your customers is important. Offer a pleasant and positive greeting. This will appeal to their sense of *sound*. Use the opportunity to convey information about your farm and your produce. Let them hear and feel the excitement and enthusiasm you have for this wonderful work you are doing.

Tell them how to handle and store the food they are buying from you. Culinary tips help, too. For instance, tomatoes are one fruit that should *not* be refrigerated. It ruins the flavor. Also, tell your customers not to put tomatoes on the windowsill in the sunlight. That also causes loss of flavor. Suggest, instead, that they put tomatoes on the kitchen counter out of direct sunlight and they will ripen just fine.

Tidbits such as this will help your customers get the full enjoyment they deserve from the produce they have purchased from you. When they enjoy something they'll return next week to purchase more. Just as importantly, they will delight in telling all their friends about you, too.

If business is good you will often be too busy to carry on much of a conversation with individual customers, especially during the rush periods when it's all you can do to fill bags and make change. Sometimes, all you will have time to do is make eye contact. Offer a smile and a few words of solicitation. This pleasant greeting will help customers overcome temporary shyness and encourage them to linger at your booth and look at what you have to offer.

In your conversation, though, make your voice loud enough for other customers to hear. As you describe the benefits of your vegetables to one customer, others will overhear and decide to buy from you. Always look for body language, too. If their eyes linger on a particular vegetable, engage them in conversation about how your grow it or how they can cook it.

In the slower times throughout the day make it a point to inquire about your customers' needs, likes and dislikes. Point out something especially attractive on your display and ask them for an opinion. Offer them a free recipe for the vegetable that seems to catch their eye. If they show interest in a particular item ask them for *their* recipe. This makes them feel special, especially when they stop by next week and see you handing out recipe sheets with their favorite one on it. Don't forget, if you use their recipe be sure to use their name as the contributor. That *really* makes them feel special. Be sure to ask before you use their name, though; it's common courtesy and they just may not want you to do it.

I cannot over emphasize the importance of conveying *information*; to your customers. Have a little spiel made up about how you grow things naturally or organically and how the weather in recent days has been affecting your crops. Whatever comes to mind, just say it. If you can keep that customer engaged in conversation for 60 seconds they will buy something. Maybe they won't purchase anything the very first time they meet you, but they will be back next week and remember how nice you were. Then they will buy something.

There are also two non-physical senses that can help you increase sales. *Common sense* is the first one. This has to do with the customers' feelings of responsibility to their bodies, and to the health of their families. Customers will recognize the value of your produce and will intuitively know that what they buy from you will taste good and be good for them.

Secondly, large numbers of consumers are now developing a sense of *social awareness*, including a newly felt responsibility to support local farmers. The public has read the stories about farm failures. Encourage your customers to help you keep your farm operating successfully and profitably. If you are offering a product that they enjoy, they will be happy to help you stay in business. You needn't feel guilty about doing this, either. You are indeed providing a real and valuable service to the public by producing vegetables that are tasty and healthy, so make the most of it.

Learning Efficient Selling

Do everything you can to appeal to each customer individually. Then turn your attention to some of the mechanics of selling that will help you speed up service. This will enable you to wait on more customers in less time. Whether you are selling at a farm stand or farmers market, you need to be able to talk to more customers each day. By doing that you will make more sales while making more new friends. Be sure to "complete" each sale, too. This doesn't need to be anything more than eye contact, a smile and a pleasant, *"Thank you, come again next week."*

Adding up orders and making change amounts to half of the time you will spend with each customer. If you can speed up the checkout it will leave you with more time to talk to more customers. Arrange your checkout so that it is efficient and quick. Have what you need on hand. I arrived at my first farmers market day with a $20 bill in my pocket, and no way to make change for customers. I had to leave my booth unattended and run to the bank for change. At the very least you will need three rolls each of quarters, dimes, and nickels. Price your produce in even amounts so you don't need to use pennies. It's hard to add odd amounts in your head and it takes too long to count pennies when making change.

You also need about 10 one dollar bills, a couple of $5s and a $10 for changing larger bills. Use a system for your change apron. Keep the coins in the right pocket and the $1s in the left pocket. If you are right-handed use your left hand to hold change or bills as you count them with your right hand. This is much quicker and more accurate, since your right hand is more nimble. Reverse the procedure if you are left-handed. Keep the $5s and $10s in either a shirt pocket or pants pocket. This will limit the possibility of giving out a $10 instead of a $1 when you are making change in a hurry, which is most of the time at the busier markets.

You can get nail aprons free or at low cost from your local lumber company to use as a change apron. Some market vendors use a carpenter's bib apron that has four pockets at the waist and more on the bib. This keeps bills separated, yet convenient. There's room for a pen, pencil or a pocket calculator in the bib pocket for quick access when adding up larger orders. It's a good idea to have two of these aprons. They do get dirty and need to be washed frequently.

Some vendors use a tackle box or money box for keeping change. I find a couple of things wrong with this idea. First, if you keep the change box on the table it is apt to get turned over and spilled, right in the middle of your big rush of customers. Second, when you turn your back somebody might help themselves to your money.

If you keep the change box on the tailgate of your truck, you must turn your back on the customer to make change. Then you lose eye contact with your customer, and disrupt the normal flow of conversation that accompanies the transaction. Finally, it takes too long to have to move back to the tailgate to make change for each sale.

If you have helpers, it also slows things down considerably if you have to wait while they have their hands in the money box counting out change. It is much better if you use an apron, and give your helpers an apron, too. Have them follow your system of separating bills and coins.

Have your helpers empty their pockets before they put the apron on. Store everything in a safe place until the market day is over. This way they won't inadvertently include their $20 bill in your receipts. It also makes it more difficult for them to put one of your $20s in their pocket, either by mistake or intentionally.

Sales In The Bag

Bagging vegetables for customers can be very time-consuming. Having the correct supplies and materials at hand is important for efficient service. You will need to have plastic tear-off "fresh produce" baggies for individual wrapping, medium size paper bags for smaller orders and large grocery bags for larger orders. I also like to have a few large grocery bags with handles for customers who buy a substantial amount of groceries. Large shopping bags are especially appreciated by customers who are walking or traveling by bus. You can buy bags in all shapes and sizes from your local paper products store. Check the yellow pages or ask local merchants where to buy them.

Having your farm name and logo printed on these larger bags is an excellent low-cost way to keep your image in the customer's eye. Your state department of agriculture may have a program for cooperative purchases of printed shopping bags, which often lowers the cost to farmers considerably.

Having bags and scales accessible to customers allows them to serve themselves.

Sometimes, the market master will have plastic bags available with the market logo and address. These can usually be purchased at cost, and help to advertise the farmers market. I don't like the use of plastic bags any more than you do. But in the vegetable industry, plastic bags are such a common item that most customers expect them. Plastic baggies are especially useful for keeping wet vegetables from leaking through the paper bags.

Have the rolls of plastic baggies on your table so the customers can pick out their selection. It takes too long for you or your helpers to bag each individual order. Letting customers bag their own order really speeds up the process. It also helps to have your scales accessible to customers so they can weigh their own purchases. Have a good supply of paper bags at each end of your bench or underneath. Be sure to keep the bags from getting wet or blowing away.

Some areas are worse for wind than others, but any strong gust can be troublesome. Always fasten your canopy, signs and banners securely. It's embarrassing and time consuming to get things put back together if your canopy falls over and strews produce all over the place. While your attention is on

Marketing is Fun

canopy reconstruction, your line of customers may fade away and head for the other booths.

At most markets there is a rule that no vendor can start selling before the scheduled opening time. This is a good rule because it is quite clear to the customers that opening time can't be rushed. *"Not my fault, Market Master says so."* Just be sure you don't dawdle and run out of time. If the bell rings and you are not ready, you lose. This first rush of customers will amount to one-third to one-half of your business for the day, so be ready for it.

Be A Good Neighbor

Be as cooperative as you can with the other growers selling in the market. If they ask you to watch their booth while they go to the bank or restroom, be accommodating. It sets a good example for the other vendors and the customers and keeps everything running smoothly. They will be more inclined to return a favor for you, too.

One day at the Boston City Hall Farmers Market I opened a bale of bags to find that the seams came apart. Without bags you can't sell many veggies, since people can't carry them. If the other growers hadn't loaned me bags I would have had a miserable sales day.

At the end of the day, be especially careful to clean up your space and the area immediately around it. It's a rule at most markets, but more importantly, it's common courtesy. Many markets are in bank parking lots or town plazas. An inordinate amount of trash left lying on the ground may discourage the cooperative use of the site in the future.

Always have a freebie on hand for the local meter-person or police. You want the uniformed people to sort of hang around. This will help keep local undesirables from trying to steal your change apron. Never count your money where anyone can see how much you have. If the local undesirables ever find out you have several hundred dollars in bills folded up in your pocket they may try to relieve you of it.

Stay friendly with the market masters. A few free veggies every week or so might encourage them to grant little favors, even steer local photographers and newspaper reporters to your booth. Twice I've had pictures of my stand on the front pages of local newspapers, and boy, what a boost for sales. It's nice to have your ego stroked once in a while, too, by having customers call you by name because they saw your picture in the paper.

Market master Alice Galloway in Brighton, Mass., saved the day for us one year by getting the local papers out to do stories on us. A snafu in the planning dates caused the market to be canceled inadvertently. We showed up anyway, but the customers didn't know we were there. The following week after the story and pictures hit the paper, we had plenty of customers, and we kept the market open and successful.

Be accommodating, even if something appears unusual. For example, I've often seen Chinese customers buy sweet corn and husk the ears before leaving the market. I have no idea why they do it, custom I suppose. If you don't have a trash barrel for the husks it creates a dickens of a mess. Don't tell them not to do it, either, it hurts their feelings. Just give them a trash barrel, tell them you welcome the husks for your compost pile, and don't make a fuss over it.

Beware of shoplifters, they come in every crowd. Often there will be lines of customers in front of your booth. It's easy for someone to help themselves to the sweet corn or tomatoes, then fade into the crowd without paying. Always keep an eye out, but don't make a scene. Just ask them to pay for the produce and let it go at that.

Sometimes, what appears to be shoplifting is just an absent-minded customer. I've had customers get so busy visiting with one another that they walk right off together, with neither one having paid me. They are usually more embarrassed than anything when I call their attention to the oversight.

Also, when there are lots of people, I've seen customers pick up goods from one stand and try to pay at another. That's OK, just take the money. When you have a free moment, pass it on to the proper stand. The grower will appreciate it, and will do the same for you next time.

Selling your produce at a local or regional farmers market can be a joyous, exciting, interesting, challenging and educational experience. Granted, there is an awful lot of work to be done in just a few hours. But spread it out, with a market every other day instead of one day right after another, and the work isn't all that bad. It gets me out of the garden and into town three or four days a week, and that is fine with me. The trip home with a pocketful of money after each market day is certainly very satisfying, too.

I think the real reason I enjoy selling at farmers markets so much is the customers. If they like my produce I feel a wonderful sense of having done something good. If they don't like my produce, which is very rare, it challenges me to do better next time. All in all, it's a very satisfying and rewarding way to make a living.

§

Restaurants, Caterers, Specialty Stores

When I started my market garden in Massachusetts, I didn't have much success with marketing to restaurants. The business is there, but I could never grow enough to support it. Nor could I generate enough self-motivation to do as much with it as I could have. My philosophy has always been that my market garden space is limited, and my time is valuable. I want to get retail prices whenever possible, and this usually isn't possible with the wholesale buyers.

More recently, with the Intervale Foundation, however, I have found a big market in restaurant sales. Farmers who are working with us are selling upwards of $100,000 annually to a group of restaurants in Burlington. They are selling the produce to the restaurants at 10 percent more than conventional produce from the wholesalers. We call this the "organic premium."

Restaurants, caterers, specialty and grocery stores purchase at wholesale, then sell at retail or value-added prices. In the earlier years of my market garden, I marketed fresh vegetables to this group at a 25 percent discount. There's not too much wrong with that, except that it takes just as long to pick a peck of tomatoes for a restaurant as it does for a retail buyer. The net return is greater with the retail buyer. Plus, in most retail situations, I get face-to-face contact with the person who will eat my produce, and that's very important to me.

On the other hand, larger restaurants, caterers and grocery stores do use huge amounts of fresh produce. They are always there when the produce is ready to be harvested and delivered. They usually pay cash on delivery, or at the time of the following delivery. I'm not totally against this method of marketing. I see it as a very viable market outlet for growers who don't have retail capabilities. The volume and ease of marketing and deliveries can often make the lower pricing worthwhile.

Profits By The Foot

Mel Bartholomew, author of *Square Foot Gardening*, also wrote an excellent marketing book entitled *Cash From Square Foot Gardening*. This book is about selling fresh produce to restaurants on a part-time basis. I recommend it for any market gardener who is contemplating this marketing system. I used his book as a guide when I set out to try it and found many of the things he said to be true and very helpful.

If you read Bartholmew's book, don't become enamored with the $5 per square foot potential that he claims. It probably is possible with very high-value crops, such as greenhouse tomatoes and exotic lettuces. However, the average backyard market gardener should expect to earn an average of $1 per square foot, based on my experience.

Sometimes, his plan to earn $5 per square foot of garden space will work. One example is Anna Eddy of Martha's Vineyard, Mass. She sells $70,000 worth of organic salad greens to Boston area restaurants annually. She has less than a quarter-acre in garden plots, and relies on a large solar greenhouse for most of the production on a year round basis.

That she has combined Bartholomew's basic restaurant sales format with daily mail order sales is even more exciting. Her biggest crop is mesclun (mixed salad greens). This exotic salad mix often sells for $16 per pound in the off-season. She gets her orders from the restaurants by telephone and ships the produce packed in ice via UPS.

Restaurant marketing is just like the other wholesale direct marketing methods. Contact the chef, show samples of your produce and ask for an order. It's that simple. Often, it's easier to sell fresh vegetables to a chef than it is to other customers. Professional cooks know good food and they will go out of their way to get it whenever it's available.

Because of the upsurge in gourmet cuisine and health-conscious patrons, the competition for tasty new meals is intensive in the restaurant industry. Chefs are always looking for a competitive edge, and fresh picked produce with that homegrown flavor really thrills them.

Cafe Budapest, in Boston, has such a keen interest in using fresh produce that it sends a car around to the various farmers markets daily during the season to pick up vegetables and herbs. Chuck Hemmerlin, master chef at Cafe Budapest for 12 years, just loves fresh produce. He feels the best way to have satisfied customers is to serve them the absolute finest and freshest vegetables available.

Perry Restaurant Group, which owns six large restaurants in Vermont, uses local produce whenever possible. It contracts annually with the Intervale Incubator and five area growers for supplies of vegetables. Perry lists these growers' names in the restaurant menus, and even named a couple of dishes for the different farmers.

Tony Perry, owner of Perry Restaurant Group, believes so strongly in the benefit of supporting local agriculture that he has provided scholarship funding for interns in the Intervale Intern Training Program. He has also given grants for research in food waste composting and other organic farming practices. He is always looking for opportunities to participate in local events that promote organic food and sustainable agriculture.

Not Too Big, Not Too Small – But Just Right

There are three lessons I've learned from dealing with restaurants. First, choose a restaurant that is not too big for your garden. Figure out how much food you can produce each week. Contact a chef or two and compare your list with what they use. For example, the Hilltop Steakhouse restaurant in Lynn, Massachusetts, uses nearly a ton of salad vegetables each day That's a much bigger customer than most backyard market gardeners can supply.

194

Second, choose a restaurant that is not too small. Small restaurants may be easier to approach for your first time and usually have a closer relationship with the clientele they serve. But, they just don't order enough to make it worthwhile. I see that as an important reason why I wasn't happy with my earlier results in restaurant food sales.

The first restaurant I chose was a little bistro that only had a seating capacity of 50. The chef was anxious to buy my organically grown vegetables, but could only use certain varieties. The menu changed almost daily. One day she would ask for fancy lettuce, the next day potatoes or carrots. Each week, she wanted something different. It was very hard for me to anticipate what I should be growing or harvesting from day to day. The biggest problem for me was the small orders, often only $20 or $30 every other day. The fact of the matter is, these small restaurants just don't use very many vegetables. I just felt the time and effort involved in such small quantities of produce was not worth the bother. I felt I was wasting time on a market outlet that amounted to less than 10 percent of my annual output.

Now that I look back I realize that I should have been working far more closely with the chef. If I had asked her before the start of the season what she wanted me to grow I could have accommodated her menu changes. If she knew my harvesting schedule, she could have planned her menu around it.

If I had followed the recommendations in Bartholomew's book *Cash From Square Foot Gardening,* I would have gone to the larger family style restaurants in town. They're not too big, and not too small, but sized so that a healthy percentage of my business could come from them.

It's easy for restaurant owners and chefs to see the advantage in using locally grown produce. It's fresh food that tastes great, and customers love the idea of supporting local farmers. The difficulty arises in the planning and scheduling of crops that will fit the restaurant's menu.

The third lesson I learned when dealing with restaurants is, don't irritate the chef. That's easy to do. I have, and it's not fun. Being a chef must be one of the most stressful jobs imaginable. With all the things they have to worry about each day, the last thing they need is a farmer who can't deliver on time, doesn't have the correct varieties or delivers produce that isn't washed or packed properly.

195

Take the time to visit with the chef during a time of day when he or she is least busy. Ask about varieties and quantities they use. Arrange a best time each week when you can call for the order, and don't make any promises you can't keep. Lack of communications with the chef will cause fewer sales or no sales.

Just remember, when working with restaurants they want it cheap, clean and on time. If you can't fill that order then the chef will look elsewhere for fresh produce. If you can work through the logistics of restaurant food sales it's a great outlet, provided you can't use one of the more profitable direct marketing methods.

§

Caterers and Institutions:

A Different Mix of Vegetables

Selling produce to caterers is a different and even more difficult proposition than selling to restaurants. Caterers usually have no idea from one month to the next how many vegetables or even what varieties they will need. This makes it very difficult for the vegetable grower to do any real crop planning.

Catering a sit-down dinner at a wedding, for example, might require the caterer to have large amounts of green beans and potatoes. Catering a barbecue might require large quantities of sweet corn, salad greens and coleslaw. If you are on close terms with a caterer and want to try selling vegetables to that market, then by all means go ahead. I would not go out of my way to find this type of market outlet, but it may be just the niche you are looking for. One trick you might try is to grow specific vegetables for local company picnics or parties. You can get the order in advance, sometimes with a deposit, and harvest the produce on the day of the event.

Institutions are a different matter entirely. Hospitals, company cafeterias, summer schools, camps and so many others could be excellent outlets for your produce. They, too, will want to buy as cheaply as possible, but the volumes they order will be large. For example, Medical Center Hospital of Vermont, in Burlington, serves over 4,000 meals per day to patients and in the staff cafeteria. They use a tremendous amount of vegetables, salad greens and fruits, and are buying nearly $20,000 in salad greens annually from local growers during the season. If you have such an establishment in your area I would very much recommend that you follow up on it. Be creative, and let your mind and imagination carry you around town to see where they are. Look for ways you can get your foot – and your produce – in the door.

We have had some success here in Burlington by providing wholesale vegetables to the local Onion River Health Food Cooperative, and the Origanum Health Food store. These specialty food stores are wholesale sales, but we get a 10 percent organic premium. They buy substantial quantities, and they are less than a mile from our farm. These are all good reasons why it sometimes makes sense to sell at less than retail pricing.

Strange as it might sound, wholesale direct marketing can sometimes be quite rewarding, personally. For some time, I sold organic vegetables to a training school for learning disabled children in Pembroke, Mass. Each Wednesday during the growing season, the school's kitchen manager left a message on my answering machine with her order for the week. The following morning, I picked the varieties she asked for and delivered them to the school. As I arrived, the kids would come running out to help carry in boxes and bags. They were thrilled as could be to help a *real* farmer bring in *real* food.

This school has a complete kitchen and makes sauces, pickles and coleslaw as training exercises for the children. They even put together small packages of dried herbs affixed to a folder with recipes. I bought these packets at wholesale and sold them retail for a decent profit. It gave me something new to talk to my customers about.

Every time I had left over cucumbers I'd take them down to the school for the students to make bread and butter pickles for me to sell. It was an excellent product and my customers loved the fancy pint jars. The pickles were delicious and I made a pretty good profit on them. My greatest satisfaction in working with this group was to help them help themselves by providing work for a very deserving group of youngsters. I didn't feel like I was exploiting the students. Instead, I felt as if I was their partner, helping them produce a product and making it available to the public in a profitable and worthwhile way. And that's what business – good business – is all about!

§

Pick Your Own Farming

At first glance, it might appear that the average backyard market gardener doesn't have room for a pick your own (PYO) market garden system. In actuality, though, PYO may be an easy way to get started in a backyard business. Examples of successful crops for this market system are strawberries, blueberries, blackberries, raspberries and even Christmas trees.

You may only have half an acre or so, but you could still earn $5,000 or more from a PYO backyard planting, especially with day-neutral everbearing strawberries. These are typically planted as an annual in May and harvested from August to October of the first year. These berries are one-quarter wild strain, and have a really sweet and intense strawberry flavor. They are very much in demand and easy to sell, but difficult to grow on a commercial basis. That's why they are a good 'niche' crop for the backyard grower who is willing to spend the time needed for best yields.

Day-neutral strawberries sell at wholesale for $1.75 per pint, and retail for $2.30 per pint. PYO, they would sell for about $1.25 per pint. The berry plants can be held over to the second year with proper care. During the second year, they will bear during June and July.

With brambles such as blackberries and raspberries, the first crop isn't ready till the second and third years. With proper care, the plants will then bear for several years.

Big letters on signs make it easy for customers to see your farm and stop to shop. photo courtesy Mass. Department of Food and Agriculture.

Dr. Booker T. Whatley, in his book *How To Make $100,000 Farming 25 Acres,* spends a lot of time discussing Pick Your Own farming. Sometimes called simply PYO, or U-Pick, the idea is quite popular in England, probably more than in the United States. Dr. Whatley, and many growers, swear it's the best possible way to sell produce.

With the shortage of field hands in many areas, I would say that it may be the *only* way to sell large quantities of certain crops, especially strawberries, raspberries, blueberries, and even apples and peaches. I'm particularly thrilled with the idea of selling Cut-Your-Own Christmas trees, which I will discuss later in this chapter.

I look at U-Pick marketing as more than just a way to avoid labor and marketing costs associated with conventional marketing methods. The U-Pick operation can be a *"come on out to the farm and have some fun"* sales pitch to get customers interested in visiting your farm.

When I first heard of PYO marketing about 20 years ago, I knew right off that there was more to it than meets the eye. The real fun is to take the kiddies out to the farm and pick a few strawberries or blackberries. The family enjoys the preparation for the trip and then the drive itself. There is the anticipation of spending a few hours or even a day out in the country. They can bring along a picnic basket, a Frisbee or a football to toss around.

Many PYO farm operators have capitalized very well on the public's fascination with driving out to the country for a visit to the farm. Some of these agricultural entrepreneurs have even earned themselves the title of "entertainment farmers." They've added fishing ponds, a petting area with baby farm animals, hay rides and even such events as "name the scarecrow" contests. There is a blueberry grower in Northern Vermont who even hires a bagpipe player to entertain folks while they pick.

One PYO operation, Nashoba Valley Winery in Bolton, Mass., has really zeroed in on successful PYO marketing. They've established a winery to make fruit wines that are for sale at the farm stand. During a visit to their farm it's fun to pick fresh fruits, then take the tour of the winery and join in the wine tasting. It's even more fun to take home a bottle of their delightful peach wine. Serve it slightly chilled in front of the fireplace after a delicious home cooked meal that includes fresh fruit dessert.

This is the real essence of U-Pick marketing. What people are *really* buying is the country outing, entertainment and rural ambiance and agrarian experience provided by the PYO entrepreneur. The number among us who are doing any appreciable amount of canning, preserving, and even freezing, is declining rapidly. Even Ball Corporation, the largest U.S. manufacturer of canning jars and supplies, has determined that this market is shrinking steadily. When you plan your backyard PYO farm be sure to add in enough fun events to make it attractive to today's fussy shoppers.

There are many circumstances where U-Pick farming might be very compatible with your future growth plans, or even your retirement plans if you are nearing those golden years. I also see PYO crops fitting in very well with the growth and expansion of an existing vegetable farm. You may have land available that is not really suited to vegetable cropping. Maybe you have an area that could be made into a nice blueberry patch, or a hillside that would be ideal for cut your own Christmas trees.

Another advantage of pick your own farming is that some agricultural entrepreneurs only want to deal with customers during a few weeks of each season. This leaves the rest of the summer free for travel or fishing. The PYO marketing system can fill these needs quite nicely.

Cash From Christmas Trees

I'm particularly thrilled with the idea of a retirement farm based on cut-your-own Christmas trees. Any piece of fertile ground on which you can walk upright is probably usable for tree crops. The trick is to not try to grow them on infertile land or without irrigation and proper attention. There is a fantastic market emerging nationwide for U-Cut trees. Oklahoma, as an example, only grows 1 percent of the Christmas trees purchased in the state each year.

The waiting period from transplanting to harvest for Christmas trees can be quite long, from 7 to 10 years. To get a faster crop you can start with the more expensive 4-year-old transplants, choose quick maturing varieties, and tend them very carefully. This way it's often possible for a beginning Christmas tree farm to start selling trees during the sixth or seventh year.

You don't need a huge parcel of land to make this operation profitable, either. U-Cut trees sell from $20 to $40 each. There are a few special varieties, such as the Silver Concolor Fir, that can fetch up to $60 or more per 6-foot tree near metropolitan areas. There can be 1,500 to 1,700 Christmas trees per acre. The well-managed Christmas tree farm can earn $30,000 to $70,000 per acre over a 7 to 10 year period. Up front costs to establish the crop can be as much as $2,000 per acre. Maintenance costs of spraying, fertilizing, pruning and shearing can add as much as $1,000 per acre each year to the total expenditures. This depends on how much labor, fertilizer, irrigation, sprays and other inputs are required to get a quality crop.

On a half-acre plot you might plant 100 trees per year for eight years. By the seventh year your first planting will be ready to harvest, if you have watered and fertilized them well. After you sell the first group of trees you can pull the stumps and start planting a new rotation. In a PYO marketing system these 100 trees per year will return about $2,000 to $4,000. With this 8- year rotation you will have a continuous crop.

I have done a considerable amount of work over the years with Christmas trees and have found them to be one of the most enjoyable of the various tree crops. First, they look so nice as they are growing, all lined up in neat rows, adding a pretty green color to even the bleakest winter landscape. Second, they don't require all that much care and maintenance or expensive equipment.

Annual maintenance work required is minimal. Mow between the rows about three to five times each year to keep the grass and weeds from competing with the trees. This eliminates the nesting sites for rodents, too. Once or twice each year you will want to apply lime and fertilizer to keep the soil healthy. After the trees begin to grow you will want to prune them each year to keep them shaping up into that classic Christmas tree form.

Insect pests can be a serious problem for Christmas tree growers in some areas, so weekly monitoring and occasional spraying will be required. The trees will require irrigation for quick growth, especially during the first years. This can be done with drip irrigation tape laid along the rows. Rabbit guards around the tree trunks may be necessary. Don't leave matted grass and weeds around the trunks when you mow, either. This attracts burrowing rodents that will chew on the tree bark and set back the growth or even kill the tree by girdling it.

Just like every other crop you might consider raising, it is absolutely imperative that you grow the finest quality Christmas trees possible. The only way to sell every tree you grow for a satisfactory profit is to provide top quality trees. Spend the time needed to guarantee a good crop. Then allow plenty of marketing time to pull the customers out to your farm.

The first group of trees will be ready for market when 50 percent or more of them have reached shoulder height. Some growers have had moderate success in marketing table model trees that are only two or three feet tall. The bulk of sales, however, are generally full-size trees. Other growers have good luck in selling live trees that are dug, balled and burlapped. It's more work, but the price is enough higher to make the extra effort worthwhile. You will need a supply of topsoil or compost on hand to fill in the holes after digging the trees. Be sure to give your customers proper instructions for tree care, though, so the trees don't all die after customers take them home. Also, be sure to have a no-return policy on live Christmas tree sales. A new idea I've just heard about is a grower in New Jersey who "rents" live Christmas trees. The customer takes the bagged and burlapped tree home for Christmas, then brings it back to the farm for replanting after the holidays. Neat, huh?

As the Christmas season gets near you can start putting out your signs and advertising cut-your-own trees for sale. Most state agriculture departments and many area newspapers publish a list of local tree farms that have trees available around the middle of November each year. Be sure to allow yourself plenty of time to be included in that list.

It's just as important to do market research for Christmas trees as it is for market garden vegetables. There may already be enough growers in your area. Or the imported trees may be good quality and very inexpensive. Then you need to think twice before planting a new plantation. And, they need to be taken care of. Don't ignore them and expect a good crop. It just won't work.

Extension agents in your county can give you some advice on which advertising methods to use and what type and size of trees are most popular in your market area. It's crucial to have this information before ordering and planting transplants. You don't want to wind up with the wrong variety and have a hard time selling them.

Certain areas of the country are more partial to pines, while consumers in other marketing areas want spruces. If you are in doubt, it's a good idea to talk to other local growers and with operators of seasonal retail lots. See what information they can give you. It's not a good idea to plant a whole bunch of Scotch Pine, for example, if the buyers in your area will be wanting Fraser Fir or another variety.

You are only going to be open to the public for about four weeks before Christmas each year. That's a good reason to consider marketing this way, especially if you have a job or other interests that keep you busy most of the time.

Francis Phillips is a very successful Christmas tree farmer in Kingston, Mass. His farm is open only four *days* each year, the first two weekends in December. He sells 1,000 to 1200 trees annually for prices ranging from $20 to $60 per tree. His Christmas tree plantation is just under 8 acres, with another acre for access roads and parking. Each spring he removes stumps left over from last year's harvest and plants 1,200 to 1,400 new trees. Then he putters around a few weekends throughout the rest of the year taking care of things, and that's about it. He has no plans to increase his annual planting beyond that level. He's happy with an above average income working a total of about one or two months per year, doing work that he really likes to do.

No doubt about it, it's the almost perfect retirement business for anyone who likes Christmas trees and has a decent site near a population center. The right piece of land is close enough to the city to attract customers, yet far enough out in the country so that land prices don't croak you. Personally, if I ever decide to retire, this is the kind of set up that I'll look for.

Bad Weather – PYO's Achilles Heel

Most PYO farms do the bulk of their seasonal business on eight to 12 days per year, according to Gus Schumacher, former commissioner of the Department of Food and Agriculture in Massachusetts. The biggest element discouraging me from doing PYO farming, whether the crops is trees, vegetables or berries, is that rain, snow or cold, cloudy weather can send your sales into a tailspin. Your customers want to come out to the country on a bright sunshiny day, when everything is perfect. If it's uncomfortable weather outside they'll stay home and clean the house or watch the game on television.

If you like the idea of PYO crops, an excellent book on the subject is *Pick Your Own Farming*, by Ralph Wampler and James Motes. First printed in 1984, this book is a valuable guide for PYO operators throughout the United States. It is available from University of Oklahoma Press.

Study PYO carefully, then talk with U-Pick farmers in your area before committing yourself to this marketing option. Whatever else you do, it's always a good idea to enter the business gradually. It would be discouraging to wait several years for a crop to mature, only to find that you have over estimated the market or failed to anticipate other problems that may arise.

I'm sure if I had more land and more time to work with it, I might quickly develop a liking for pick your own farming, especially if I could incorporate U-Pick marketing into my other endeavors to round out the marketing program to attract more customers to my farm. Under the right circumstances, it could be very profitable, and certainly a lot of fun. In fact, we are getting ready to give it a try here at Intervale Farm with a pick your own pumpkin patch.

§

Producers Cooperatives

There are some market gardeners who may not be successful at direct marketing. They may not have the desire, enthusiasm or personality that it takes to be financially successful dealing with the public on a daily basis. Some folks simply cannot force themselves to meet people, let alone ask them to buy something for money. They will forego a business idea entirely rather than become a direct marketer.

It's also true that certain parts of the country just don't have enough retail options to go around, particularly those areas that are far from city population centers. Or the established growers in your area may have already snapped up all the available direct retail and direct wholesale markets. This leaves you trying to compete from a weak position. It may even cause you to think about giving up your market gardening idea altogether.

If you are too far out in the boonies for successful retail marketing, you can consider starting or joining a producers cooperative. There are some problems with a co-op, but it may be your best or only option. Larger commercial growers, particularly, may have no other choice than to sell their farm crops this way.

At first glance, a producers cooperative sounds like a fine marketing idea. Just get a group of growers together, grow truckloads of vegetables and hire a manager to sell them. This way, several growers together can supply a bigger market more regularly. These types of associations are not new, and many have grown very large over the past two decades. Agway and Welch's are two examples. Ocean Spray is another.

There are, however, several drawbacks to a vegetable growers co-op. To begin with, the cooperative is a wholesale oriented marketing organization. It can only sell your output for 50 percent or less of its retail value. Then, as a way to pay for the co-op manager and for the co-op warehouse, you will be charged a fee of about 10 percent of your sales. Next, the cooperative will tack on transportation charges from the cooperative warehouse to the inner city supermarkets. This costs you another 10 percent.

Because the cooperative is usually wholesaling to large outlets, the growers have to pack everything in brand new, expensive boxes, which can cost another 5 percent of your sales. By now, you are receiving less than 25 percent of retail value for the food that took you months to grow.

As if that weren't bad enough, the cooperative's grading standards will be very strict. They aren't doing this because they want to be mean to you, but because they are competing with large and ultra-large growers from other parts of the country. With today's food industry grading standards, produce that is only slightly blemished, slightly misshapen, or under- or over-size by fractions of an inch may be rejected.

Tomatoes are a good example of skewed attention to industry grading standards for size, color and shape. In my area there are only three acceptable wholesale tomato packs: 1) Greenhouse gourmet varieties in 10-pound boxes, 4 rows by 5 rows, single layer. 2) Field tomatoes in 20-pound boxes, 4 rows by 5 rows, two layers. 3) Field tomatoes in 25-pound boxes, 5 rows by 6 rows, two layers. To fit these packing requirements, all the tomatoes have to be pretty much the same size and shape. I don't know who came up with those rules about tomatoes having to be the exact same size to be acceptable. I've never *not* been able to sell a tomato because of its size!

When you get through grading for size and appearance, you will sometimes lose half your crop. The remainder of the over- and under-size fruits will have to be sold as seconds (if you can find a market), lie in the garden to decay or wind up in your compost pile.

Now that's bad, but it gets worse. The tomatoes have to be picked at exactly the right degree of ripeness (actually greenness) called the "breaker" or "mature green" stage. This is an industry term used to designate when the tomato is starting to show the very first faint blush of white and pinkish color in the skin.

At this stage, less than 5 percent of the potential flavor is starting to develop in the fruit. But the supermarkets insist that you pick tomatoes at this stage, maybe one day before or one day after, period. If you miss this critical window your fruits will not be accepted.

It's not just tomatoes, either. The large wholesale and supermarket buyers treat *everything* that way. The least bit of tip burn on a few lettuce leaves or a few flea beetle bites on the spinach can cause a whole truckload to be rejected. Then what do you do with it?

There are still more problems with producer's cooperatives, such as scheduling. What happens if you get a flat tire on the way to the co-op warehouse and miss the tractor-trailer shipping schedule? Or, what about odd lots and extra produce? If the cooperative's marketing staff doesn't have a buyer already lined up for it they won't take it.

Another big problem for cooperatives is competition from growers in the South and West. One day you may get a decent price for your crop, the next day the price falls dramatically, because one or more of the large commercial growers has flooded the market. It happens all the time.

There are many sad tales about $14 per crate on Tuesday but only $2 per crate on Wednesday. During the height of the 1990 season here in Vermont, for example, the price for organic lettuce dropped out of sight when Western growers flooded the market with conventional lettuce. Martin's, a local chain supermarket, was pricing iceberg lettuce at 9 cents per head for an entire week! It's hard to sell organic lettuce for 75 cents per head when you've got that kind of competition.

Selling at wholesale levels requires, nay *demands*, top quality and expensive packaging. Then there's the cost of transportation, which is always high. You have no control over the market. You wind up risking your all on only one or two major crops. The more you produce, the less you get paid per unit. It's the law of supply and demand, you know.

The bottom line for most wholesale growers is that they have to pay for their land, buy expensive specialized equipment, hire field labor and pay for expensive cooling and packing facilities. Then they have to pay huge costs for picking, grading, packing and shipping. After all these costs, many commercial growers will often earn 10 percent or less per acre of what is possible in backyard market gardening.

In fact, many large-scale commercial vegetable producers are averaging less than $500 per acre in net income from their fields. Market gardeners can earn that much in their backyard with just 100 tomato plants.

It *is* possible for you to make some money as a *small-scale* wholesale grower. The way to do it is to concentrate on selling your crops to other gardeners who have an established retail market. They can use your produce to supplement their supply. For my retail outlets I've purchased wholesale from other growers frequently over the past few years. We've found it to be a mutually beneficial way to do business.

Likewise, a small independent grocery store or specialty store in a nearby village might be a good outlet for your produce. Smaller retail outlets don't usually ask for expensive packaging, and grading standards become less of a problem. These smaller, locally owned stores will be more likely to buy field run vegetables and not worry about specific grading standards at all.

The wholesale and producers cooperatives situation is becoming less bleak each year, however. More grocery stores are responding to the requests from consumers for more locally grown produce. Major city supermarkets are becoming more willing to accept field run grading standards. In some cases, they will even agree to guarantee a season-long wholesale price to get more local produce on their shelves.

However, organic produce in the supermarkets amounts to only 1 percent or 2 percent of the $370 billion-a-year retail food industry in the United States. But it's a step in the right direction. If this trend continues, it will open wonderful marketing opportunities for individual growers and producers cooperatives in many areas of North America.

CHAPTER 5:

The New Gold Rush

From the 50 cent egg 140 years ago to baby lettuce today, entrepreneurial farmers continue to make direct marketing the key to financial success.

by T. L. Gettings

The citizenry of San Francisco has been feasting on the labors of Sonoma County farmers since the Gold Rush days of '49. "In the 1850s, farmers were getting 50 cents an egg," says Greg Nilsen, co-owner of Wine Country Cuisine in Santa Rosa. "Back then, the Petaluma River was a highway to the Bay Area for farm produce. We don't go by river these days, but we are still very much in the business of supplying San Francisco with quality food. Vegetables are the new cash crop of Sonoma County. You can gross as much on one-tenth of an acre of the right kind of vegetables as you can on a full acre of apples, yesteryear's cash crop.

"What makes us unique here is the mild climate and volcanic soil that allow us to produce a wide variety of crops that we can constantly change to meet the food demands and needs of the Bay Area," he explains. That mix includes baby vegetables, edible flowers and "mesclun," a colorful blend of young, tender salad greens that has become the new golden eggs to be ferried down to the grateful citizens in the city by the bay.

The New '49ers

Nilsen started his specialty produce business in 1985 to service the top four chefs in Sonoma County. "We'd pick from gardens locally in the morning and deliver in the afternoon. We sell all our produce directly to restaurants. By 1988, we had 150 customers, nationwide. We've moved more than $2 million worth of produce in four years. We ship cheese, nuts, berries, fish and fruit in season. All in all, we handle over 600 items," Nilsen says.

"We are even shipping produce overnight express to exclusive New York City restaurants like the Milrose. We can deliver 400 servings of our salad mix of vegetables to New York City for $1 a serving. They charge $8 for the salad. They are making money and so are we. Right now, 85 percent of our sales are to the Sonoma County restaurants and the San Francisco area, but we are intent on increasing our out-of-state sales in the future."

Mesclun, the salad mix that Wine Country Cuisine makes fresh every day, accounts for about 33 percent of the company's sales. Vegetable greens make up another 50 percent. "We turn over the produce so quickly we can purchase garden varieties that are better tasting than ones that are commercially grown," Nilsen adds. "We buy seed and supply it to our growers so that we get exactly what we want. It is essential to our business that we sell only quality, wholesome plants that are damage-free and have exciting flavor and texture that will survive the restaurant fare.

"Our salad mix is made up of individual baby lettuce plants, chicories and other greens such as kale and Japanese mustard plants. The mix changes from summer to winter, according to the availability of fresh greens," Nilsen explains.

Salad Magic

Mesclun. The name sounds mysterious, exotic. Maybe even illegal.

What is .i.mesclun;? "It's a field blend of young, tender lettuces, chicories and other salad greens. Mesclun is a French word derived from the Latin word for mixture. It's an old product in France that's been around more than 1,000 years," explains Greg Nilsen of Wine Country Cuisine in Santa Rosa, Calif.

Nilsen markets his mesclun as a ready-to-serve convenience item for swank restaurants, clubs and banquets all over the country. Food service professionals faced with labor shortages and wage increases really appreciate that, he adds.

Over the course of a year, as many as 30 or 40 different items may be used in mesclun. The basic ingredients include:

Lettuces – Red and green salad bowl, red and green perella, lollo rosa and boindo, Tango and red romaine.

Chicories – Belgian endive, radicchio and frisee.

210

Greens – Russian red kale, roquette, mizuna and red mustard.

Price varies during the year from about 55 cents to 80 cents per serving. Restaurants typically charge $4 to $5 for one mesclun salad. "On several occasions, a major hotel or a club has used our product for as many as 2,000 people at one serving," Nilsen says. "We think it is going to get bigger and bigger."

Nationwide Demand

"Restaurants all over the country are in the market for exciting and entertaining fare. Farmers in the East, farmers anywhere can grow salad greens, baby vegetables, edible flowers, fresh herbs, ripe fruit and direct market them to restaurants – just as we're doing." Nilsen observes. "There's no secret. Grow what you like, but always grow for the market and grow what grows best on your land. What we are selling here will sell everywhere – flavor. Shelf-life doesn't pay. Mass marketing is out. Niche marketing is in. Every city in the country has restaurants that sell the eating experience as entertainment. That's the niche."

One of the real pioneers of today's Sonoma County gold rush is Warren Weber, who started his Star Route Farm in 1974. "There were all these natural food stores that didn't have any produce. The movement was kind of like an army with no kitchen," Weber recalls, while taking a break from field work on his certified organic farm near the small town of Bolinas. "In the early days, we grew whatever would grow in our coastal climate; potatoes, onions, garlic, cucumbers, beets. In 1983, we began to specialize in selling leafy greens to restaurants, then branched out to include herbs and edible flowers. Our business has grown 30 percent every year since I started farming 15 years ago.

"Our specialty salad mix (mesclun) is the result of years of trying different varieties. We have tried 80 varieties of lettuce to come up with the eight that we sell," Weber says. Don't ask for his mesclun recipe, though. Weber won't talk about it. Same with his machinery and greenhouses, all of which are strictly off limits to photographers.

It's no surprise that Weber guards his farming systems so jealously. Last year, Star Route Farm grossed about $600,000 from just 35 acres of cultivated land. Weber, who will talk freely about organic philosophy and markets, believes that organic operations like his have a bright future. "Organic farmers will continue to gain a larger share of the market because consumers will continue to want to upgrade the food in their lives," he opines. "People also want to have faith in what farmers are doing. They want to know that the earth is being kept in stewardship. There is a real and growing fear of pesticides and chemicals by consumers and, after all, we are in business for the consumer."

Hundreds of thriving small farms throughout Sonoma and Napa counties prove this point. One such farm is Forni-Brown Gardens, which consists of five cultivated acres in four different locations scattered around Calistoga. "I made my first sale to a restaurant in 1981 when I was delivering elephant garlic to a co-op and a chef happened to be there. He saw that garlic and ordered 200 pounds of it for his restaurant," explains Lynn Brown, who started his operation in 1980 to service area co-ops. "The light bulb was lit. Now we're growing more than 200 varieties of vegetables using a modified French-intensive system that is exclusively organic because this is where we work.

"Each of our locations has its own soil and weather conditions, so we plant different varieties in each site at different times of the year. We plant by hand, broadcasting the beds every week so we get five crops a year out of the land. We fertilize with rice hulls and chicken manure. We are particularly proud of the horticultural techniques we developed over the years, most of which allow us to grow intensively weed-free, which keeps our quality high and picking easy. Our only piece of power equipment is a 10-hp BCS rototiller. It's easy to transport to the various garden sites and fits our goal of high-performance, intensive methods."

Sales Soaring

Forni-Brown Garden's business doubled in each of its first five years. "We are one year away from a $250,000 year," says Barney Welsh, a partner in the business. Half of Forni-Brown's sales are handled by a distributor, who sells their mesclun salad greens to San Francisco-area restaurants. Direct sales to Napa Valley restaurants and overnight shipments to New York City restaurants account for the other half of the business. "Direct shipping is an exciting feature," adds Brown. "From our soil to the New York City restaurant, it takes 18 hours with no middlepeople, so there's no extra markup. It's amazing what computers and overnight delivery have made available to farmers. The whole country is an open market to us."

Although it might mean increased competition, it's a way of farming that Brown and Welsh say they would like to see adapted by farmers throughout the country. "This is not a fad because food isn't a fad, and it's not a trend because these foods have been eaten by royalty in Europe and Asia for hundreds of years. It's just now more of us can partake," says Welsh. "Baby vegetables have been used in French cooking for hundreds of years. It's not new. What is new is the mixing of Oriental greens with traditional vegetables."

There is a new emphasis on direct .i.marketing;, too. "More farmers should be dealing more directly with customers, especially restaurants," adds Brown.

Selling directly is not as difficult as it might sound. "We have chefs that call and then make up their menus according to what we have that is ready to be picked. We tell chefs, "Don't order for five days at a time. You call and we'll pick to order. The best place for a plant is in the ground, so we don't pick until it's ready to be sold.'

"The purple garlic chive flower we sell was developed from one flower Lynn found in his garden. It's a real favorite edible flower for our chefs. They also can't get enough of our French wild mountain strawberry that we developed from one plant a chef's mother gave to us. Working directly with chefs is a special relationship. We once had a hailstorm and a local chef we supply called to make sure his salad greens were protected. That's special!"

$62,000 From 3 Acres

This special way of farming has also given birth to some very special tools, namely Stu Corwin's pedal-powered "weedmobile." "I'm into tools. My education is in engineering," explains Corwin, who grows 3 acres of baby lettuce with his wife, Simon, in Sonoma County. "When I look at our successful fields, I see order. And when I see it look perfect, I'm satisfied. That's why I invented the weedmobile so that our weeding operation could be the best it could be."

Meticulous weeding is especially important in the Corwins' operation. "We plant every seven days so there is always a crop to be harvested. Every week, I'm cultivating, planting and harvesting on some piece of ground. We harvest three times a week, from the end of March through January. The last two years we sold all our harvest to Wine Country Cuisine. Before we hooked up with them, we sold directly to restaurants. But I liked working with one distributor so you can be on a schedule to meet their needs," Corwin says.

In 1989 the Corwins grossed $62,000 on their 3 acres of organic baby lettuce. "We could farm 30 acres instead of three, but we limited ourselves because Simon and I don't want to hire labor because that complicates things too much," Corwin says. "We decided on growing baby lettuce exclusively after experimenting with a variety of crops. We fertilize with blood meal and sodium nitrate and the only pests we have are rabbits that I keep under control by going on daily dawn and dusk hunts. It takes all the daylight hours to keep up, but it's not stressful. In fact, it's enjoyable because when the lettuce looks good, you get a lot of positive feedback."

Demand Beats Supply

Carl Stillman grows 25 varieties of baby vegetables under 10,000 square feet of cold frames year round. "We grossed $30,000 on half an acre the first year," he says. "It's easy to forecast a $50,000 gross for an intense full year of production."

The sorrel Stillman grows in the well-ventilated and irrigated cold frame will be harvest 20 times during the year. "We sell herbs directly to a number of upscale supermarkets and gourmet shops. We are new and we are going to increase our volume. If I had more product, it would still be easy to sell, especially in the winter months. The cold frame allows us to grow on a constant schedule all year around. The baby bok choy, flamboyant radishes and Tokyo market radishes are good examples of baby vegetables that sell at a premium price, and you can never have enough ready to be harvested. What surprises me is that more young farmers aren't growing for this market, not just here in Sonoma County, but all across the country."

Mobile Marketing

This grower goes the distance to satisfy customers.

by Bob Hofstetter

HUSTONTOWN, Pa. – Parking a dusty old pickup full of warm produce on a hot asphalt parking lot is *not* Jim Crawford's idea of farm-to-city sales. He knows how to do it right.

Every week from June to March, Crawford's fleet of three trucks – each carrying up to 5 tons of fresh vegetables, fruits and other farm products – brings a taste of the country to five Washington, D.C., neighborhoods.

"I've been a customer ever since Jim first parked his truck a block from our home 16 years ago," says D.C.-resident Jane Miller. "He brings more than good food at good prices. His truck is like the village well where all the neighbors congregate."

Nurturing such a loyal clientele has helped Crawford expand from just a handful of crops in an 8,000-square-foot market garden 20 years ago to 40 crops on 20 acres today. Crawford's perseverance and fine-tuned management skills have made his New Morning Farm a thriving operation during two decades when many entrepreneurs with similar visions have gone out of business.

High-Demand Vegetables

Crawford was a law student with a part-time office job back in '71 when he decided to try growing and selling vegetables. "A farmer-neighbor of mine asked if I thought I could sell some of his tomatoes at the office," he recalls. "I tried it and was successful. I'd always liked gardening, so I decided to grow a small assortment of vegetables to add to my neighbor's tomatoes." Pretty soon law school was out, and he's been growing ever since.

Crawford concentrates on high-demand vegetables that customers can find in any grocery store, such as tomatoes, beans, peppers, sweet corn, summer squash, and fall brassicas. He prefers proven varieties with multiple-pest resistance, and doesn't bother growing unusual specialty crops. "If I have to spend time educating the public about a new product, it's probably not worth the effort."

Crop rotation and careful attention to soil fertility help Crawford grow high-quality crops without chemicals. To help check insects and disease, he avoids planting similar crops in the same place in consecutive years. Composted or aged poultry manure (from his own flock of free-range chickens and other local sources) is his primary nutrient source. Annual soil tests help ensure adequate application rates.

On acreage harvested by mid-September, he rototills or disks, then broadcasts a mix of hairy vetch (25 lbs./A) and winter rye (2 bu./A). Vetch is slow to establish in fall, so after mid-September he'll plant only the rye as a late-season soil protector. Crawford kills covers with a PTO-driven rotary field mower, usually by early April, followed by a disking.

"To tap early markets, we plant warm-season crops such as tomatoes, peppers and cucumbers into black plastic mulch and then protect them with Agryl-P17 row covers," he says. "We've been harvesting crops a full week ahead of bare-ground plantings with this system." A Holland mulch-layer makes it easy to place the plastic.

Crawford cultivates as needed to control weeds in unmulched rows. Typically, lettuce is hand-weeded just once, because close row-spacing helps plants to shade out weeds.

Market Locations Critical

You might think that Crawford's reasonably priced, consistently fresh, high-quality produce would sell itself. But that can't happen if there's no one around to buy it. New Morning Farm is located in the scenic but economically depressed Tuscarora Mountain area of south-central Pennsylvania.

"There aren't many people or jobs here. We tried selling at local farmers markets, grocery stores, restaurants and roadside stands. But they didn't work out. The demand and prices weren't good enough," he says.

Determined to succeed, Crawford sought and found markets elsewhere – in the neighborhoods of the nation's capital less than three hours away. "I remembered when I was a youngster growing up in Massachusetts, some farmers delivered produce door-to-door. So I had leaflets made up telling potential customers who we were, what we were doing, and when and where we'd be selling near them."

This approach to marketing takes time – and patience – to be successful. "If sales don't increase after two or three tries, you move to a new neighborhood," says Crawford.

To increase your chances of hitting the mark when choosing an off-the-truck marketing site, Crawford suggests:

• Select areas where people know their neighbors and are sociable and family-oriented.

• Avoid congested areas, where your presence could be a nuisance to traffic or people.

• Don't pick commuting zones, despite their high-volume appearance. Commuters are always in a rush and rarely give you a second glance.

• Conform with any permit requirements or other regulations in your marketing area. Check with city hall *before* selecting locations.

• Don't assume affluent or ethnic neighborhoods will necessarily provide more sales. "Two of our best market sites are in the inner city. Our customers at these sites come from all walks of life and are of no specific age group," Crawford points out.

A Regular Presence

Crawford makes the five-hour round trip to Washington twice a week (Tuesdays and Saturdays) from early June through late November. From December through March, he markets just on Saturdays and only at four sites. He makes no deliveries in April and May. Crawford has used the same sites for more than 15 years, so he doesn't need to use advertising fliers as often as before.

During the growing season, Crawford's customers select from an assortment of vegetables and a few small fruits, such as strawberries and raspberries. Winter offerings include root crops, winter squash, salad greens from the farm's 1,500-square-foot greenhouse, and eggs (about 110 dozen weekly). Crawford also sells apples, cider, maple syrup and baked goods produced by his neighbors.

Winter marketing is important because it generates off-season income and keeps him in personal touch with customers, says Crawford.

Crawford made do with two pickup trucks until 1978, when he bought two 12-foot trucks. By '83, those weren't big enough to hold all the produce, so he traded them in for two 16-footers. Now, most market days, it's a three-truck convoy that can carry up to 15 _tons_ of goods. The trucks aren't refrigerated, but two walk-in coolers at the farm provide almost 3,000 cubic feet of cold storage. Highly perishable produce is harvested, and cooled, then carefully packed to maintain freshness enroute to market.

Helping Hands

Crawford has a full-time production manager, equipment operator and delivery coordinator, plus four interns for the growing season. On delivery days, his wife, Moie, their 13-year-old son, Arlo, and one other person run one neighborhood site from 8 a.m. to 1 p.m. (Their 8-year-old daughter, Jane, also helps with chores around the farm.) Meanwhile, Jim delivers to the other four sites. "The markets are in the same general part of town. So it only takes 5 to 10 minutes to move from site to site," Crawford says.

"I usually bring along one person from our farm staff," he continues. "And I hire four or five high school kids from the delivery-site neighborhood. They meet the truck at our first site and continue on with us to our other sites." Crawford usually rehires the same neighborhood helpers for three or four season, so they're familiar with his system.

An innovative and talented marketer, Crawford knows that keeping customers happy is what keeps the business prospering. "I've gone to many grower and marketing meetings, and often hear the consumer referred to as a 'target.' But I don't agree with that. You need to respond to your customers' likes and dislikes. And treat them as you would like to be treated as a customer. "Don't be pushy, either. Instead, be honest and forthright. If consumers respect and trust you, they'll listen to you."

---
§

The Corporate Connection

They're feeding The Washington Post with vegetables now instead of words

by George DeVault

DOTT, Pa. – Most people would say they had it made. Both Ward Sinclair and his partner Cass Peterson had reached the peak of their profession, covering important beats for *The Washington Post's* elite national desk. He covered agriculture, rocking the halls of USDA headquarters and constantly crisscrossing the nation's back roads to get the real story directly from farmers during the depths of the farm crisis during the 1980's. She was *The Post's* watchdog on the environment and natural resources, a job that took her from toxic waste sites in Georgia to oil spills in Alaska. Sinclair was named farm writer of the year in 1984 by the Newspaper Farm Editors of America. Peterson was nominated for a Pulitzer Prize in 1989 for her exposé of environmental problems caused by nuclear weapons plants.

But, after a combined total of 21 years at *The Post*, they gave all that up. They resolutely walked out of the newsroom and away from the power, intrigue and glamour of life in the fast lane of Washington's political life, trading it all for bloody knuckles, sore backs and knees, sunburned necks, frozen fingers and 14-hour work days. The rush of adrenaline that comes from scooping *The Des Moines Register* or *The New York Times* on a major story was replaced by the gut-wrenching financial uncertainty that comes from being in business for yourself. Sinclair and Peterson chose one of the most unpredictable, uncontrollable and, in recent years, most unprofitable businesses known to man.

They became full-time farmers, moving from Arlington, Va., to a 65-acre farm in south-central Pennsylvania about 100 miles northwest of Washington, D.C.

Growing A Market

Although Sinclair and Peterson are no longer on *The Post's* payroll, they still receive pay checks of a sort from the newspaper. That's because instead of feeding the front page with words, they now feed editors, reporters and other newsroom employees with fresh organic vegetables, fruit and even free-range eggs. Sales in 1990 to some 125 *Post* employees totaled more than $20,000. The newspaper is just one of several markets that help the farmers gross more than $50,000 from their 15 cultivated acres.

Such success didn't happen overnight, however. Sinclair and Peterson bought their farm at an estate auction in 1983. It came with an old farmhouse, a barn and an assortment of tumbledown chicken houses. They called the place Flickerville Mountain Farm and Groundhog Ranch, "a name chosen to lure and amuse farm-market customers," Sinclair says.

Their machinery lineup consisted of an old, secondhand Troy-Bilt tiller, a riding mower, a backpack sprayer and various hand tools. They worked their share of mandatory weekend shifts at *The Post* during winter so that they could have Fridays off to farm in summer. Thousands of vegetable transplants were started under grow lights in a bedroom of their home in Virginia.

"We changed our direction a number of times. One of the original ideas was to have an herb farm," Sinclair explains. "We planted a lot of herbs. It was a wet year ('84). They did pretty well. We had all of these herbs that we didn't know what to do with. Cass had an idea to put an ad in *The Post* house organ, 'Fresh Herbs For Sale.' A few people called us, not a lot.

"One of the reporters there said, very casually, 'Do you have any veggies?' We said, "Well, yeah, we do.'

"'Well, why don't you bring me some?'

"We brought in more veggies week after week. Word got around that we were bringing in vegetables and it got up to 25 or 30 people by the end of the year. We put together bags of whatever we had and wrote up little invoices. One was $3.17, another $6.12. Crazy little numbers like that," Sinclair says.

For the next five years, Sinclair and Peterson continued to work full-time for *The Post* and farm on weekends, holidays and vacation. "It grew in '85. I suppose we had 35 people. Each year it went up," Sinclair adds. "People said, 'Can you bring me stuff?' And we said, 'Of course.'

"It just grew and grew. We never did advertise. Word got around that pretty good veggies were available and the prices were apparently right. Some people complained that our prices were too low, especially on raspberries, which we were selling for $3 per pint." They now charge $2.50 per half pint for raspberries.

In addition to sales at *The Post*, Sinclair and Peterson had a stand at the farmers market in Hagerstown, Md., on Saturdays. They also started selling excess production to Organic Farms Inc., a now defunct organic foods distributor in Beltsville, Md.

As demand for produce grew, the farmers developed a detailed 5-year management plan, which called for doubling production each year. Using their off-farm income, they started adding equipment and improvements to the farm. First a Farmall A tractor with mid-mounted cultivators. In 1985, they bought a new 19-hp, four-wheel drive Ford 1310 diesel tractor, a 54-inch PTO-powered rotovator and a rotary mower. Other implements included a plastic mulch layer, bedshaper, two-bottom moldboard plow and a manure spreader. Then came a commercial-size delivery van. Two greenhouses, the largest of which was completed in 1990, now produce more than 80,000 transplants from 1,880 square feet of growing space. A new well was dug to supply an extensive drip irrigation system. They also built a 9-by-11-foot walk-in cooler and a bunk house for interns.

"By '88, which is when I left *The Post* (Peterson left in May '89), we were up to 75 customers. So many people asked us if they could get on the list that we didn't have enough stuff to fill more bags," Sinclair says. "We decided then that this was a very lucrative market to be tapped if we could do it right."

'Good News, Bad News'

The number of customers grew to 125 in 1989. Collecting money from so many people every week became a nightmare. In 1990, the farmers said, "OK. bookkeeping is a terrible problem. It takes a lot of time. Let's raise prices and offer them a 10-percent discount if they pay ahead of time."

Flyers explaining the new program were sent to all existing customers and likely prospects, about 200 people in all. "The bad news is our prices have gone up," the four-page brochure explained. "The good news is your prices have come down – if you take advantage of this offer which we are making to streamline bookkeeping."

Then the farmers waited, not knowing quite what to expect. "Our bank account was down to zero when suddenly in April, seven or eight thousand bucks just came rolling in here," Sinclair exclaims. "The overwhelming majority of our subscribers that year paid for the whole year. Customers said, 'That's terrific. That's a good idea. It's a pain to remember that every week.'"

They offered produce in three different size bags: small for $6.50, medium for $10.50 and large for $16. Assuming everyone pays in advance and receives the 10-percent discount, Peterson says a normal weekly delivery looks like this:

- 52 small bags at $5.85 for $304.20
- 51 medium bags at $9.45 for $481.95
- 25 large bags at $14.40 for $360

"The total is $1,146.15 per week or $20,630.70 per year. It's an 18-week market, which is a little on the short side," Peterson adds. "But it is a guaranteed market, regardless of weather and with no set-up. Whether it's pouring down rain or so hot nobody wants to come out, we can count on it every week."

Looks Easier Than It Is

"It's not easy money," Peterson emphasizes. "You just can't throw whatever you happen to have excess around the farm in a bag and expect people to be delighted. If you're going to throw kohlrabis in there, you have to tell people what it is and how to use it.

"You need to pick, wash, pack, weigh or count them and separate them into bags. Make sure you have the exact numbers and that the portions are different according to what size bag you're packing. It's a headache. You get out there early Tuesday morning, start loading the truck and find that you're two zucchinis short. It means a hike out to the zucchini patch.

"You need to be realistic about this," Peterson adds. "There is one woman on the list who does not want any squash, eggplant or tomatoes. This causes a problem in September when we have a lot of squash, eggplant and tomatoes. It's always a challenge every week to try to fill her bag and give her money's worth and a variety and not give her things she won't eat." That's one of the reasons the farmers discourage subscriptions from people with gardens.

"If you only have 20 units of sugar snap peas, 80 people are going to be disappointed. Everybody wants items like sugar snap peas and raspberries. We have a good raspberry patch, but you can only pick the day before and the patch does not necessarily provide a pint for everybody on the list. When they first start coming in, only the large bags get raspberries. Then the medium bags get them the next week. Then as production increases, the small and the large bags. You've got to make sure that the most coveted items get spread around or you're going to find people feeling cheated."

While all of their produce is certified organic by the Organic Crop Improvement Association, Peterson says that is not a big selling point. Most people just want fresh produce – and convenience. "It's a farmers market for people who don't have time to go to a farmers market," she adds. "They want fresh produce...delivered to their desk. They can carry it home on the subway tonight and think, "I don't have to shop. I don't have to worry about it.""

Creative Marketing

Flickerville Mountain Farm now produces 70 different crops, including 42 different varieties of tomatoes, 20 kinds of herbs and 40 different flower varieties for drying or fresh-cut sales. Some standouts include mini and violet eggplant, heirloom tomatoes like MORTGAGE LIFTER, and JENNY LIND cantaloupe, which although unattractive is prized by customers for its spicy, green flesh.

"If there are weird things, the food writers get those," Sinclair says.

To add variety and bulk to their customers' bags, the farmers also package custom items like "Salsa Tonight," little bags containing hot peppers, garlic, tomatoes, cilantro and onions, plus directions for making your own Mexican hot sauce. "It took a lot of time to do that, but it made a big hit. Everyone loves it," says Sinclair.

Other packaging innovations like "Bag-O-Peppers" – seven small peppers of different colors for $1 a bag – can help ease weather-related problems. Only a reporter from Iowa recognized the gourmet mini peppers for what they really were – drought victims.

Corporate Liaisons

"Management is extremely tolerant, probably because Ben Bradlee (*Post* executive editor) is on the list," says Peterson. Other notable customers include cartoonist Herblock, Investigative News Editor Bob Woodward, the managing editor, deputy managing editor, restaurant critic and food writer.

Working at *The Post* while setting up their farm was a definite advantage. "Our success is due in part to the fact that we were all colleagues. Many of the people who subscribed did so because they wanted to see us succeed," Sinclair says. "They got a vicarious thrill out of helping us do what we're doing. They would like to do the same thing."

But they are convinced you don't have to work for a company to successfully sell farm produce there. "It just might take a little longer is all," Peterson observes.

Personal friendship, they explain, is becoming much less of a factor. There is a high turnover rate in the newspaper industry. Newsroom personnel now sign up even though they don't know the former *Post* writers, says Peterson. "They want fresh vegetables and they recognize it as a good deal," she adds.

Demand is so great, in fact, that Sinclair and Peterson say they have to turn many would-be customers away. The farmers have limited themselves to about 125 customers because they deliver to *The Post* on Tuesday, the same day they deliver to two Washington restaurants. Their van just can't hold any more produce. Adding more customers at the newspaper would require a bigger truck or a second delivery there. That last option is something neither farmer wants to think about right now, since they already drive about 900 miles a week making deliveries and going to farmers markets around Washington. "Some weeks," Sinclair groans, "I feel like I'm running a trucking company more than a farm." Despite its problems, though, Peterson says the corporate connection "has been a great marketing tool for us. We're very pleased with it, even though it's not easy."

How To Score BIG With Consumers

Provide "safe" food and make them feel part of your farm.

by T. L. Gettings

Many of the brave and hardy souls who made their way west on the Oregon Trail in the mid-1800s put down new roots in Oregon's Willamette River Valley. The area quickly became known for its productive and diversified farms, and as a haven for those with a pioneering spirit.

Today, 150 years later, there are new pioneers in the valley: organic farmers. Oregon Tilth, one of the oldest and most innovative organic grower groups in the country, lists no less than 30 of these new pioneers in the valley in its directory.

Intent on improving their soil and using farming methods that are in tune with nature, these growers are finding new ways to use and improve the rich resources around them. Close to the Portland and Salem metropolitan areas, many growers are selling their produce directly to city folk through custom pick, U-pick and subscription farming operations that offer lower prices.

But saving money is only one thing that attracts customers. The growing desire for chemical-free food has led many consumers to rekindle the farmer/consumer connection that has been absent in most of America for decades.

"It is now time for the consumer who cares about good food to find new farmers who want to produce it," Gene Logsdon writes in *Ohio* magazine. "This is the new age we are headed into. People will boast about their favorite farm the way they now boast about their favorite restaurant."

225

Meet some of the new farmers in the Willamette Valley:

Subscription Farming

"Have you ever wanted to own a family farm? Here is your chance! Three Rivers Farm provides our members with unforgettable farm experiences and top quality organic produce." So begins the brochure for Three Rivers Farm, which produces 40 acres of certified organic fruits and vegetables alongside the Willamette River.

"In the spring, we sign up our subscription members for the year at a fee of $25 a family," says Martha Schrader, who runs the farm with her veterinarian husband Curt. "They calculate their needs for the year from our produce list, which offers broccoli, cantaloupes, carrots, corn, peppers, potatoes, pumpkins, shallots, squash, strawberries, tomatoes and watermelon. We then plant according to their requests. We have learned to *over plant* because our members tend to want more than the original order. They also tend to pick more if they pick their own at our discounted rate of 15 percent, rather than have us pick for them.

"Our goal is to have 200 farm families. We have 75 this year that are real involved and that's the kind of subscription member you want," explains Martha. "One of our greatest sales tools is selling the ambiance of the farm. We keep sheep and have restored the barn as a sales point that also creates the atmosphere that keeps our members wanting to spend the better part of a day any number of times a summer at what they like to think of as *their* farm. The sheep are a family farm crop, too! We sell 40 to 50 lambs a year."

The subscription idea comes from deep in the heart of Dixie, all the way from Alabama and small-farm guru Booker T. Whatley, author of *How To Make $100,000 Farming 25 Acres.*

"We tried the U-pick route first, but we aren't in an ideal location for drive-by customers, so we switched to a subscription operation," explains farm manager Doug Roberts. "Customers are more interested in how things are grown than even a year ago. The subscription family membership format together with our commitment to biologically safe farming is a perfect fit.

"Our credibility to our customers is in our certification. Most, if not all, of our members are very interested in organic produce. That's what led them to us in the first place," Roberts adds. "Our 8 acres of strawberries yielded 40 tons (in 1989). It's our top money-maker. What we don't sell to our members, we sell wholesale. Finding more than one market is essential to being profitable with berries. We sell whatever is left to Cascadian Farms, the organic food processor in Washington.

"All the vegetables we grow are ones that look like the ones in the supermarket. We select our varieties for taste, not shipping or handling, but still we want familiar-looking ones to our members. We don't want funky or unusual crops," says Roberts.

From The Orient, $1 A Square Foot

Fred Oerther, who operates the Oerther Family Farm in Clackamus with his wife Deborah, saw his first raised bed garden in Vietnam in 1968. "I watched a family actually farm half a block of raised beds just outside the Saigon city limits. They were marketing their goods directly to city residents.

"I was a physician in the war. I ran an artificial kidney unit. When I got to Oregon in 1975, I did a flat garden. The soil here has so much clay in it it's like concrete in the summer and floods all through the winter. The flat garden wasn't working. So, the next year, I dug 18 100-square-foot beds like the ones I'd seen in Vietnam. Now we have 40,000 square feet of raised beds. We don't till anymore. We plant on top of our mulch beds. We can gross $1 a square foot a year.

"For the seven years I was practicing medicine in Oregon, I invested in land, instead of German sports cars. One of the advantages of farming close to a city is there is so much waste. I started making compost at the same time I dug those first 18 beds. At the end of the first year, I had 4 yards of finished compost. The second year I made twice as much, but it still wasn't enough. I decided I needed to add 6 inches of finished compost to each bed to regenerate the soil properly.

"We collect the compostable materials from municipalities, tree services and private citizens. The fertilizer value of the biodegradable solid material generated by this municipal area could provide the nutrients to grow one-fourth to one-third of the food consumed by the people living here. Each time a truck pulls in I think they are bringing me gold," Fred grins.

Deborah is the marketer. "We market as many ways as we can," she explains. "Fifty percent of our sales are here at the farm, as a 'you select, we pick' operation or at the local farmers market. We also sell directly to restaurants, wholesale to health food stores and, recently, we've started to service Fred Mayer and Safeway supermarkets. The local stores are real interested in putting organic produce in their stores."

The Oerthers don't just grow vegetables, though. "I could sell 500 young frying chickens this year to the Oriental-American community in this area, if we had them," observes Fred. "We have 300 organically raised layers now. The next thing we do will be to upgrade our facilities to raise those fryers."

2-Acre Eden

Margaret and Dale Dennis already had a big garden. And lots of friends – and friends of friends – coming by to sample the great taste of their homegrown produce. So they decided to turn their 2 acres of mixed vegetables into a U-pick farm.

"It's the perfect size for a one-person operation," says Margaret, who greets each customer, personally.

"Our pole beans and peas are unique. People travel a long way to buy our shelling peas. We switched from pod peas and found that shelling peas were a real hit. We joined the Tri-County Farm Fresh group to let people know we were in business and then joined Oregon Tilth to be certified organic and get more publicity.

"We've always been organic and our biggest drawing power is the taste of our produce. It keeps bringing them back. One couple comes all the way from upstate Washington to buy hundreds of pounds of tomatoes. They have always been our biggest seller."

U-Pick – At First

"I came here in '71 from San Francisco when I worked night and day as an airplane mechanic to swing enough income to buy this 30-acre spot," says Len Saunders of Hopewell Farms in Salem. "When I first started U-pick was a savior. It was a major means of marketing until I learned all the ins and outs of wholesale marketing. Picking just at the right time, having the right trays and boxes, and being professional enough to supply steady quality and quantity are all essential for making it in the marketplace."

Canadice grapes and 18 varieties of squash thrive on his farm, but peaches – 15 tons last year – are Saunders' main crop. "We pick for the early market and supply natural food stores in Salem, Portland and Corvallis. Our wholesale price is 70 cents a pound, but we still depend on U-pick at half the wholesale price after our major harvest is finished. We put an ad in the local stores announcing our U-pick season and they come from as far away as Portland. U-pick only amounts to 10 or 20 percent of our total sales these days because of the effectiveness of our wholesale effort. Still, in the beginning, it was what got us going and kept us going and I still look at U-pick as an important part of our marketing scheme."

§

Higher-Value High-Value Crops

Income triples with crops that pay the most.
by Craig Cramer

UNDERWOOD, Minn. – Back in 1984, Ron Roller and Katy Olson's Linden Tree Farm consisted of little more than a 4,500-square-foot market garden and a 10- by 10-foot roadside stand. Since then, the couple have roughly doubled their farm income each year, and are on the verge of realizing their dream of making a good living from less than 10 acres of high-value crops.

How? "We more than triple our income by focusing on *higher-value* high value crops," say Roller. In 1989, they grossed about $30,000 growing organic vegetables and ornamentals on just 7 acres of marginal, sandy soil. Roller is gradually cutting back on his off-farm job to devote more time to the operation.

"When we first started, we planted lots of tomatoes, sweet corn, squash, pumpkins, potatoes and other crops that were easy to grow," he recalls. "But just growing regular produce gets pretty old after a while. You have to handle a large volume, and the profits really aren't that high."

Grow Less, Make More

For example, they used to grow premium-quality pickling cucumbers that sold for $14 per bushel – $6 more than their competition. "Even with the good price, it just wasn't worth all the time, effort and grief to pick and sort them," says Roller.

Now, instead of picking and sorting bushels of pickling cucumbers, they sell 2-foot-long Chinese cucumbers to local restaurants for about $1 each, or at local farmers markets for about 50 cents. "You can make as much on 30 row-feet of Chinese cucumbers as you can on 100 feet of pickling cucumbers," observes Roller.

The same goes for root crops. "Most root crops, like carrots and potatoes, are actually pretty low-value crops," says Roller. "It's tough to compete with larger growers. So we only grow them as a special service to customers who specifically want organic and will pay for it." The one exception is Daikon radishes. The couple sell the half- to 2-pound radishes for $1 per pound at farmers markets.

Roller and Olson have also cut their tomato plantings in half, and only grow early-season, determinate varieties. "When the main crop of local tomatoes starts coming in, we're just about done," says Roller.

They wholesale just 10 percent of their produce. Of the remainder, about two-thirds is sold through their roadside stand and at local farmers markets. The rest is sold directly to restaurants. Regardless of the buyer, everything has to be top quality. "Buyers can return anything, no questions asked," says Roller.

"Rather than trying to compete in the wholesale market, we're reducing our marketing costs by developing our on-farm market," says Olson. They plan to cash in on recent improvements to the hard-surface road that passes their farm by selling more from their roadside stand. "That should double or triple the traffic and our stand sales. So we'll spend less time hauling produce to town," notes Roller. To keep a wide selection of produce available for their customers, they will contract out standbys like sweet corn, melons and pumpkins to sell along with their higher-value crops.

Risky Business

Roller and Olson's search for higher-value crops eventually led them to ornamental crops – like gourds, Indian corn, pumpkins, dried flowers and everlastings – which make up about three-quarters of their plantings. "Anything you can't eat, you can make money on," says Roller. "It's ironic people will pay more for crops they look at than food they eat."

Kale, which has taken over most of the acreage they once devoted to broccoli and cabbage, is a good example. The couple gross $4 to $5 per plant for the nutritious greens, which are seldom eaten. They mostly serve as backgrounds on salad bars and dinner plates at local restaurants. But that market is fast drying up, says Roller. One of his biggest kale customers, the manager of a nearby chain restaurant, was told by his superiors to stop buying from local growers. "So now we have California kale here year-round, while ours goes to waste in the field," he laments.

Focusing on even higher-value crops works for ornamentals as well as vegetables, says Roller. "I can get $50 for a crate of small ornamental pumpkins. But you've got to carry a lot of big jack-o-lantern pumpkins out of the field to make that much," he observes.

While kale and cucumbers are profitable, the couple's real moneymakers are dried flowers and everlastings – like statice (Limonium sinnatum), straw flowers (Helichrysum bracteatum), globe amaranth (Gomphrena globosa), larkspur (Delphinium ajacis) and cockscomb (Celosia cristata). "Those five make up about three-quarters of our plantings, but we grow about 40 different everlastings altogether," says Olson.

"Cockscomb is probably the most profitable of the dried flowers we grow on a large scale," she continues. "We should gross about $12,000 on our half-acre planting." On a per-acre basis, larkspur can gross 20 percent to 25 percent more, she notes.

Also keep in mind that dried flowers are a risky crop to grow, says Olson. While many kinds can thrive on poor soils, they are easily damaged by weather. Despite drip irrigation, yields were reduced during the '88 drought. Part of the '89 crop was damaged by hail, and some was hit by frost before maturity. "You don't have federal crop insurance to fall back on, either," notes Roller. Many species are also particularly susceptible to fungal diseases. "We've suffered some severe losses because we refuse to use fungicides," he recalls. "And that's a hard choice to make."

Dried flowers and everlastings are also extremely labor-intensive to grow, notes Olson. Two acres is enough to keep the couple, their 8-year-old daughter, Cedar, and two interns busy the entire season. Extra help is also hired during the peak harvest season. Plus, input costs for dried flowers are substantial – about $2,000 per acre. Most of that pays for seed, plastic mulch and drip irrigation tape. "If you count labor, you're up to around $4,000 per acre," says Roller.

Lots To Learn

Still, Roller and Olson do all they can to keep production costs low. They raise their own transplants in three plastic-glazed greenhouses they built themselves. The greenhouses measure 30, 40 and 60 feet in length, and are 12 feet wide. "We used a lot of recycled materials, so they didn't cost much to put up," says Roller. "It's a low-tech system with wood heat that anyone could put together. But they still work well."

"If you want top-quality plants, you're probably going to have to raise the transplants yourself," adds Olson. She's also considering using the greenhouses to raise bedding plants to sell at the roadside stand to help with spring cash flow.

The couple use black plastic mulch to control weeds, warm the soil, conserve moisture and speed growth during their relatively short growing season. Water is provided through drip irrigation tape under the plastic. "We started out using 4-mil tape, but that was too light," notes Roller. "We had leaks all over the place. Eight-mil worked better. But I'm thinking of moving up to 15-mil tape and reusing it for two or three years."

The transplants are set in holes punched through the plastic. A cup or so of diluted fish emulsion helps avoid transplant shock and gets the crop off to a fast start.

Roller and Olson are concerned about the effects of intensive cropping on their sandy soils. So they have begun to experiment with rye cover crops to prevent erosion and build soil organic matter. "We also don't like using so much plastic," says Roller, who notes that they carefully roll up plastic mulch and take it to a local recycler each year. "But with peppers and tomatoes, plastic and drip irrigation triples production, and you get them to market three weeks earlier."

"The same goes for flowers," adds Olson.

To try and end their dependence on plastic mulch, the couple are comparing four mulch systems with the help of a grant from the Minnesota Department of Agriculture's Sustainable Agriculture Demonstration Program. The four systems are 1) bare ground, 2) plastic mulch separated by bare ground, 3) plastic mulch separated by living grain rye mulch, and 4) straw mulch separated by living rye mulch.

"The first year, the plastic and rye looked the best," observes Roller. "The straw was not as effective in controlling the weeds and the yields were lower. But we want to see the effects of the straw on the soil over several years before we decide which is best." To make laying straw mulch less time-consuming, Roller is modifying a silage wagon to help spread straw more evenly. Because recent droughts have made straw hard to come by locally, he plans to grow an acre or so of sudax to chop for mulch.

"Some of the flowers did prefer the straw," observes Olson. "But what I really liked was the rye cover between the rows. It helped keep the crops cleaner because there was much less splash. During harvest, I could set bundles of flowers down on the rye without getting them dirty. And when you're tired, it's just nice and cool to flop down on it."

After the flowers are hand-harvested, they are bundled into standard-sized bunches for both wholesale and retail markets. Then the season ends where it began – in the greenhouses – where the bundles are hung to dry. Black plastic is used to screen out light that would otherwise fade the flowers.

Value Added

Marketing the dried flowers is no problem, says Olson. "Our flowers are sold before we plant them." In '89, about 6,500 row-feet of the couple's flowers were committed to the Minnesota Everlasting Co-op, a marketing group of nearly 100 growers in four western Minnesota counties. The couple also sold about 5,000 row-feet themselves at their roadside stand and at farmers markets.

"The dried flowers we're marketing through the co-op are replacing imports from Europe," says Olson. "We're by far the largest growers in the co-op. But some of the growers raise as little as 50 row-feet." Since the flowers can gross $5 to $10 per foot, even such small plantings can be a profitable way to gain experience before going ahead with commercial-scale production. "There's a lot to learn if you want to grow quality flowers," says Olson. "Everyone knows when to pick a ripe tomato. But with flowers, it's a different story."

To add even more value to their already high-value flower crops, Olson spends winters in her studio assembling them into wreaths, bouquets, decorative containers and baskets. She markets them through her own Prairie Spirit craft line to retail outlets in five Upper Midwest states. "We're focusing more and more on the craft line and less on wholesale. Growing bulk for wholesale is very exacting – every bunch has to be perfect and the same weight. With the crafts, quality is still important. But aesthetics are what counts.

"Plus, I've basically created a job for myself beyond just growing the flowers," she continues. "Because I produce my own raw materials, I get paid twice. And they're better quality than I could ever buy, because they haven't been shipped and banged around."

Selling Ideas

Roller and Olson hope to add yet another unique crop to their existing enterprises: new, high-value crop farmers. They've started an internship program to train prospective growers in the art and science of organic vegetable and flower production. "In a season with us, we can save someone five years of trial and error," says Olson. "And it helps us with the labor crunch, too."

"We enjoy farming," adds Roller. "But we'd rather promote and sell ideas – about the skills needed to grow good food and create jobs that can rejuvenate rural economies – not just peddle crops."

But skills, alone, aren't enough. "You can't get started without that outside source of income," says Olson. "You've got to start small and experiment until you find out what you like to grow, what grows well and what you can market."

And go slow, she continues. "We were fortunate because we had to clear brush from our land as we went. That slows you down. So does capitalizing the operation with off-farm income. We didn't just sit down with the banker and say, 'We want to start a 25-acre truck farm and we need $100,000.' "

You don't need great soil and lots of capital to make a living on the land. "Our land is marginal, but it hasn't held us back," says Roller. "Anyone can enjoy this kind of life, if they want to work at it."

§

CHAPTER 6:

Plan to Succeed

There are three ways to increase profits in a market garden business; cut costs, increase sales or raise prices. - Andy Lee 1991

What does the grower selling $12 per square foot of display space per day do differently from the grower who is only averaging $5 per square foot? Marketing skills, choice of varieties, and a dozen other things contribute to increased sales, but they all begin with the business and marketing plan.

Choose your markets as if your very life depended on them. Indeed, your economic life does. Study these markets carefully and create a production and marketing plan specifically tailored to the idiosyncrasies of the population that you serve.

Each sales location will be different, so it's really important to do your homework. Design just the right plan to account for all the variables. Always keep an open mind, so you can make improvements or changes as the season progresses or when the need becomes apparent.

Treat this exercise with as much energy and forethought as you would with any small business enterprise. Don't leave anything to chance. Include every possible expense you can imagine.

A market garden is a business. It requires basic business management skills, including a working knowledge of bookkeeping and record keeping. If you are like me, you may find the nuts and bolts of accounting and record keeping to be dull and uninteresting, except as it affects the bottom line. If that's the case, you can work with a local business or individual specializing in these functions. Let them do the detailed paper work, so you can concentrate on the fun of growing and marketing food.

This administrative assistance will be an expense against your income. You can arrange a barter situation with an accounting friend, as I did, to lessen the cash cost to your company. Trade food for accounting knowledge. In this chapter we'll delve into some records your business should keep. There are a few ways you can minimize the expense, aggravation and complexities of becoming a small-business owner.

Plan to grow as many different varieties as possible, but with particular emphasis on high value varieties that you know will sell well at the market. It's good to include a few less well known veggies in your cropping plan. Treat these as novelties, which they are. Use them for crowd-attracting displays, but don't expect to make a fortune because you are the only grower in the market to have them on sale.

Outline in your growing plan what you are going to do in terms of irrigation, sprays, fertilizers, cultivation and whatever else that needs to be done to grow quality produce. Be as specific as you possibly can.

This is even more critical if you only have a few hours each week away from your regular job to tend your crops. You will need to be efficient, well organized and in control of the cropping and marketing schedule. This can only come about by creating an efficient working business plan.

Know from one day to the next what to expect from insects, pollination requirements, irrigation requirements and so forth. Schedule from the beginning what weeks you should plant each variety to have it mature as your marketing schedule needs it. Learn how to plant successive crops to have a continuing supply throughout the season.

It won't do you any good at all to get a jump on the season if all your crops reach maturity at the same time. For example, having 9,000 ears of sweet corn all maturing on the same day would be disastrous.

One year, I had two whole beds of lettuce, nearly 2,000 heads, reach maturity the week *before* the farmers market was ready to open. Fortunately, I peddled it to the local food broker, but for less than half price. When the farmers market did open I didn't have any lettuce to sell. Maybe I was overly sensitive for the next couple of weeks, but it seemed that every customer who came to my booth asked for lettuce.

When you design your marketing plan use direct or subscription marketing techniques to by-pass the middlepeople. Go directly to your customers with your product, and directly to your bank with the profits.

This Game Called Business – The *"Gambler's Paradigm"*

In Booker T. Whatley's book *How to Make $100,000 Farming 25 Acres,* there is an interesting chapter about a computer program called the *Gambler's Paradigm.* The author, David Ehrenfeld, professor of biology at Rutgers University, uses the program to determine the probability of becoming a winner, both at the card table and in farming. By betting different levels of assets on the outcome of several trial runs, the farmer can predict the farm's probability of success or failure.

In the computerized trial run the farmer who borrowed heavily against farm assets to invest in a new farming venture lost after only three trial runs (seasons). The careful farmer, who invested 10 percent of farm assets on each trial run, was still in the game after 18 seasons. By leaving a solid asset base to carry through lean years, the farm managed to double net worth during the 18 seasons. Similarly, the gambler betting heavily on the first few hands in a poker game lost quickly. The more conservative professional player won more hands than were lost, subsequently building wealth steadily.

Just as in any game, you will begin your home-based market garden business with a number of assets and liabilities. These are analogous to the rules of a card game; playing options, wild cards, and one or more opponents or obstacles. The object of the game is to take the hand you've been dealt and play it with all the energy and skill you can muster. The object of business is to use your start-up capital and a well conceived business plan to overcome the obstacles and setbacks. The goal is to arrive at a profit, thereby becoming the winner.

This is, of course, a completely whimsical over-simplification of the sometimes difficult process of starting and managing a profitable business. The similarities between owning a business and playing a game however, are startling.

For example, compare your start-up business to a poker game where you have to "pay the pot" as a form of investment capital. Then, take your cards and play them carefully, adding or taking away investment capital as needed. As a card player, you might have to drop out of the round if your chances for success are bleak, just as you might cut your business losses by dropping a product line that is not selling well.

You can use business investment strategy to further your chances for succeeding, and even bluff the competition into believing you have a better product than they do. A wild card may be a big asset, or a total liability for your hand. Wild cards occur in farming all the time. Examples are political changes, heavy rain or lack of rain, or a brilliant idea for a new product that is a sure winner.

I'm not suggesting that you run your business as if you were competing in the casinos, although some businesses do give that appearance. I'm merely pointing out that you should adopt the attitude of having fun with your business. Play with it, derive some pleasure from it and allow yourself to enjoy the journey.

Taking our lead from successful gamblers and successful small-business people, there are certain undeniable characteristics apparent in all successful home businesses. For one thing, the entrepreneur started with a plan.

You've probably already heard the story about Apple Computer's first business plan. It was sketched on a napkin during lunch. That story may be true. That sort of success does happen, occasionally. But it's not the type of well conceived and well documented business plan that will generally lead to a significant business success.

More commonly, the real business plan, the type that wins financing approval from sophisticated bankers and supporters, is more than just a few ideas jotted on a paper napkin. It is, instead, a carefully worked out series of questions and answers. These solutions to problems lead the business to a state of usefulness to the community, hopefully resulting in a condition of *profitability*. From that position, the business earns the right to expand its services or products to the public. Ultimately, the business will provide more jobs, pay more taxes and offer valuable support to the community that sustains the business.

What is contained in a complete business plan?

Most of us only write a business plan when we need to borrow money, usually because the bank asked us for one. The real value of your business plan is much broader, however. It serves as a guide and counsels you on upcoming business decisions. It provides a framework or structure for your new business endeavors. Without it you will have no clear goals or any realistic plans with which to achieve your goals.

What are the elements that a business plan needs to address and for which a financier will look for answers? Here are some clues:

- What are your personal goals?

- What type of business do you want to start?

- Why do you want to start and own this business?

- How will your new business help you achieve

  personal goals?

- Who will the business serve?

- Where will it be located?

- What will it produce?

- Who will help with various elements,

  especially financing?

- Where are the markets?

- How will you approach the markets?

- How will the business grow?

- What is the probability of success?

- How will the business affect the quality of life of

  the businessperson and family?

- Will the business be fun to own and operate?

Every successful company uses a business plan that asks, then answers, questions like these. The successful mom and pop store on the edge of town, or the multi-national conglomerate with many individual enterprises will have a business plan. It is the central theme for any start-up enterprise or company expansion. To forego this step will invite disaster. Without a plan you will be like a ship without a rudder, floundering around making little progress, eventually grounding on a reef or sinking with all hands.

What's the "Big Deal" about a Business Plan?

Writing a business plan is not as intimidating as it might first appear. I think most successful small businesses start with probably no more than a few pages of well thought out and well balanced ideas. In the several businesses that I am familiar with, the longest plan I've read is 17 typewritten pages. The shortest is just two paragraphs.

Simplify your message when introducing your new business idea to various people. It will be advantageous if you can condense the *essence* of your business plan into just one small paragraph. Better yet, one long sentence. For example, the title and subtitle of this book captures the vision in just 11 words. The *goal* of this book is *to help people learn how to grow food where they live, and sell it profitably.*

If you plan to borrow start up money, try describing your new business idea to friends, family and business associates before you go see the banker. You only have about 10 seconds of their brain time to give them enough information to help them like it. So, condense the excitement, energy and challenge of your vision or mission into one long sentence or a very short paragraph.

When describing your market garden plan to a first-time listener, keep it crisp and clear. Don't go into a long-winded spiel about how, *I'm going to start this big garden and grow vegetables for anyone who will buy them. I hope I can make some money doing it.*

Instead, try a short, concise and excitingly simple description of exactly what you intend to do: *I'm growing organic vegetables in response to pent up consumer demand for chemical-free produce.* In one sentence containing 15 words, you have just told your listeners most of what they want to know to form an opinion of your business plan. If they like the idea they will take an interest in your plans and ask questions to give you a chance to fill in the details.

By saying *I'm growing organic vegetables...* you have told them that it is possible to raise vegetables organically, that land is available and the practice can be successful. When you tell them you are doing this in response to *pent-up consumer demand...,* you are telling them that there is a market for these vegetables. It is profitable because there is enough demand for fresh garden produce that you can sell what you are growing. You have very succinctly stated that you have located a profitable market niche in your community.

The steps involved in creating your business plan are very similar to the steps I followed in writing this book. Begin with your mission and personal goals then add the list of problems and how you plan to solve them. Next, develop a list of important elements, divide the group into sections, eliminate superfluous information and add critical information. Always look for outside help and suggestions, and format the plan so you can read it and follow it.

The business plan should be complete with budgets and narrative. A cash flow plan showing your projected income and expenses month-by-month is a very important component of the budget. The cash flow projection points out weaknesses in your working business plan and helps you keep from over-spending during low-income months. Keep the business plan where you can refer to it frequently. Update and improve it as needed to keep abreast of changing conditions, both in the marketplace and at your gardening site.

Make the plan as complete as necessary to give a thorough understanding of the dynamics of the business and how it fits your personal and monetary goals. Write your plan by the season or by the year, for at least two years into the future.

The old school bankers may want to see a business plan stretched out to five years. It's hard enough to predict one year into the future, let alone five. It is helpful, though, if you can at least offer a vision and basic growth plan for up to five years.

To establish parameters for writing your business plan, you might start a list of the limiting factors. These will contribute to the organization and operation of your business. In market gardening, potential limiting factors are:

- Amount of start-up capital you have available.

- Time you can dedicate to the business.

- Land available for crops.

- Other resources: labor, water, climate, soil types,

  equipment, buildings, etc.

- Market potential in your area.

- Impact on quality of life and lifestyle for you and your

family.

Over estimating market size and income potential is a
common and recurring problem in many small businesses. It
would be futile, for instance, if you grew truckloads of produce
and only had one or two neighbors to sell it to. It wouldn't be
any better to try supplying produce for a small city if you only
have enough land to grow crops for a few families.

For example, around Boston, Mass., there is a market
population of more than 1 million people. Because of the
environmental awareness of a major part of this population,
this is an excellent upscale market for fresh garden produce.
Market potential is definitely not a limiting factor in this
metropolitan area.

When I started my market garden, I wanted to operate from
my home, but I had less than one acre for growing food. I could
have rented or borrowed nearby land for an expanded
cropping plan. But I lacked start up .i.capital; to buy
equipment and supplies and to hire labor for a larger site. So,
my first market garden was on land that I had available, and I
relied on savings to pay operating costs. These were the two
limiting factors that dictated the scope and size of my
business.

It would have been possible to borrow start up funds from
friends or family, or the bank. But my intent was to enter this
business slowly and carefully, and let it grow through
reinvestment of earned capital. I stayed within the
restrictions of my limiting factors of land and money. I had to
ignore the huge untapped market for organic produce in the
Boston metropolitan area. My business plan, however, did
include expansion and growth plans. These were to carry me
to a higher level of retained earnings as my business grew to
match the market.

Because of these limiting factors of money and land, I couldn't
earn a full time income from my new business at first. This
then became a limiting factor. I needed an outside income to
meet my year-round needs, 20 to 40 hours per week to earn a
full-time living. Time (or lack of it) to work in the market
garden and to market the produce became another limiting
factor.

It was clear what resources I had and how I could use them to
fit the limiting factors. I knew I could enter the business
without fear of losing my shirt, and could anticipate an

excellent return on investment. I created a part-time job that was satisfying, both monetarily and aesthetically, as well as being emotionally fulfilling.

I now feel it would have been OK for me to borrow money to start my business on a larger scale. Then I could have started with a more sophisticated and aggressive plan. By doing so, I could have taken advantage of certain economies of scale in buying supplies and equipment, and in hiring labor. However, the opposite could have been true. I might have over expanded, like the first farmer in the Gambler's paradigm farming game, and gone out of business quickly.

Conserving Capital, and the Wise Use of Credit

Conserving capital and the wise use of credit and business assets are central anxieties for all business people. Almost every business failure gives lack of operating capital and lack of management expertise as the main reasons they didn't succeed. They may have started out with sufficient capital and experienced unexpected losses, or they may have been hopelessly under-capitalized from the very beginning.

Often, insufficient capital results from overspending on non-necessities. At other times, the problem is lack of a valid budget to address cash flow management situations. Don't let this happen to you. Be wary of falling into any of these traps. They could result in your new business failing.

If you do lack sufficient capital to carry out your master plan then consider it a hidden benefit. You can design ways to do the job better with less money. Down-size your first year plan and goals to fit your budget, even if this means starting on a part-time basis.

If your plan is *very sound* (and there aren't many fool-proof business plans), you might consider borrowing operating capital. Before heading down this road of possible no return, you must first reconsider every aspect of your business plan to see how it fits the vision and master plan. Locate places where you can save money. Go through each step with a fine-toothed comb, and pull out the fluff.

Think of spending money as either vital, essential or nice. In the first year, focus on the vital elements of your business plan. These can sustain your immediate future. Leave the essential items for the second or third year, and don't buy the nice items until your business is solidly established.

For example, don't buy a new tractor or rotary tiller if you can rent or borrow one in the short term. Don't buy a new truck if a used truck will work just as well. You need to save money, so be as inventive and innovative as you can to keep your expenses at a manageable level.

What About all that Boring Business Stuff?

Certain business management basics are necessary for all businesses. The home-based market garden is no exception. This doesn't require an academic degree in business management, but you do need to pay close attention to the facts of business life.

For example, you must follow local, state and federal government regulations about taxes and insurance. Failing to do this can result in surprising and annoying side effects.

Years ago, I didn't file proper year-end tax papers and wound up with a stiff penalty of $400. This was money that I sorely needed elsewhere. Similarly, a business associate friend of mine didn't pay workers compensation insurance premiums. He later had to pay a $1,100 hospital bill for a worker's injury. Don't ignore the rules. The consequences are not only annoying, but can sometimes be devastating.

Beginning at the federal level, you are responsible for reporting income and expenses accurately. This means filing quarterly reports and annual returns, withholding taxes from employees and self-employment taxes for yourself. You have to provide safe and comfortable working conditions and suitable hours of operation for your employees, and carry workers compensation insurance for employees.

The state also requires that you pay unemployment insurance for your employees, and collect sales tax on sales of taxable items. At the local level, you may need to deal with building permits, excise taxes and zoning ordinances to name just a few.

Granted, this mess of bureaucratic red tape is a pain in the neck. Unfortunately, we have little choice. I don't like it any more than you do, but the laws are clear. Trying to avoid them can cause nagging annoyances to turn into big time problems.

These range from simple embarrassment, to fines and penalties, and even business closure in extreme cases. Just grit your teeth and do what you have to do. It is expensive to run a business properly. Just pass the cost along to the consumer like everybody else does.

I get impatient with all this paperwork stuff, too. If you don't have the time, skills or patience needed to check it out personally then hire a professional to do it. A knowledgeable accountant or attorney will have most of the answers you need. Membership in your area small business associations will help and a visit to your local Small Business Administration office will be very useful.

Use Knowledge to Help You Achieve Your Goals

Specialized knowledge is a combination of passion, skills and confidence. Each breeds the others. - Andy Lee, 1992

Knowledge can be categorized in three distinct levels, each as important as the other. Generalized knowledge, of course, is the information we have that helps us get through the basic undertakings of life, such as feeding ourselves and driving a car. Infinite knowledge gives us the ability to dream dreams. It helps us to know and understand that we can be successful if we try hard enough and work smart enough. Specialized knowledge is the one that will allow us to bring our dreams to reality in our chosen field.

Specialized knowledge deals specifically with the intricacies and variabilities of our particular field of endeavor, be it gardening or conducting a symphony orchestra. Some examples of specialized knowledge that apply to the market garden would be planting methods, schedules, and marketing techniques. This part is pretty easy to understand. We just need to know how to find the information when we need it.

As you advance with the writing of your business plan, you will see the need for a tremendous amount of specialized knowledge. As a market gardener you will learn to wear a dozen different hats, all at the same time. You need to know how to improve soil, design a cropping plan, grow crops, harvest and pack produce, and market the crops profitably.

These, combined with record keeping, financial management, labor management, time scheduling, crop scheduling, market

246

scheduling and seemingly a zillion other things, may at first appear to be overwhelming. Just take one step at a time and write it down as you gather information. You can construct a realistic and workable business plan that eliminates the confusion of starting a small business. The plan provides the map you need to bring your business vision to reality.

One reason I made a smooth transition from table gardening to market growing was my long-term passionate interest in gardening. For years I have felt compelled to learn every aspect of it. I have collected literally hundreds of articles and books dealing with gardening and selling fresh food. Over the years I've attended many seminars, workshops and meetings to learn about market gardening and have kept copious notes and records to fall back on.

I keep a daily journal of my activities and jot down anything that seems important. In my office, I have several cardboard boxes full of information that I've collected over the years. I group the cardboard boxes by subject matter. When I need a particular tidbit of information I can usually put my hands on it quickly. I know there are better filing systems than mine, but it seems to have worked so far. After all, I'm a vegetable grower and marketer, not a file clerk.

Where does all this information come from? Well, to begin with I subscribe to two dozen publications about farming and operating small businesses. Probably 75 percent of the information I find most useful comes from these periodicals.

Over the years of searching for organic market gardening information, I've gained the most assistance from magazines such as *Rural Enterprise, Ford's Enterprise Farming* (no longer published), *Small Farms Today, NEW FARM, ,Organic Gardening, The Mother Earth News, National Gardening,* and *Harrowsmith Country Life* (see appendix for addresses). If you aren't subscribing to these publications then you may want to purchase sample copies and see what you think of them.

An especially useful and entertaining monthly newsletter has recently become available from Fairplain Publications, Box 365, Auburn, Kansas 66402. It is entitled *Growing For Market; news and ideas for market gardeners.* The annual subscription rate is $24. Publishers Lynn Byczynski and Daniel Nagengast are experienced market gardeners with a well-developed outlook on commercial gardening as a way to make a living. Their newsletter fills a niche for up-to-date information and solid inspiration for beginning and established market gardeners and small-scale farmers.

Libraries and used book dealers are sometimes good sources of agricultural and gardening books. However, the industry is changing so quickly that much information in the older books is dated, and of little value to me. The exceptions to this rule have been the writings of Louis Bromfield, Edward Faulkner and Peter Henderson. All of these writers were visionaries and years ahead of their times. They lived the type of farming that should today be considered conventional.

Attending meetings, workshops, seminars and other functions can be very helpful in gleaning useful information. Field days and workshops sponsored by the local growers' associations, universities and the USDA can be very fruitful. The Cooperative Extension Service can be particularly useful to a beginning market grower. Their staff includes trained specialists in such areas as home economics, nutrition, vegetables and small fruits and berries, livestock, land management and even Christmas trees. They have reports on almost all aspects of agriculture, even solar greenhouses.

While the USDA's informative bulletins and news releases about small-scale farm management are often useful, I've often criticized the Extension Service. Sometimes their less than positive attitude towards organic gardening and farming annoys me. I feel this is primarily from the older agents trained in the nation's land grant universities. These colleges rely to a very large extent on grants and scholarship money from the wealthy and influential chemical companies that manufacture and sell agricultural chemicals. It then follows that the teaching emphasis is on how to grow crops and solve cultural problems synthetically rather than organically.

I sense, however, that many Extension agents are becoming more enlightened, particularly in areas of composting, integrated pest management and low-input sustainable agriculture. In the past two years I've seen more university trained professionals teaching sustainable agriculture techniques. I sincerely hope this trend continues and expands. Meanwhile, I'll keep using the many excellent ideas and publications that they do have available.

State agriculture departments are also valuable information sources for the beginning or expanding vegetable producer. As an example, the Massachusetts Department of Food and

Agriculture is very aggressive in promoting statewide farmers markets. It also publishes a monthly newsletter called *Fresh Connections*, which links local growers with restaurants.

During the growing season, the department publishes a fresh produce market report that keeps market gardeners informed on pricing and availability of locally grown produce. The report shows how pricing for locally grown produce compares to area supermarket produce sections.

Additionally, the department has just released a new *Green Book*, which lists wholesale growers statewide who are looking for markets. This is a real asset for market gardeners and vegetable farmers, because it helps food outlets locate local growers.

The department has had tremendous success in promoting events to connect regional food writers with local food growers for articles about the availability of homegrown produce. One such function, a *Peak Of The Season* luncheon at the famous Old Colony Restaurant in Boston, featured *Massachusetts Grown and Fresher* produce from eight area growers.

The menu for the luncheon included salad greens, herbs, edible flowers, mushrooms, baby vegetables, rabbit, chicken, lobster, fruit dessert, and locally bottled wine. More than 50 area newspaper and television personalities including Julia Child were on hand to enjoy this sumptuous feast.

Look for publications and events like these in your state. They have a very positive effect in heightening consumer awareness of the vast range of agricultural products available. Increasing public awareness will increase sales and profitability for all market gardeners and small-scale farmers.

Ways to Increase Your Specialized Knowledge

Joining state-wide vegetable and fruit growers associations is an excellent way to obtain specialized knowledge for growing and marketing garden products. There are trade organizations in every state of the nation. They serve as support groups for beginning market gardeners and established growers.

These associations and cooperatives provide leadership, co-op advertising, group purchasing and sometimes group insurance packages. They usually have a monthly or quarterly newsletter to inform members of political happenings, new growing and marketing techniques, agriculture related human interest stories and grower success stories. Sometimes these newsletters provide the only available way to advertise products and services. Vegetable growers can advertise to buy and sell equipment, find workers and sell products in these publications.

A beneficial service of these trade associations is to sponsor meetings and workshops. Members, particularly new business owners, can come together informally to exchange ideas and information. Some of my best marketing tips and growing techniques have come firsthand from these evening and weekend meetings.

In your search for specialized knowledge, don't overlook the research farms. There are several state and federal experimental farms in this country that are doing a great job in breeding and testing new varieties. They are also using new techniques, and new ways of putting old ideas together to create more functional systems.

Experimental farms around the country offer day-long, weekend and week- long courses or seasonal apprenticeships. Some have publications and research papers that are of immense benefit to both new and established growers.

Schedule a block of time daily to increase your specialized knowledge. Read books and journals on market gardening. Keep a personal daily journal, and maintain a good filing system that will help you retain information from one season to the next. Make friends with other nearby growers and be willing to exchange information with them frequently. Look in the gardens of your neighbors and see what they are doing successfully. Call on the more experienced gardeners in your area. You will find most folks who enjoy growing things also enjoy helping others get started, so don't be shy about asking for their ideas and support.

CHAPTER 7:

Small Is Beautiful

And Profitable

These days we hear a lot about "intensive farming." Sometimes I question what it really means to produce vegetables intensively. Farmers of all kinds have been trying to do it for years, often with a great deal of success, but usually at great harm to the environment.

It is almost always possible to make plants grow faster and yield more. Unfortunately, it's not always practical and it's not always profitable. Anytime there is a great increase in outputs it almost always relies on increased use of expensive and environmentally questionable inputs. How much does intensive production really increase yields and what is that greater yield worth when compared to the greater inputs costs and labor required? And what about being *too* intensive? Doesn't this sometimes result in an exploitation of the farm or the farm family?

If you are striving for intensive production then it makes just as much sense to rely on intensive marketing, too. One aspect of intensive production has to do with the food value and dollar value of the crops grown. Grow the higher value crops, bypass the middlepeople and look for ways to earn retail prices for your produce.

Some of us rebel at the idea of intensive production. It sounds too much like a lot of hard work. Think of it as grace and efficiency, then it becomes less hard work. Some things that intensive production can mean are year-round greenhouse production, cold frames, equidistant spacing, boxed raised beds, retail versus wholesale, interplanting and succession cropping.

From my viewpoint, intensive production means greater yields from smaller pieces of land. I commend this because as population expands there will be less and less farmland to grow food for more and more people. It is possible to upgrade fertility on small parcels almost immediately. One way to intensify yields is to take the resources from a broader area and use them to enrich a specific area. One way to do this is to compost leaf and yard waste from your community to make your garden fertile and to increase yields. This results in more food from less land. These concentrated inputs will result in greater yields, and less sprawl. Smaller parcels of land are easier to encompass, manage and understand. Putting it all together in small packages is less daunting, easier to start and manage, and less disruptive to larger parts of the world that can then be allowed to rest.

These smaller parcels are often cheaper to rent, sometimes even no rent at all. Smaller parcels are almost always easier to find, too. In many cases unused backyards and vacant land can be found closer to the market center. This enables farmers to get their crops to market sooner, fresher and with less expense. This can result in higher prices that lead to higher profits.

Costs of intensive production are always higher. Specialized tools are often required that are more expensive than ordinary tools. For example, a tractor-powered spading machine that is built to replicate double-digging by hand can be very expensive, as much as $2,000 more than a tractor-mounted rotary tiller.

Market gardening in any form is only profitable because we manipulate the soil and the climate. Intensive production often calls for us to further manipulate each end of the season, with such things as row covers and plastic mulch. But is it more profitable when you factor in the cost of the materials and the labor to install and remove them at each end of the season?

Learn to work smarter, not harder. Use a good rotation plan to build soil and control weeds, pests, and disease cycles. Get multiple crops from your garden and make every square foot pay for itself. But only do this if you are not at risk of over-producing on your land. Add value to everything you can. Use trellises, intercropping and companion planting.

The results of intensive production techniques can be quite impressive. John Jeavons, author of *How To Grow More Vegetables From Less Land,* can produce many times more carrots per acre than the national average. In my market gardens I can out-perform national tomato yields by a factor of eight.

The bio-intensive gardens at Ohio University in Athens, Ohio, managed by Steve Rioch, have been well documented since 1987. During the first year the yield from one-eighth acre of land was only 2,000 pounds. The following year the yields increased to 6,000 pounds. During 1991 the yields shot up to 14,000 pounds of food, on only 4,000 square feet of garden space. All of this is the result of intensive management.

Lay out your garden efficiently. This takes a good amount of forethought. No matter what size garden you have, 1,000 square feet or 40,000 square feet, it is easier if you plan and plant in beds. They don't have to be raised beds, but the planning and planting goes easier if you plant 4-foot crop strips separated by paths. I make my paths 24 inches wide, but I have plenty of land. If you have limited space you can cut your paths to as little as 12 inches.

Position your beds in a north to south direction. This way you will get maximum solar exposure from the morning and afternoon sun. Also, prevailing winds in most parts of the country are from the northwest or southwest. These winds are less likely to flatten crops in north-south beds. They can funnel the wind, rather than have to stand broadside to it.

Long growing beds are more efficient than short beds. When I first started out as a market gardener my beds were only 25 feet long. I reasoned that I could use the cross paths at each row end to get to other areas of the garden quicker. After I fine-tuned my operation, I found that it made a lot more sense to choose one bed to work on and stay in one area until the work there was finished. This saves all that time lost in frequently moving from one task to another.

Also, short beds are inefficient for plastic mulch, row covers, drip irrigation, and for crop planning. I converted the gardens to 100-foot beds in my second year. Today, we use beds that are 300 feet to 700 feet long.

The truly sustainable garden system will have at least one-seventh of its area dedicated to green manure cover crops each year. Base your crop rotations and marketing plan on the remaining space. Once you have determined your garden layout there is never any need to change the plan. Just rotate the crop plan along the beds in the direction you've established. Using this system, it will be seven years before any crop gets back to the bed it was in during your first year.

You may want to intersperse the beds of cover crops throughout your garden, rather than group them together as a block. The block approach is more efficient, but scattering the cover-cropped beds will attract more beneficial insects and look pretty as the cover crops set flowers. High growing cover crops such as sweet clover, however, tend to lodge and fall over. It's best to have these higher growing varieties grouped together so they can hold each other up. In the block approach it's a good idea to cover crop the paths between the beds, too. The cover crop roots will help reduce soil compaction. The top growth will help smother weeds and will harbor beneficial insects that help break disease and pest cycles.

Your compost pile can take up two or three of the empty beds in your garden each year. This is an easy way to quickly get nutrients into your soil. Probably better, and certainly faster, than cover cropping. Facilities such as greenhouse, cold frame, tool shed, washing shed and walk-in cooler should be as close to the middle of your garden as possible. Every day begins and ends in one of these buildings. By having them at the middle of the garden you will be able to work in any bed, yet still be close enough to the tool shed for tools, or close enough to the greenhouse and cold frame to keep an eye on things as the daily temperature changes.

If you have workers reporting to the garden you can leave instructions on a bulletin board in the tool shed. Having the tool shed nearby eliminates those tiring and time consuming trips to go get tools and supplies during the day.

Similarly, a centrally located wash stand is easy to get to from all the beds. The produce doesn't have to be moved too far to be washed, packed and stored in the walk-in cooler. Also, it's easier to return wash water to the garden from a central location.

City Farm Grosses $238,000 On 1/2 Acre

by George DeVault

Ah, the sounds of early morning at Kona Kai Farms. Heavy traffic and truck horns on I-80 a few blocks to the west. The whistle of an Amtrak passenger train one block to the south, and the click of quick footsteps on the sidewalk as office workers hurry by, carefully sipping their morning coffee. If all this seems more like morning in the middle of the city, it's because that is exactly where this farm is located. Kona Kai occupies slightly less than half an acre at the corner of Hearst Avenue and Fifth Street – near the heart of downtown Berkeley, Ca., population 103,328.

Kona Kai's neighbors are a stained glass shop, an Audi and Volkswagen dealer, The Nature Company, Spenger's Fish Market & Restaurant, nondescript warehouses and manufacturing plants and a few badly weathered, two-story frame houses. Most of the wooden fence on the property immediately to the west has fallen down. The yard there is dotted with rusting junk cars and chest-high grass and weeds.

Real Urban Renewal

"There are small places like this in any metro area," observes Michael Norton, who founded the farm in 1983. "You probably couldn't do it as profitably in other places, because we have the ideal climate and customer base."

But, he stresses, it is possible to do somewhat the same thing just about anywhere in the country. In fact, Norton says one of his personal goals for the farm is to inspire others to set up similar operations around the country. So far, three former employees have gone off to start their own garden-farms. "We get a lot of visitors, too," he adds. "People just show up. People come by and say, 'I knew farming could be like this.' One man from North Carolina said, 'I had four things to do in California and visiting you was one of them.'

"It would take about $50,000 to get started on this scale," says Norton. He feels it could work on up to 10 or even 40 acres. But – whatever the scale – you'd darn well better know what you're getting into first, because it's not just a simple matter of sowing a few seeds and raking in the profits. "Twenty percent of this is farming, 80 percent is marketing, transportation, and communications," Norton stresses.

"Farmers don't seem to be good salespeople. I was always a good salesman, but never had experience as a farmer. I figured I'd better sell things, rather than grow things. Many farmers view themselves as production people. The second goods leave their property, their involvement is over with. By adding to their responsibilities they add value to their product. I think there is a role for small, specialty producers. I think there is a demand for produce that justifies it. A produce brand name is worth a fortune."

That's why Norton handles the marketing and administrative side of the business, while a hired farm manager concentrates on running the farm organically. There are more than 30 varieties of fancy lettuces with even fancier names like RED GRENOBLOISE, REINE DES GLACES and MERVEILLE DES QUATRE SAISONS. Kona Kai's offerings also include salad greens like mizuna and red mustard, chioggia beets, radishes and a nearly round, 19th century French heirloom carrot.

"We specialize in baby lettuce and the various salad greens that are available in the finest restaurants worldwide," proclaims Kona Kai's marketing literature. "We ship regularly (via overnight air freight) to Hong Kong and Japan and daily to the Midwest, New York and Hawaii. In the industry, we are known for having the highest quality products. Our standards for consistency and service have no equal.

"Each day we cut a variety of our lettuces and salad greens and incorporate them into what we call our 'market pack.' This is a mixture that is pre-cut, washed and air-dried for your convenience. We can ship six cases of 2 pounds each delivered to your door for $104. This equals about 104 salads at $1 per salad. An alternative to this is five cases of 2-pound market packs with radishes and/or onions and flower garnishes. This is $125 delivered and produces about 85 salads at $1.50 each. These mixes create a visually spectacular salad that awaits only your favorite dressing. We cater these packs to your individual desires."

Locally, Kona Kai also delivers three times a week to fancy restaurants throughout the San Francisco area. "We have one restaurant that likes their greens particularly small, about 2 inches, instead of the standard 3 to 4 inches," says Farm Manager Viki Von Lackum.

Profitable Sideline

Norton first got the idea for his garden-farm from a TV feature on Alan Chadwick, the guru of intensive gardening in double-dug, permanent raised beds at the University of California in Santa Cruz. "I saw that and talked my ex-wife into growing herbs. We had a lot next to us. A friend had a lot. We formed a business to grow herbs. A hundred dollars a month was a big month," he recalls.

Herb production continued as a sideline for about 18 months, while Norton kept building his main enterprise, a coffee plantation on the Kona Coast of the Island of Hawaii. "It took more money and time than we thought," Norton says of the coffee business. He gave up on herbs and started growing lettuce. "We needed the money. We needed $25,000 by September. We were up at dawn, three years in a row. We lived six months off of coffee and six months off of lettuce."

The coffee business also provided Norton with a vital marketing edge. "It gave me a presence in the gourmet food world. It meant that we could call any of the fancy hotels in New York, the Waldorf or the Plaza. Instead of saying, 'I'm some hippie with lettuce in my backyard,' I could say, 'I'm from Kona Kai, the largest processor of Kona coffee. We also grow many specialty lettuces. Let me send you a sample. See if this might not be the product for you.' Another person doesn't have that advantage.

"The concept of marketing scares a lot of people," he adds. Norton may have been a bit bashful, at first, too. "But, after going to the fanciest restaurants in San Francisco three times and having them go ga-ga over the greens, we had a little more self-esteem."

In 1988, its best year ever, the little farm grossed $238,000. Next year's gross was down to about $150,000, but only because production and marketing were scaled back. "There's not the pressure for the money now that the coffee business is doing better," Norton explains.

A Lot From A Little

"We fell into this property," Norton says of the present location. "There were two houses that had deteriorated to such a state that they had to be torn down. And in Berkeley, a house

257

has to *really* deteriorate to be torn down. If you couldn't push it down by hand, you rebuilt it. You could push these down by hand." A third house, built around 1870, was a little sturdier. It became the headquarters for Kona Kai Farms, with business offices on the second floor and packing shed on the ground floor.

Kona Kai has no tractor. There is not even a garden tiller, just racks of well-used hoes and other hand tools for freshening and smoothing the 69 permanent raised beds in which all of the crops are grown. The only power tool on the farm is a circular saw used to cut boards that frame the beds.

The beds are nothing fancy, just functional. They're made of 2 x 10s and 2 x 12s, braced with 2 x 4s. All beds are 5 feet wide, but they vary in height from 12 to 24 inches, and in length from 25 to 48 feet. There is just enough space between them to accommodate a wheelbarrow. Irrigation pipe, sprinkler heads and garden hoses are everywhere.

Each bed is easily converted into a mini-greenhouse using 9.5-foot lengths of quarter-inch fiberglass rods and sheets of plastic. The plastic is kept over the beds for a few days after seeding to help speed germination. It also protects the plants at night during cold weather. At first, Kona Kai used three-quarter inch PVC pipe to support plastic covers, but the pipe was too bulky to store and broke easily.

Beds are filled with clean topsoil enriched with mushroom soil and compost made from straw, chicken manure and other organic materials, including crop residues. Fish emulsion also is applied, following label directions.

At first, the beds were kept slightly rounded in the middles in hopes that would help them heat up and drain better. Now, they are smoothed flat with a large landscaping rake to save on labor. "Our costs are labor, seeds and dirt. Labor is so high, so we look for ways to make labor easier and better," says Von Lackum.

"We work this ground hard, a lot and fast," she adds. "We get a tremendous amount of growth out of a little bit of land without much (in the way of inputs) at all."

Every five weeks in summer, a crop is ready for harvest. That slows to seven to eight weeks in winter. "In the winter, we really pick through the beds to hold onto as much as we can.

In summer, we're too busy. We just compost the leftovers," she explains.

Other than a few aphids and a few weeds, which are mostly volunteer lettuce plants, Von Lackum says, "We really don't have much of a pest problem. We turn the beds often enough that we break their life cycle."

Birds were her biggest problem. "The birds would steal seed right after we seeded the beds. You could never really tell how much seed was left," Von Lackum explains. At first, bird netting was draped over the beds, but that was too labor-intensive. Now, the entire farm is covered with bird netting suspended on cables.

There is no special crop rotation. "We just don't put the same crop in twice, but it doesn't seem to make a lot of difference," she says. "We put a lot back into the soil. If we have trouble with lettuce in one bed, we don't plant lettuce there."

Success Breeds Success

Norton just started a second farm on a vacant lot in San Francisco, right off of U.S. 101 near Candlestick Park. "It will be in full production by October," he says. "We're gearing it to make up for the slowness of the winter growth, so that we do not lose any customers. Then we'll make a big push next spring."

In addition to the same leaf crops, he's also growing cut flowers. "We think we might have a niche selling to florists and restaurants. Some flowers are really difficult to get to market, because they are too delicate to be packed in traditional ways. We're growing just a few types of flowers (Icelandic poppy and bearded Iris) that would be atypical. The things that aren't there are what's valuable.

"The marketplace will tell you what you can do to make a profit," Norton concludes. "Give it the opportunity to talk back to you."

'Do What No One Else Is Doing'

Savvy crop selection keeps this grower a step ahead of the crowd.

by Craig Cramer

VIROQUA, Wis. – Richard de Wilde has a rough rule of thumb about which crops to plant: "Don't grow anything that doesn't have the potential to bring in at least 50 cents a pound or row-foot, retail," he suggests. "And I prefer to get a dollar. I'm not getting any younger, and the crops aren't getting any lighter to carry out of the field."

De Wilde admits he doesn't always follow his own advice. But when things go right, most of the dozens of high-value crops he grows on 20 acres of silt loam bottomland meet the 50-cent test.

Choosing the highest-value crops helps. And adding value to some after harvest boots his bottom line. But de Wilde also pays special attention to every detail of production, harvest and transport to make sure his products are the best money can buy. They are also organic – certified organic by the Organic Crop Improvement Association.

"We focus on growing the highest quality. We grade hard, and use refrigerated transport to give us that extra edge in quality," says de Wilde. While spending more for refrigeration is important, that quality edge comes only by doing a lot of small things right. For example, a simple shade-awning on the wagon keeps the harvest from overheating (not to mention the harvesting crew) en route from the field to the cooler.

Slightly more than half of de Wilde's sales are made at farmers markets in Madison and La Crosse, Wis. He sells the balance to area food co-ops and restaurants. "I don't get as much, but those deliveries help pay for the trips to the farmers markets," he says.

"I emphasize specialty vegetables and greens," he continues. "But at the farmers markets, people want to buy everything in one stop." So to keep those customers happy, de Wilde still grows more common fare – but with a slight twist. Instead of ordinary potatoes, he distinguishes himself by growing Yukon Golds. Likewise, de Wilde doesn't just sell plain old yellow sweet corn. He sells bicolor and white sweet corns. "I always try to do things no one else is doing," he says. "I'll grow just about anything you want. But not for 20 cents a pound."

$7/lb. Salad Mix

One of de Wilde's hot new items is his baby salad mix – a combination of lettuce and other greens harvested when they are about 3 inches tall. "It's a West Coast phenomenon that we're trying to introduce to the Midwest," he observes. "I've got a couple-day advantage over California growers in freshness. And I have a price edge because I don't have to pay a broker."

Normally, de Wilde enjoys sharing information with other farmers. "Doing that pushes me to stay a step or two ahead of the crowd," he says. But for now, at least, the exact composition of his baby salad mix isn't public information. "Besides, I improve it each year," he says.

In '90, the second year de Wilde tried the mix, he seeded an early crop on April 3, covering roughly three-fourths of the space in two 42- by 12- foot hoop houses. On April 28, he harvested 50 pounds and sold it at the farmers markets for $7 per pound. "We kept cutting it, and it kept regrowing," he recalls. "We got about 50 to 60 pounds a week from those two houses, until the end of May."

Two or three cuttings are possible when the weather is cool. But once it warms up, regrowth becomes bitter. So for later-season crops, de Wilde seeds the mix every 7 to 10 days and harvests it just once.

Some of de Wilde's other specialty crops include:

• **Chilies** – De Wilde sells strings of about 30 dried chili peppers for $4.50. "They're good for spring cash flow," he says, noting that many customers buy them as much for decoration as they do for cooking. "People want something – *anything* – that time of the year. And they don't nickel-and-dime you on ornamentals." De Wilde strings the peppers in winter when the workload is light.

• **Flowers** – De Wilde grows about one-half acre of fresh-cut and dried flowers. He markets fresh-cut larkspur and Bells of Ireland to distributors in Chicago through a friend who takes 30 percent of the gross. "They're still more profitable than vegetables," he says. Dried strawflowers, statice, acroclinium, gomphrena and others are used in garlic braids and ornamental arrangements.

• **Garlic** – When braided and decorated with dried flowers and herbs, de Wilde's garlic brings up to $10 per pound – more than three times his normal retail price for unbraided garlic. Selling common fresh herbs like oregano, thyme and marjoram to restaurant customers hasn't been as successful as de Wilde would like. But more unusual offerings like cilantro and arrugula have paid off well, he says.

Direct Seed & Flame Weed

Cropping practices on de Wilde's Harmony Valley Farm are just as innovative as his crop selection. Many growers transplant crops or rely on plastic mulch to control weeds. But de Wilde direct-seeds whenever possible. Only about 20 percent of his crops are transplanted. "Why transplant 1,000 plants an hour when you can direct seed 1,000 in five minutes?" he asks.

Still, de Wilde transplants crops when there are distinct advantages. To get a jump on the season, he transplants his first lettuce crop. And he transplants cucurbits to avoid cucumber beetle damage. De Wilde also starts cucumbers in the greenhouse to transplant in July to help fill the late-summer production slump. Onions, leeks, celery root and tomatoes are also transplanted.

De Wilde uses a pair of Stanhay belt seeders to direct seed on two-row beds. The units – which list for about $1,500 each – allow de Wilde to space plants precisely. "They save me a lot of time and money because I don't have to come back and thin," he observes. "But you have to have excellent weed control first if you're going to direct seed." De Wilde bought the units used, but feels that even at the full price they would quickly pay for themselves. For the salad mix and large-seeded crops where thinning isn't needed, he uses Planet Jr. planters.

Tobacco growers in the area taught de Wilde the key to better weed control. "They say to never let any weeds go to seed. We've stuck to that rule for the six years we've been here. And we've noticed that our fields have gotten incredibly cleaner. There's a lot less hand-weeding to do now."

De Wilde's second rule is to use a chisel plow whenever possible. "A moldboard plow just turns up your old sins, causing more weed problems. I only use it when I absolutely have to." De Wilde sometimes chisels a second time, then disks at least twice and cultipacks to prepare the seedbed.

One way de Wilde helps direct seeded crops get a jump on weeds is to use a flame weeder to kill weeds between planting and crop germination. His flamer was set up by Thermal Weed Control Systems, 3403 Highway 93, Eau Claire, Wis. 54701. Pregermination flaming works particularly well for slow-germinating crops like carrots, parsnips and larkspur, says de Wilde.

When flaming, timing is critical, he continues. To predict the best time to flame, de Wilde sets a pane of glass over the row after planting. The crop seeds under the glass germinate several days before uncovered seeds. When they come up, de Wilde knows it's time to flame the early weeds that have sprouted, before the rest of the crop germinates.

Timing is even trickier with fast-germinating crops, like spinach and lettuce. De Wilde admits he's had less success flaming these crops. His strategy is to prepare the ground, then delay planting for four or five days to give the weeds a chance to start sprouting. He direct seeds the main crop, then flames the field three or four days later. Without the delayed planting, weeds and the crop would germinate simultaneously, making flaming impossible, he explains.

De Wilde also flames potatoes. "They're tough. They can take a flaming even after they're up," he observes. In '90, potatoes that he flamed as they emerged and cultivated just once required no additional hand-weeding.

To work close to the rows without throwing too much soil, de Wilde equips his midmount cultivator with narrow, 1-inch-wide "snake points" set as close as 2 or 3 inches from the row. Narrow, 3-inch-wide shields make it possible for him to cultivate young crops without burying them. Wider, 4-inch shovels kill weeds between the rows. De Wilde feels a combination of Bezzerides' Spyders cultivating tools and torsion weeders will help him cultivate closer to the row and further reduce hand-weeding.

De Wilde limits mulching primarily to tomatoes and strawberries, mostly to keep the fruit off the ground. He greenchops overgrown rye cover crops and augers the mulch out of the chopper box along the tomato row. Garlic is mulched in fall with a manure-sawdust mix trucked in from a local livestock breeding operation and stockpiled for six months before being applied with a manure spreader. In addition to suppressing weeds, de Wilde likes how the mix helps hold moisture and supplies nutrients.

Carpets Of Cover Crops

Cover crops play a big role in de Wilde's cropping system. Normally, they carpet about 17 of his 20 acres over winter. His most dependable cover has been a rye/vetch mix. He drills the mix wherever it's possible to get it in by mid-September. Where he knows that won't be possible – on peppers and fall cole crops, for example – he prefers to broadcast red clover and annual ryegrass at final cultivation.

De Wilde chops cover crops the following year before working them with his chisel plow. "The downside of covers is that if they get away from you, you have to plow them with the moldboard to get rid of them," he cautions. With a wet spring in '90, that happened more often than de Wilde would like. Rye, especially, got out of hand. So more and more, he is replacing rye with oats. Seeded alone, oats winterkill, making them an excellent cover where early spring crops will be seeded. Seeded with vetch, the winterkilled oat mulch protects the legume over winter. Then the vetch can be left to regrow in spring before incorporating for later crops.

De Wilde also broadcast annual ryegrass into his asparagus. The asparagus is planted deep enough that he can disk any ryegrass that doesn't winterkill. He also flames asparagus residue in spring to kill asparagus beetles.

To try to keep quackgrass from creeping into the asparagus from the field edge, he's planting a border of rhubarb. "An old gardener friend pointed out to me how you never find quackgrass in a rhubarb bed," he recalls. "So I'm going to try to take advantage of that to keep quack out of my asparagus."

Cover crops also help de Wilde reduce insect damage. He often lets narrow strips keep growing through the season so that their blossoms will attract beneficial insects into the field. Every few years, he'll also work up his semi-permanent picking roads and seed them to white clover, which also attracts pollinators and pest predators. The picking roads divide his fields into long strips, about 70 feet wide. Crops that need daily picking are planted next to the roads to reduce the distance they need to be carried and to minimize field traffic and compaction.

In addition to his two hoophouses, de Wilde has a 14- by 40-foot greenhouse where he grows transplants. He built a new 30- by 60-foot greenhouse last fall, primarily to extend production of his baby salad mix.

De Wilde uses Reemay floating row covers to keep flea beetles off of late crops of the baby salad mix and other mustard-family crops that are direct-seeded in the field. He's found that a double layer of Reemay can protect tomatoes, zucchini and other frost-sensitive crops down to temperatures as low as 23 F. After the threat of hard frosts is past, de Wilde removes the top layer and leaves the bottom one in place until the weather settles.

De Wilde also runs a 40-ewe sheep flock on an additional 20 acres of land too marginal to crop. "The sheep aren't a big money-maker. But they make use of the steep hillsides and they supply some compost for the crops," he observes. "There's a good marketing overlap with the crops, too."

Besides composting sheep manure, he buys composted turkey manure. At least a little compost is broadcast on almost every field each year. De Wilde has also applied calphos, potassium sulphate, high-calcium lime, kiln dust and trace mineral products. He determines fertility needs based on annual soil tests.

With his emphasis on greens, de Wilde carefully avoids spreading raw manure because of the potential for nitrate accumulation in the crop. "I feel just being organic isn't enough," he says. "You have to be responsible, too."

Are Raised Beds Worth The Effort?

One way to increase yields in the garden is to use double-dug raised beds. In hard packed soil with a lot of clay the raised bed system may be the only way you can achieve good yields, especially with root crops. I have found, however, that in a sandy loam soil, crops do just as well in wide rows separated by paths. In a sense, this is something of a raised bed, because the path will get traveled enough to compact it, thereby leaving the surrounding area raised.

It is simple to make raised beds with the walk-behind rotary tiller if your garden is too large to double dig by hand. Just add a hiller-furrower and till the pathways. The furrower pushes soil up on the beds and leaves a narrow walking path. This doesn't really "raise" beds, so much as it digs a ditch on each side of the bed. The ditch becomes the path by default.

It is easy to rent or buy a rotary tiller to prepare the soil. Unfortunately, a rotary tiller, even the big ones, can't dig deeper than about 7 inches. Rotary tilling also tends to create a plowpan at the bottom of its digging range. Another drawback is that excessive rotary tilling can destroy the tilth of soil by making too many fine particles. These fine particles tend to pack harder from rain and traffic on the soil. This causes crusting which sheds water rather than allowing it to be absorbed. The tilling action also tends to break down organic matter too rapidly, causing a loss of soil fertility and structure. The only way to prevent this destruction of soil tilth is to limit the number of times you use the rotary tiller, and to till shallow rather than deep.

In most parts of the country the freeze/thaw action helps in keeping the soil loose and friable. Earthworms and other soil dwelling critters will do a good job of loosening the ground to a deeper depth, too. However, if you are taking over abandoned farmland that has been intensively row cropped for any length of time you may find a plowpan or hardpan at about 10 inches below the soil surface. This can be broken up with a chisel plow pulled behind a tractor. Other tools for sub-soiling include a single-shank subsoiler or even deep moldboard plowing.

It takes about 30-horsepower and 4-wheel drive to pull a single shank sub-soiler that breaks up hardpan down to 24 inches deep. Single shank subsoilers are available for less than $200 from most farm equipment dealers. Chances are you can rent a neighbor's tractor and chisel plow, or hire someone to come and do it for you.

Alternatives, if there are no farmers in your area with chisel plows, would be to double dig by hand. This intensive and laborious practice can add days or even weeks to your spring start-up chores. Double digging is to move the top seven to 10 inches of soil one spade width, then work it smooth with the spade or fork. The underlying seven to 10 inches is loosened in place with a potato fork. Once the hardpan is loosened it can be worked each year with the U-bar. This device loosens soil without moving it up or down in the profile.

The problem with double digging raised beds is that it's very labor-intensive. If you have no alternative but to double dig by hand then by all means start your land preparation a year before you want to grow crops for market.

In average soil a healthy person with a sharp spade and a sturdy potato fork can probably double dig a 4- by 100-foot bed in about two days. For a half-acre market garden that amounts to about 80 days of work. That is most of a summer. If your garden site is rocky or heavy clay you may even have to double that time estimate. Yes, your crops will yield more, but I wonder if it really makes enough difference to be worthwhile.

A better alternative is to plant cover crops noted for their deep and vigorous rooting systems. This, plus the freeze/thaw action and earthworms, should be enough to soften all but the worst hardpan. In extreme cases your only alternative may be to haul in topsoil and compostable materials and build garden beds above your rock or clay problem.

There are spading machines available from importers that will replicate the double-digging method. These are quite expensive, ranging in price from $6,500 to $10,000, and require a large tractor in the 30 to 60-horsepower range. A 4-foot wide spading machine will require at least 30-horsepower and 4-wheel drive. There are also spading machines made to fit walk-behind tractors in the 14 horsepower range. Spading machines can only dig 7 or 8 inches deep, however, so their value for subsoiling isn't as great as double digging. Their real advantage is that the spading action is much less stressful on the soil than rotary tilling. They incorporate crop residue into the top 5-inches of soil and provide a smooth planting surface while leaving larger particles in the lower profile.

In the long run, it is probably more cost effective to haul in more compost or cow manure to build up a deeper loam level over the hardpan. This will give you good soil instantly, and alleviate the backbreaking work of double-digging and subsoiling. Try the rotational bed idea, and each year spend a week of your off-season time double digging the beds where the carrots and potatoes are going to be planted. These are the two crops that require the loosest soil. As you move along the rotational cycle year after year, you will eventually double dig all of the beds.

The idea of using permanent beds isn't so bad, except that it's a lot of effort to keep the beds intact and separate from the paths each year. Just the normal foot and cart traffic on the paths will not compact them so much that they can't be loosened again next year. It is a good idea not to walk on the beds, though. In loose soil, a footprint can sink several inches deep. That not only looks unsightly, but will interfere with root growth.

Cages

One of the easiest ways to double or even triple yields of tomatoes is to grow them in cages. With this system you will get nearly three times as many tomatoes with less than one-third the work associated with trellising or staking. You can start with fewer tomato seedlings, less greenhouse space, less cold frame space and a lot less labor. These cages can be used for other vining crops such as cucumbers, peas, snow peas, pole beans, small winter squashes, gourds and baby pumpkins.

The cages are expensive to build, about $3 each. But, they will last for 10 to 20 years. Store them outside stacked at the edge of the field on pallets to keep the wire from resting on the ground. If you are really fastidious, you can spray paint the wire cages with rust inhibiting paint to prolong their life and make them look better. Green is a good color that blends in well with the vining crops as they grow.

Put black plastic mulch on the beds to warm the soil, with the drip irrigation tape installed underneath the plastic. After the soil is warm, spread a thin layer of straw over the plastic around the cages so that soil borne diseases can't splash up on the lower leaves. Clip a section out of the bottom of each side of the cages to keep the wire rim from pressing down against your irrigation tape and pinching off the water supply.

Plant a single line of tomatoes in each bed. Secure the cages to each other with baling wire. Drive a steel post every fifth cage to hold them upright. In a windy location it may be necessary to drive short stakes at each cage to hold them up. Most of the prevailing winds are from the southwest or northwest. If your rows are north to south chances are your cages will be able to withstand a pretty good wind before toppling. If a 70 mph wind is threatening, however, you might want to add a steel fence post to *each* cage.

A 12-foot width of Reemay will fit nicely over the tomato cages, pinned at the bottom with wooden clothespins. To vent the cages on a hot day just loosen one side of the Reemay and fold it back over the cages. Then lower it and refasten it at the end of day.

Put a 12-inch strip of tar paper around the inside of each cage to help deter slugs and cutworms. It will also gather heat and block winds from young seedlings, keep dirt from splashing in from the aisles and keep wind-blown dust off the leaves and fruit.

These cages can be used year after year if stored in dry place for winter. They will deter groundhogs and rabbits, dogs and cats. You can get an early crop of lettuce inside these cages, as well. By the time the tomatoes need the room, the lettuce will have been harvested, weeks before your neighbors and other market gardeners are harvesting theirs.

Trellises

Another way to use 5-foot wide construction wire for trellising is the vine shaded bed method. With this method you put a post every 5 feet on the *east* side of the 4-foot bed. Then cut sections of construction wire to 8 foot lengths. Use the cut wires on one end of the fence panel to anchor it in the soil on the *west* side of the bed. Then bow the panel so that the other end can be tied to the top of the fence post on the east side of the bed. This makes a quonset shaped half-bow roof over the bed, beginning at ground level and curving up to the top of the posts. The 5-foot wide panels can be anchored at each corner to the steel posts.

Start your plants on the west side of the bed. Tomatoes, pole beans, cucumbers, peas, mini-pumpkins, gourds or New Zealand spinach will climb the trellis and form a shady roof over the bed.

During the hot sunny days of summer, you can grow cool-loving plants under the leaf canopy of the trellis. They will get enough light from the morning sun for photosynthesis, but will not be overheated by the afternoon sun. Because of the openness of the trellis, there will be enough air movement to facilitate pollination.

Harvesting from this trellis is a breeze. Just walk along the east side of the trellis and reach under to the vegetables that are dangling down ready to be plucked.

This type of fence panel trellis is more expensive, because steel posts and wire cost more than other trellising methods. But, the saved labor will more than offset the cost of fencing and posts. The panels are easy to store, since they will lie flat and stack at the edge of the field on pallets at the end of the season.

Cages will do a better job of containing the plants, but the half-hoop trellis will work if you spend a few minutes each day training the tendrils and vines to follow the curve of the hoop.

Another kind of trellis can be made by simply using 5 by 10 foot wire fence panels and hooping them over the whole bed, anchoring them in the soil on each side. With this hooped panel you can get a quonset-hut shaped structure about 3-feet high in the middle. This is ideal for covering with Reemay or clear plastic as a season extender. However, the chore of training vines to the hoop and then reaching through the panel to pick the produce is a little more labor intensive than either the cages or the half-hoop, vine-shaded systems.

Irrigation: It's one thing you can't do without

Irrigation for the garden is absolutely essential. Don't try to be a market gardener without it. When I started out I used a lawn sprinkler mounted on a step ladder to soak the garden. This works, but not as well as other systems.

Overhead watering has several serious drawbacks. Mainly, it uses way too much water. Because there is no way to apply precise amounts of water, a lot evaporates before it reaches the soil. Overhead watering splashes the plants and the ground. This causes ground crusting. That inhibits the soil's ability to absorb water and leads to runoff.

Overhead sprinkling also splashes soil-borne diseases onto the plant leaves and can help a disease spread through the garden. In addition, the hoses and sprinklers have to be moved periodically. This is a chore that takes a significant amount of time over the season. Moving heavy garden hoses among growing crops causes a lot of plant damage and frustration. Finally, with overhead watering, it often means you can't water the vegetables while you are picking or doing other garden chores.

Sometimes, you need overhead sprinkling. Moistening a bed for seed germination is one example. Also, spraying water on small fruits such as strawberries can keep them cool on a really hot day. It can also keep fruits and some vegetables from freezing in a light frost.

A much better irrigation system is to use soaker hoses or drip tape in the beds. This uses less water, there is no splashing, it requires less maintenance and gives a measured amount of water to the plants as they need it. Workers can come and go in the field without worrying about getting wet, walking in soggy ground or picking wet fruit that will degrade rapidly.

My favorite drip tape watering system is Roberts Ro-Drip, available from Zimmerman Irrigation in Mifflinburg, Pa. This light 8-mil plastic tape has openings (emitters) every 8 inches for water to drip out. To install it, simply unroll it in the middle of the bed. In healthy soil with a good amount of organic matter one drip line in the middle of the bed is enough. In sandy or poor soil conditions you may want to have two lines per bed, about 24 inches apart.

The supply line (header hose) is a blue 1.5-inch diameter "lay flat" hose called Vinylflow. It looks like a small version of fire hose. It is light weight and easy to unroll, and easy to roll up and store.

The first year I used drip tape in my market garden the annual water bill dropped from $256 to $86. I was impressed. (Growers in the Intervale now farm more than 10 acres in vegetables, flowers and strawberries, using nearly 10 miles of Ro-Drip. We like it.)

The key to the drip tape irrigation system is the fittings used to connect the Vinylflow to the drip tape. These are plastic fittings that simply plug into holes in the Vinylflow and screw tight. The other end of the fitting slides inside the drip tape. Secure it by screwing the collar tight. These fittings are leak free. Be careful not to drive the tractor across them, though, because they do break. The tractor can drive over the Vinylflow supply line with no damage, however.

Plastic connections attach the drip tape to the lay flat hose. They are inexpensive, easy and quick to install and they don't leak.

It is important to keep the water pressure at 5 to 8 pounds per square inch. Use a pressure regulating valve to keep the pressure just where you want it for slow distribution of water. The drip tape should release about one or two small drops of water per second over a long period of time. In a hot, dry summer we often leave our drip tape system running overnight about three nights each week.

The pressure regulating valve protects the system from too much water pressure while providing sufficient flow to irrigate the crops.

As the drops of water come out of the hose, they fall gently on the soil and migrate to the sides and down. This forms a wetted area in an upside down mushroom pattern. If the soil is fairly moist, it can be held that way for long periods of time. If the soil is really dry, it may require the drip tape to be on for several days. This brings the soil up to field capacity, about 75 percent moisture content.

If the drips of water come out of the hose too quickly, a drilling effect takes place. The water doesn't have time to use capillary action to migrate sideways before going straight down. Even with the pressure regulating valve you will need to experiment with different settings to get it right, because the number and length of drip lines you have on any patch will vary. With just a few drip lines, the pressure will build up immediately. With an acre of drip tapes, you may have to wait 20 or 30 minutes for all the drip lines to fill with water. Once filled, back-pressure causes the gauge to register.

After a few times turning the water on and off and watching the drip tape working, you will get a feel for it. In my gardens, I can tell when the pressure is right as I listen to the water hissing through the supply hose fitting. It is sort of like tuning a guitar, you can "feel" it when the pitch is right.

If you turn the water pressure on full blast, it will fill the lines and rupture them. The ruptures usually occur at the middle of the grid, at the ends of the drip lines. Turn the water on gradually. As water fills the drip lines the trapped air will have time to escape through the drip emitters.

The 8-mil drip tape comes on 7,500-foot rolls, which is enough to put one drip line on each 4-foot bed in a 1-acre garden. The cost of the material is so low that if you want to you can throw the hose away at the end of the year. However, I use the hose two and sometimes three years in a row. I roll it on cardboard rolls and store it in the barn out of direct sunlight and away from the mice. The drip tape has to be handled carefully, since it springs leaks very easily. Hoeing can cause punctures. So can stepping on the hose with a rock underneath. Even severely bending or stretching the hose can cause a leak.

Installing drip tape is very easy. Slip a rod or hoe handle through the hole in the center of the roll. Place the rod across the wheelbarrow handles. Then take the loose end of the tape and walk down the bed, allowing the tape to settle in the middle of the bed with the holes facing down.

Close the ends of the drip tapes by cutting a 2-inch section to be used as a rubber band. Then fold the drip tape end back on itself twice, and slip the 2-inch section over the end as a holder. When you want to drain the lines just slip the band off, and the hose is fully open.

The drip tape is so light that the wind will blow it off the bed in nothing flat. You can tie the end of the drip tape to a hoe handle and walk along the bed with the tape held down near the soil. As you walk back to the starting point use the hoe to drag a bit of dirt over the drip tape every 10 feet or so. This will keep the wind from blowing it.

The lay-flat Vinylflow header hose comes in 330-foot rolls. You can add as many drip tapes to it as you like. Make the holes for the drip tape fittings with a special pliers that cuts a neat round hole in the lay-flat. Then use the special plastic fittings for the connections.

The lay-flat can be connected to a garden hose for water supply from your well or faucet. A special reducing fitting for joining the different size hoses is expensive, but will last forever with proper care. The lay-flat, fittings and drip tapes needed to irrigate a 1-acre garden will cost less than $500. This is money well spent in terms of your peace of mind, better yields, healthier and more disease and pest resistant plants and lower water usage.

The only problems I've encountered with this irrigation system were mostly from inexperience. I had to learn to respect the fragility of the system, and stop treating it like rubber garden hose. The one problem I can't correct is that the drip tapes can't be used up and down hills. The water pressure can't build up enough to push the water up a hill. The openings at the lower part of the hill will squirt water, while the ones at the top of the hill don't get any water.

In my market garden in Massachusetts, I solved that problem partially. I used a longer header hose to deliver water to the top of the slope, then let it into the drip tapes. This worked moderately well, though the drip tape on the lower part of the slope still had more water release. This is caused by increased hydraulic pressure in the lower section of the line, causing a hammer effect in which the water will spurt out of the emitter holes rather than drip out.

There are more expensive types of drip tape available with pressure regulating emitters. These pressure regulated drip tapes can move water up and down slopes, but they are more expensive. They do last longer (up to 12 years), though, so their cost can be recovered over several years. They are particularly useful for watering orchards and Christmas trees on sloping land. One manufacturer of pressurized drip emitting hoses is Netafim. Information is available through Gardener's Supply.

Irrigation Made Easy

A step-by-step guide to drip irrigation you can install yourself.

by George DeVault

EMMAUS, Pa. – Spring 1988, the year of THE DROUGHT, was not the time for me to plant another 100 blueberry bushes, 24 antique apple trees and 500 raspberry plants. But I had no way of knowing that when I ordered all those trees and plants over the winter.

Small-farm guru Booker T. Whatley said I should install drip irrigation lines on everything as I did my planting. I knew that was sound advice, and I told Booker I would get an irrigation system, but not just yet. Ordering all that nursery stock had drained my farm savings account. And besides, I rationalized, southeastern Pennsylvania usually receives adequate rainfall throughout the growing season. Irrigation could wait.

As I finished planting the last of the raspberries, it started to rain. And, as the days grew longer and warmer, everything started growing like crazy. The rain came regularly through the rest of April and into May.

By mid-May, though, it was becoming increasingly obvious that I was in trouble. The faucet in the sky had been turned down to barely a trickle. Booker was right; "Weatherproof your farm, at least as far as is possible, with both drip and sprinkler irrigation."

Busy As A 1-Man Bucket Brigade

Then the rain stopped altogether. By June, the only thing standing between my new plants and the broiling sun was a heavy mulch of rye straw. My plants had to get a drink – and fast. But the phones at irrigation supply houses around the mid-Atlantic area were already ringing non-stop. When I finally did get through, no one had much time – or equipment – left for a small grower. Larger growers were making a run on big-ticket items like traveling guns and enough high-pressure hose to resupply every fire department in the country. One supplier, I later learned, sold more than 10 million feet of drip-irrigation tape that summer.

Determined to save my nursery stock, I roped three 55-gallon drums in the back of my pickup, grabbed four 5-gallon buckets, connected 400 feet of garden hose to the faucet at the back of the house and headed for the fields.

For five weeks, all I did was come home from work, haul water, finish up after dark and do it all over again the next day. It was a 3-day cycle: 1) water the blueberries, 2) water the orchard, 3) water the raspberries. The cycle repeated itself again and again and again.

Lesson Learned

The system worked. The apple trees and blueberries survived just fine. Only a couple of raspberry plants died. My children, Don and Ruth, had fun playing in the barrels of icy water in the 100-degree heat. And I learned my lesson, vowing to have a proper irrigation system installed *before* the start of the next season.

I spent all winter studying irrigation catalogs and working up an irrigation plan. In early April '89, I drove two hours to Zimmerman Irrigation in the center of the state. (Be sure to get a copy of their catalog.) On the return trip, my truck was loaded with 900 feet of blue, 1 1/2-inch Vinylflow supply hose, 8,000 feet of drip tape and all of the necessary fittings, valves and gauges. To be on the safe side, I even bought an "irrometer" to monitor soil moisture and a 7 gpm fertilizer injector.

When everything was hooked up just right, I turned on the water. It rushed through the layflat supply line with a roar like a firehose being charged. The drip tapes wriggled like long black snakes, then straightened out and swelled up. Water began dripping out of the lines in the raspberries, blueberries and the orchard. I could now water everything, just by opening a faucet and adjusting a few valves.

Then it started raining. And through April, May, June, July and into August, it kept on raining. After one of the driest summers in history, we were entering one of the wettest seasons ever. It was so wet that some of my raspberries in a low spot actually drowned.

I only needed to turn on the irrigation twice. That was during an especially hot, dry spell in midsummer, just when the pods were starting to fill on about 600 row-feet of trellised sugar snap peas. The extra water saved the peas, which are our main cash crop.

Always Next Season

Ah, such is farming. At least I'm ready for the next drought.

I could have installed a more permanent system with buried plastic or metal mains and standpipes. But I like this above-ground system because it's extremely flexible and easy to install. The only tools you need are a flathead screwdriver, a sharp pocketknife and a special hole punch. The punch costs about $45, but it's worth it. You don't want to try making holes in supply lines without it.

Maintenance is a breeze. For example, one of the first things I did after laying down a 500-foot supply line was chop a jagged hole in the middle of it with the mower. Just because this hose is called "layflat," don't get the idea that it stays flat, especially when you drive over it with machinery. All I did was cut the damaged section out of the hose with my pocketknife and then cut a piece the same length off of another roll of hose. Using two plastic connectors and four hose clamps, I had the whole repair job done in less than five minutes.

After the season is over, I just drain the supply lines, disconnect the tapes, roll up the supply lines and store them in the barn. This isn't the cheapest drip system around. A 300-foot role of supply line ranges in price from $105 for 1 1/2-inch hose to $271 for 4-inch hose. The plastic fittings cost from 50 cents to $1.45 each. But growers I know who use this system say it will provide many years of relatively trouble-free service. With reasonable care, even lightweight 8- to 10-mil drip tape can be used in vegetables for several seasons. Heavier tapes made of 16- to 20-mil material can be left in raspberries or blueberries for five to 10 years.

Intensive Production In Your Greenhouse

The greenhouse is an important part of your market garden. You will use it to start seedlings, as a field tunnel for growing early tomatoes or other high-value vegetables or flowers and as a workplace for seeding trays and for storage.

My first greenhouse was a 9- by 12-foot lean-to against the front of my house. Since then I have graduated to larger greenhouses, such as the 12- by 20-foot and the 12- by 30-foot Sun Tunnels that I now use.

The greenhouse can be any size you can afford. It does need to at least be big enough to grow your seedlings for warm weather crops like tomatoes, peppers and eggplants.

For a half-acre market garden, a 12- by 20-foot greenhouse containing 240 square feet is about minimum. Cost is about $1,000 to $2,000, depending on accessories and whether or not you install it yourself. In most areas the greenhouse needs to be double-glazed (two sheets of plastic inflated by a small electric blower).

In a 12- by 20-foot greenhouse, you can build a bench down each side with a path in the middle. The benches can be 4 1/2- feet deep, and 20 feet long. This is enough bench space to handle 120 trays of seedlings. After you move the seedlings to the cold frame for hardening off, you can remove the benches. Dig up the floor and transplant a greenhouse tomato variety for early and late tomatoes. These can be trellised to overhead wires that are tied to the greenhouse structure.

The Sun Tunnel greenhouses we use have roll up sides for extra ventilation in summer. A shade cloth stretched over the house and secured with earth anchors will provide plenty of shading for hot summer days. For irrigation, take your pick of an overhead misting system, a watering can, spray nozzle on the garden hose or drip tape.

Greenhouses come in all shapes and sizes. They are often the most profitable component of the backyard market garden business.

With this intensive greenhouse system you will get about 8,000 seedlings if you only grow one cycle. These have a wholesale value of about $1,200. The early crop of tomatoes from 75 plants will yield about 1,600 pounds of tomatoes worth $2 or more per pound in the early and late markets. Each year, you will gross more than $4,000 from a structure that costs less than $2,000 to build.

The smaller the greenhouse, the larger the "per square foot" cost. You may want to consider building a larger greenhouse than you need for your own plants. Use the extra space to grow extra bedding plants for sale at your roadside stand or farmers market.

Six-packs of flowers sell for about $2, as do 6-packs of vegetable seedlings. If you have a 480 square foot greenhouse you can have all the seedlings you need for your garden, plus another 720 six-packs to sell for an extra $1,400 gross. Plus, you will have room for a larger tomato crop that can bring in an extra $3,000 or so.

This 480 square foot greenhouse will cost about $3,500, but you can grow about $8,000 worth of crops in it per year. These are gross figures, of course. The net income you earn will be affected by costs of heating, ventilating, seed, potting soil, trays, fertilizer, sprays and your labor.

Still, you can net as much as $2,000 annually from this size greenhouse and have a lot of fun doing it. It's easy to see that the greenhouse will usually earn more money per square foot than any other single thing you can do in your garden.

With this protected tunnel for tomatoes you will enjoy vine-ripened fruits about one month earlier than from field-grown tomatoes. This is a real big jump on your competition, allowing you to be the first in the market with your customer's favorite veggies. This early season crop will help you build customer loyalty.

In this artificial environment, it is easy to attract pests and diseases to your tomatoes. Avoid this by good soil fertilization and keep the greenhouse clean and properly ventilated. Put up sticky traps to monitor pests. Spray when you need to, don't wait. Spray is cheap. Waiting too long will cost many times more in lost produce. A disease-infested greenhouse is hard to clean out for future crops.

Soil fertility in the greenhouse has to be at ideal levels if you plan to grow in the ground there. Double dig, if needed, to break up any hardpan. Use well-balanced compost frequently. Apply a 1-inch layer of good compost when you work the soil, then another 1-inch layer for mulch. Use drip tape on the tomatoes to keep the soil moist.

The Gardeners Supply tiller works well for preparing greenhouse soil. It is small enough to maneuver easily in the confined spaces, digs about 5-inches deep, and stirs the soil very well. Just be sure to roll up the greenhouse sides and run the vent fan while the tiller is running. Otherwise, exhaust fumes from its gasoline engine can give you a headache.

Because your greenhouse soil is fertile you can plant your tomatoes closer together than in the field. I use 18-inch spacing for two rows on each side of the door, one row down the middle and a pathway at each end for easy access. In a 12-by 30-foot SunTunnel we have five rows of 15 plants each for a total of 75 plants.

For really early tomatoes in the greenhouse, I use a trellis system. Just run wires overhead above the greenhouse cross-supports. Then tie a length of untreated twine loosely to the base of each plant. Attach the other end to the overhead wire. Leave several feet of extra twine so that the plant can be lowered and layered as you remove the lower fruits and leaves. Plants can be trained up the twine as they grow, but be sure to wrap the vines in the same direction each time or they will simply unwind. It is faster and gentler on the vines to use special greenhouse clips that attach the vines to the twine. These special clips are sold by greenhouse companies for about 15 cents each and can be used for several seasons. Use untreated twine so that it can be composted with the vines at the end of the season. Otherwise, you will have the extra work of separating the twine from the vines.

Lowering and layering the vines gives you greater yields over a longer season. After the tomato vines reach the overhead trellis wire, pick off the lower leaves and fruits. Then lower the twine with plant intact, so that the stem of the tomato plant is resting on the floor. Then re-tie the twine to the support wire. This keeps the foliage upright, so the sunlight reaches the fruit and leaves. The bare trunks of the tomatoes can be "layered" in such a way as to rest on the ground without crowding their neighbors. You can extend the life of your vines by one or two months this way.

In this artificial environment the tomatoes will taste as robust as field- grown tomatoes and they will be blemish-free and fetch good prices. You will need to assist pollination by vibrating the plants each day. How? Just twang the twine. Often, this is incidental to pruning and training the vines. Make sure each plant gets shaken each day. Otherwise, the blossoms won't set fruit. Too vigorous a shaking, though, will cause uneven pollination or even cause the blossoms to fall off the plant before they set fruit.

The greenhouse structure will last for decades, if treated properly. The plastic film glazing will need to be changed every three or four years, because its gradual yellowing will reduce the amount of sunlight that can reach your plants.

Potting soil is an expensive item for the greenhouse. You can only use it one time. Buy the best that is available. Buying in bulk is about the only way to get the price down. Check the vegetable growers associations in your area and see if they have a bulk order system. Or buy a two year's supply of potting soil to get the price down. If you buy it in bulk, be sure to store it up off the ground on pallets and out of the weather.

One year, I purchased a cubic yard of compost-based potting soil from Foster Brothers Dairy in Middlebury, Vt. The potting soil was poorly blended and the compost material was phytotoxic. It was still composting and giving off gases that killed the seeds or grew stunted and unusable seedlings. This fiasco caused the loss of 12,000 seedlings. I had to start all over again, and was a month late getting seedlings started and transplanted. I now buy potting soil from Karl Hammer at Moody Hill Farm in Amenia, NY., and have the best looking seedlings I've ever grown.

Seedling trays are also expensive. Fortunately, they last for years with proper care. We just clean them thoroughly at the end of each season and bath them in a 10 percent bleach solution to eliminate any harmful bacteria. We use three sizes. The 150-cell tray is for starting cole crops and salad greens that only need three or four weeks in the greenhouse and cold frame before going to the field. The 72-cell tray is for the warm-season crops such as tomatoes, peppers and eggplants that will stay in the greenhouse for seven or eight weeks. Once the tomatoes get up about 6-inches high I transplant them to 36-cell trays for a couple of weeks before sending them to the cold frame for hardening off. This greater soil mass in the 36-cell tray gives a really nice root ball for the tomatoes. This makes a sturdier plant that will be healthier, transplant easier without shock and have a greater yield.

To keep the seedlings going along nicely in the greenhouse I spray foliar fertilizers such as Sea Crop, Sea Mix or Folio Gro. This provides the nutrients that the plants often don't get from the potting soil. Sometimes plants have a hard time extracting the nutrients from the soil as they need them, so the foliar fertilization helps them get off to a good start. The blend of compost, peat moss, mineral additives and foliar feeding provides all the nutrients the seedlings need for vigorous growth.

A Homemade 'Greenhouse' For $100

by Bob Hofstetter

A friend of mine suffered a vegetable grower's worst nightmare a few years ago. He had ordered several thousand tomato plants from an out-of-state supplier, and the shipment was lost in the mail. His entire planting schedule was disrupted. Even worse, the varieties he needed were not available locally.

Problems like this don't happen often. But when they do, they can be almost as costly as an outbreak of pests or diseases. The solution is fairly simple: Grow your own transplants.

The most common structure for doing that, of course, is a greenhouse. But you don't need to borrow money and put up an elaborate, glass building just to start your own high-value transplants. For less than $100, you can build a hothouse big enough to start transplants for 1 or 2 acres.

Keep It Simple

Your structure will only be used for three or four months, so there's no need to be elaborate. For myself and many other farmers I know, a simple lean-to with a grass floor is ideal. It can be attached to a wall of any building with south, southeast or southwest exposure. And all you'll need to get started is a level area next to the building and a few basic pieces of lumber – much of which you probably have lying around the farm.

First, cut or find two 2 x 4s or 2 x 6s of identical length for the base and the header. Bolt or nail the header to the wall of the building that will serve as the back of the lean-to. The header can be as high as necessary for your own convenience. About 10 or 12 feet is good. Drill holes into the baseboard and peg it firmly into the ground. Diagonal support rafters are then nailed or screwed to the header and base. You may want to miter the ends of the supports, but it's not necessary.

The supports don't need to be very sturdy, since they'll only be supporting a plastic cover. The angle of the supports, and the spacing between them, is more important, especially in areas where snowfall is common. In snowy regions, greenhouse consultants recommend a 60-degree angle with 4 feet between the support rafters. A 45-degree angle and 6-foot support-rafter spacing is fine in areas where snowfall is of little concern.

While we're on the subject of snowfall, never attach your lean-to to a side of a building where the roof slopes down. It doesn't take much imagination to realize what would happen to your plants if heavy, wet sheets of snow slide off during warm spells and the covering gives way.

Finally, frame out a door on both end walls (or a door on one end wall and a movable window on the other). This type of structure can rapidly build up heat on sunny winter days, and having these openings allows you to hook up a portable window fan to dump the hot air quickly.

Covers Last 3 Years

Cover the frame with a durable plastic. Polyethylene film is the most popular type. It comes in thicknesses of 2, 4 and 6 mil. Price ranges from as little as $55 for a 4-mil, 10-foot-wide roll to as much as $135 for a 4-mil, 24-foot-wide roll. Count on spending about $30 more for a 6-mil roll.

When covering your lean-to with plastic, start at one of the end walls and "scroll" the material all the way over to the other end. Staple or tack it to the support rafters, using some type of "washer" on top of the plastic to prevent the fastener from ripping it (I prefer waxed cardboard, but a piece of felt will work, too). Used drip tape works great, too. And, it's <u>free</u>. Tack wooden furring strips on top of the plastic and supports for added strength.

If you don't mind replacing the cover every year, you can use 2- or 4- mil polyethylene without a UV inhibitor, which is a chemical treatment that keeps the sun's ultraviolet rays from decaying the plastic. While these films cost only about 5 cents a square foot, you will find they quickly become brittle and break up. Your best bet is 4- or 6-mil polyethylene with a UV inhibitor. These types usually last three or four years.

Unfortunately, you can't buy only what you need. Greenhouse coverings are sold in rolls of 100-foot lengths. Purchase a roll slightly wider than the length of your diagonal supports. For example, if the supports are 20 feet long from header to base, buy a 22- or 24-foot wide roll. If you buy an 18-foot-wide roll, it won't cover the frame from top to bottom. You'll have to put on a second piece overlapping the first, which can cause leaks and weak spots.

Besides, you'll want some extra polyethylene on-hand to replace or repair torn sections. There are many elements around the farm that can damage glazing: cats that insist on climbing up anything they can dig their claws into, chickens that peck at a material until they get a reaction, or youngsters who think it's fun to bounce sticks or stones off the resilient glazing.

In almost all of these cases, puncture holes are created allowing warm air to escape and cold air to enter. You can easily cover small holes with clear, waterproof mending tape (when possible, tape the hole on both sides). But if the holes get too big to fix with tape – and they just might, if left unmended on a windy day – you'll have to replace the entire cover. Using heavier-mil plastic is the best way to reduce the chance of punctures in the first place –other than threatening the kids with hard labor, giving away the cats and butchering all the chickens.

The cost of your lean-to depends entirely on the size of the area to be enclosed. You can build one covering 200 square feet – enough to produce from 5,000 to 10,000 plants – for as little as $75. You may be able to spend even less if your framing materials are recycled or come from your woodlot.

Fungus-Fighting Fans

There are other expenses. While you won't need artificial lighting, you will need a portable heat source to keep the inside temperature around 60 F on cold, cloudy days. Such a unit need not be expensive. A common household space heater – preferably an electric one with a self-contained circulating fan and thermostat – should do the job just fine, experts say.

Some farmers use kerosene space heaters, but young seedlings can be sensitive to the fumes given off by these devices. Unattended open-flame heaters can also be a fire hazard, especially if your lean-to is built against a wooden wall. If you must use a kerosene heater, get one that's thermostatically controlled.

Cold spots may develop whether you use a kerosene space heater or an electric one. The best solution is to run a small portable fan to keep air circulating. This also will help you avoid inert warm and humid pockets of air, which are ideal areas for fungal disease to take hold. Cold air coming in at the base of the lean-to can also be a problem. A row of hay or straw bales pressed end-to-end along the base provides good insulation.

Inside the lean-to, set flats of transplants on blocks and planks about 2 feet off the ground. Not only will you have to stoop less, but you can use the space beneath the planks for storing extra flats and other supplies.

Complete your makeshift "greenhouse" by building a simple cold frame to harden off early plants or to free up space in your lean-to for late-season plants. Take some used lumber or bales of hay or straw and create a large box or frame on the ground. To provide headroom for larger plants, make the structure at least 12 inches high. Cut several 1 x 3s or thin scrap boards about 12 inches longer than the width of the structure. Place these on top of the box 3 feet apart from each other and tack your leftover polyethylene onto them. When you need to get into the cold frame, simply roll the cover back and replace it when you are finished.

§

The *NEW FARM's* Greenhouse Guide:

Smart shopping can help you to make more from your high-value crops.
By Bob Hofstetter

In Iowa, an organic grower produces $5,000 worth of spinach and lettuce before other growers even get their crops in the ground.

A central Pennsylvania dairyman boosts his cash flow by planting tomatoes in February. He starts harvesting vine-ripened tomatoes in early May. His seconds sell for $1 a pound!

A chemistry teacher and his wife both work away from home, but earn $25,000 with the help of a greenhouse covering one-seventeenth of an acre.

What's their secret? In a word, greenhouses.

Between you and clear-roofed profit, however, are many decisions that demand careful consideration of resources, markets, skills and location. What type of structure should I build? What size should it be? How will position affect its operation? What am I going to grow?

Recent economic research by National Greenhouse Manufacturers Association (NGMA) has shown that on the average, 2,500 square feet of greenhouse production space is necessary to show a profit for a one-person retail operation. Twice that space is needed for a wholesale operation. The purpose of a greenhouse is to provide an environment for optimum crop production. Knowing how to control this environment is as important as knowing how to grow and market your crops. Because sufficient start-up space and equipment can get expensive ($5,000 and up), you must do your homework.

Get catalogs, talk to experienced growers, contact greenhouse manufacturers or suppliers to find out what's out there. Unless you are an experienced greenhouse producer, you may be overwhelmed by information and the decisions that await you. But you can make your start a good one by keeping your resources and capabilities in mind, and by keeping your personal goals clearly before you.

Structural Options

There are several types of greenhouse structures. The main ones are the hoophouse, arch roof (a hoop house with vertical sides) and gable frame. While the hoop house or quonset-style frame is probably the least expensive and easiest to erect, some of its floor space may be unsuitable because of its sidewall curvature, depending on your production system. Waist-high tables will leave inaccessible areas along the wall base, for example. You can overcome that problem and use virtually all of your floor space by using a structure with straight walls of at least 4 feet in height. A straight sidewall structure with a center height of 11 feet should be considered if field equipment is to be used in prepping the greenhouse floor. This will allow you to till closer to the wall with moderate sized implements. Kits in this form can be purchased in either a gabled or arched-roof frame.

Along with size, each of these styles is adaptable and can be built with several different materials. The commonly used materials are galvanized steel, wood and aluminum. It is not unusual, however, to see a combination of these materials in one structure. Galvanized steel and aluminum are virtually maintenance-free and are the most commonly used materials in greenhouse construction today. But wood is still the choice for framing out the end walls and around ventilation system fans and vents. Wood can also be used for framing a gable-frame structure. However, these units can be expensive to erect and maintain.

Protecting wood from moisture will require periodic coats of paint or copper based wood preservative. Never use creosote or pentachlorophenol in the greenhouse. Both substances are highly toxic to plants and humans.

Greenhouse covering material, referred to as glazing, is available in glass, plastic panels and plastic sheeting. The most versatile and commonly used is polyethylene film, which is available in rolls 10 to 40 feet wide and 100 to 150 feet long, specially folded for easy installation. Visqueen manufactures a co-polymer film called NUTRI GRO. It is available as a one-year covering in 2 to 4 mil thicknesses and a three-year covering in 4 to 6 mil thicknesses. A thermal, three-year covering that is available in 6 mils only is THERMAL 3, which the company claims provides as much as 20 percent more in energy savings than the conventional two-layer, air-inflated system.

While glass houses are long-lived and feature excellent transmission of sunlight to plants, few new glass greenhouses are being erected because of their high costs for both initial construction and maintenance.

Other materials used in the manufacture of greenhouse coverings are polyvinyl chloride, both film and rigid, and panels of polyvinyl fluoride, fiberglass reinforced plastic and extruded polypropylene, acrylic and polycarbonate.

There are pros and cons for all glazings. Like greenhouse structures, there isn't one best glazing, but rather the best-suited glazing for a particular situation. At present, the most popular greenhouse glazing for hoop houses and arch-roof structures is the three-year U.V.-treated polyethylene plastic film. It's readily available from all greenhouse suppliers, easy to install and inexpensive.

The plastic-over-hoops combination provides a season-beating growing space at a modest price for growers getting started or those who are mainly concerned with cutting transplant cost for their own field operations. Chip and Susan Planck of Purcellville, Va., grow 40 acres of vegetables from transplants produced in two 12- by 100-foot hoop houses. "Hoop houses (quonset design) are cheap to put up. It's an inexpensive way to grow your own transplants" Chip says.

The Plancks' low-tech production system requires careful attention and management during weather shifts. "We don't have an automated heating and ventilation system. When it gets cold, we fire up the wood stove, which is fabricated from a steel 55 gallon drum. When it gets hot we open up the doors on both ends of the greenhouse or lift up the polyethylene cover a foot or so on each side of the structure," Chip explains.

Joe Maxson, a horticultural extension specialist for Oklahoma State University with expertise in small greenhouse production systems agrees with Planck's summary of quonset design's advantages. "I tell people to start small and stay within their budget," says Maxson. "A quonset greenhouse with 600 square feet (20- by 30-feet, for example) of growing area should be able to generate approximately $10,000 in gross sales by marketing flowers and vegetable transplants through wholesale channels," he adds.

Meeting the Challenge

Deciding which structure or material you should buy will depend on more than just durability, size or expense. If you are looking at a long-term enterprise, a greenhouse has to be built to last. You have to be aware of the three most common stress factors, called design load, that need to be considered in your framework design.

Wind resistance concerns all greenhouse growers. Unit structures should be able to resist a minimum wind velocity of 80 mph. The NGMA states that an 80 mph wind hitting a pipe-frame greenhouse can produce an uplift force of 220 pounds per foot of greenhouse length. A pipe-frame structure, especially one which is composed of aluminum, is quite light and has little resistance to the uplift. Solid anchorage is necessary to combat this potential problem.

Snow Load must be considered for any location that receives even the smallest amount of accumulation. For snow loads, a minimum value of 15 pounds per square foot of covered area should be used. Your figure will be based on annual accumulation for your area, whether or not the greenhouse is heated, and the degree of your roof's slope.

A heated greenhouse kept at 50 F will usually cause sufficient snow melt. "If snow or ice builds up quicker than it can melt, have a few 2x4s cut to length and use them as prop supports under every third hoop or where the buildup is most severe," says Bill Reidel, a southeastern Pennsylvania greenhouse grower. He produces bedding plants and poinsettias in poly-covered hoop houses.

Both wind stress and snow load are termed "live load" factors. A third factor termed as **dead load** refers to the structure frame, glazing, ventilation and heating equipment, hanging plants or anything else permanently attached to the greenhouse frame. This dead load adds weight to the framework, which in turn may make the structure a bit more stable under high-wind conditions. A word of caution: purchasing inexpensive, light-weight framework (small-diameter aluminum) hoop house and hanging it full of "dead load" items to aid in wind resistance can cause excessive damage to the hoops, allowing them to buckle or collapse under a wet snowfall.

Siting Your Needs

In the end, selection of the proper structure system, size and suitable building materials will depend entirely upon what you expect to get out of your greenhouse. Don't overburden yourself with more than you can handle in labor and expenses. While it is best to start small, be sure you have enough room to enlarge your greenhouse in case the learning experience was pleasant, or at least profitable.

But choosing the right greenhouse structure isn't enough. Before you spend a single penny on your new greenhouse, you have to consider **site selection**. Proper location can be critical in making a greenhouse environmentally efficient.

An ideal location is a level spot at the base of a south-facing slope. This gives access to good winter light and protection from north winds. If you're not blessed with such a spot, however, you need not scrap the project. Placing your greenhouse slightly more than 100 feet from existing tree lines and outbuildings also will help break the wind. If you don't have a natural wind break, plant your own. To maintain maximum benefit of daylight and to prevent uneven plant growth, the greenhouse should be situated with its end walls facing north and south, giving the sidewalls maximum exposure to the morning and afternoon sun.

It is also essential that the location has soil with good surface and subsurface **drainage**. In areas of heavy rainfall or on poorly drained soils, it may be advisable to mound up the structure site so that water will go around, rather than through, the greenhouse. If raising the structure site isn't possible, drainage ditches should be built around the greenhouse to direct surface water away. Drainage ditches should be seeded to a perennial grass or lined with stone to lessen chances of erosion.

A Real Hothouse

Of course, your goals for your greenhouse will determine one other structural necessity: heating and ventilation systems. If your main goal is to use your structure as an oversized cold frame, or giant row cover for cool season crops, there should be no need for a permanent heating system. The same holds true for getting a jump on warm-season vegetable production. An unheated structure should allow you to plant tomatoes and peppers four to six weeks earlier than the recommended outdoor planting time.

If you want to produce vine-ripened tomatoes three to four months ahead of the field-grown crop, however, you'll have to start them in the dead of winter. Greenhouse producers in southeastern Pennsylvania set their plants in December in order to begin marketing in April. Planting at that time of the year requires a dependable heat source. The size and design of the greenhouse, as well as the type of production system you will be managing will determine the proper size heating unit. Oil, gas, coal or wood heating units can be located in the greenhouse. Gas and oil-fired units are most common. "The most economical is a single unit hot-air heater with an output of 200,000 Btu. Anything smaller than that won't be efficient in a house of this size (2,500 square feet)," says Bill Reidel.

Reidel's gas-fired burner has three ducts on the top of the unit. Hot air blown out of the ducts is directed to the sides and center of the greenhouse. The center duct can be positioned to blow hot air upward into a polyethylene tube with holes sized and spaced to provide even distribution of heat. The tube is hung just below the center purlin and runs the length of the greenhouse. "Positioning small window-fans very 40 feet or so around the greenhouse will help eliminate cold and stagnant air pockets," says Reidel.

Nighttime temperature should run about 60 F to 65 F with daytime temperatures averaging 15 F to 20 F higher.

Clearing the Air

Ventilation systems are as important as the heating systems. They consist of fan assemblies and louvered vents. Like heating systems, they are thermostatically controlled. Both fans and vents must operate simultaneously. When the temperature moves above the preset maximum, the fan turns on and the louvered vents open. This allows fresh, cool air to be pulled in and humid hot air to be expelled. When the minimum temperature setting is reached, the fan and louvered vents shut down. The number and size of fans will vary according to greenhouse size and design.

When ordering your structure, consult with the manufacturer or supplier on specific heating and venting systems for your intended production system. These systems are the heart of your greenhouse production system. Don't skimp. Inadequate delivery of heat or fresh air may put all the contents at risk.

But then, don't skimp on anything, especially your homework. Deciding on the right kind of greenhouse can be a nightmare, and guessing on your needs can be disastrous. Seek professional advice from greenhouse manufactures, suppliers and growers. Many of these companies have been around for decades, some for a century, and are in the business to keep the grower in business. Take advantage of any information your university Extension service has to offer such as seminars, greenhouse tours, and periodicals. If you've done your homework, a greenhouse operation can be quite profitable. However, if your are averse to physical and mental labor, this will definitely not be your cup of tea.

Three Growers Find Profit Under Cover

Ronald and Margaret Jones of Mifflintown, Pa., used to produce only grain, hay and milk from a 53 cow dairy herd on their Juniata County farm of 240 acres in the steeply rolling hills of central Pennsylvania. Then they began searching for an enterprise that would provide a stable cash flow and include effort from all 11 family members, including their four daughters and five sons ranging in age from 4 to 20.

Vine-Ripe Tomatoes - in Early May!

"We have some friends who are in the greenhouse tomato business. After talking with them about growing and marketing, I felt it would be worth a try," says Ronald. "Diversifying with greenhouse tomatoes increased my gross income by $10,000 to $12,000."

The friends advised starting with a growing area of less than 4,500 square feet to keep crop management and marketing under control. "We put up a hoop house 148 feet long and 28 feet 6 inches wide. This gives us about 4,100 square feet of growing area," says Ronald.

He opted not to grow his own transplants but to buy them from another grower. He uses JUMBO, a special greenhouse type, set directly into the ground. "We don't use artificial growing medium or anything like that. We plant right into the greenhouse floor soil," explains Ronald.

In late August or early September, the greenhouse floor is conditioned with a tractor-driven 60-inch tiller mounted on a three-point hitch powered by a 40-hp International 454 field tractor. Following immediately is a seeding of cover-crop oats at a rate of 4 bushels per acre. The planting goes rapidly. "After it's attained a height of about 12 inches, we come in and spread approximately 600 bushels of cow manure. This is incorporated right away, again with the (tractor) tiller, and then seeded with another crop," Ronald says.

This time it is grain rye seeded at 4 bushels per acre. The rye is allowed to grow until mid-February just prior to tomato planting, when it is tilled down. To ensure good incorporation, the tractor-mounted tiller is used twice. Then a pass is made with a rear-tined, walk-behind tiller in the area to be planted as four-row planting strips. About 1,200 plants are hand-set 12 inches apart in staggered spacings which form a diamond pattern. Between the strips is a 3-foot walkway.

A half cup of phosphorus-calcium mixture is placed in each hole just ahead of the plant. "It takes ten of us about two hours to do the fertilizing and transplanting," says Margaret. Four people experienced with the system could do it in about four hours," she estimates. When transplanting is done, drip irrigation is put into place. After the plants are established but before they are a foot high, black plastic mulch is applied over the entire greenhouse floor. The mulch film is laid gently on top of the crop. Each plant is carefully worked through a slit made in the plastic. It takes about two hours for four people to do this job.

To anchor the plants for their vertical climb, twine is tied from the base of each plant to an overhead support wire that runs the length of the greenhouse at a height of about eight feet. A slip knot at the wire allows adjustment as plants grow.

As they stretch upward, plants are wrapped around the twine, not tied to it. "We wrap the plants about once a week over a six-week period. At the same time, we also pinch off the suckers," Margaret says. "Be sure the twine is not stretched too tight, or you'll pull the plants out of the soil when you're wrapping them. Also be sure to wrap the plants around the twine in the same direction (each time), or they'll unwrap." Initial tying, wrapping and suckering can take three people from four to six hours. Less time is required for later rounds when no new tying is done.

$1.50 – A Pound

When the plants begin blooming, the Joneses lightly tap the support wires to cause optimum pollination. Plants shaken too hard cause problems. "You'll get uneven pollination which causes unevenly shaped fruits," says Ronald. This process is done every day when the plants are in bloom, usually from March until May. It takes two people about half an hour, Margaret says.

Harvesting ripe tomatoes begins in early May from the earliest plants. "Seventy-five percent of the crop is sold retail right from our house at $1.50 per pound," says Ronald. The rest is wholesaled to a local grocery chain for $1.25 per pound.

The Joneses advise anyone who is thinking about going into the greenhouse business to start small and obtain as much information as possible. "A house this size (4,100 square feet) is all two people can handle if one of them has an off-farm, full-time job. If your sales are strictly wholesale, you could probably run two or three houses (this size)," Ronald says. Selling a tomato with several days' shelf life to retailers usually means both harvesting and marketing happen only twice a week, whereas retail sale of ripe fruit demands picking every other day – with sales nearly every day of the week.

As they look back, the Joneses warn newcomers that the first year in business may be disheartening. However, once the word travels that there is a local source of fresh-picked, vine-ripened tomatoes – *available in May* – you will have a steady flow of customers, they say.

Change Brings Success in a Shifting Market

"You should be able to gross $100,000 to $250,000 with an acre under cover. If you're not doing that, you won't be in business very long." says Ted Benson, owner and general manager of Benson's Greenhouses in eastern Pennsylvania.

Benson is a second-generation greenhouse grower whose family has been selling plants since 1930. "Ninety-five percent of my sales are wholesale and delivered to retailers within a 50-mile radius. A few additional deliveries go a bit farther to Philadelphia and into New Jersey." His greenhouses are in full operation eight months a year and provide ample work for three full-time and 10 part-time employees.

While the business has been profitable in recent years, Benson admits "We've experienced some hard times in this business. Twenty or so years ago, you wouldn't find very many bedding and potted plants here. It was practically all vegetable plants." A rapid market shift to landscape and flowering species caught his company by surprise. Suddenly, the public no longer wanted to plant large vegetable gardens, but cared intensely about aesthetics – how things looked. This would seem to have been good news for Benson's thriving cut flower section, but foreign imports spoiled the bloom of that enterprise. "Large football mums were coming into this country at four stems for a dollar. It practically cost us that much to grow a single bloom," Benson recalls.

"You need to stay on your toes, especially if you plan to make this your sole source of income. If you don't follow the trends in this business, you'll go bankrupt," he says. Staying ahead of the pack is what keeps Benson at the top. By the time one crop of plants is being delivered, next year's plantings are already planned. Keeping his customers satisfied takes more than 40 varieties of bedding plants plus potted plants, such as tulips, hyacinths, daffodils and poinsettias, as well as greenhouse and field-grown chrysanthemums. "We offer plants for all occasions, including popular religious holidays and others you've never thought of," Benson says.

'Buy Smart – Not Cheap'

"Start small" is his advice, too. To be successful with wholesale bedding plants you have to work long, hard hours, keep meticulous production records and be a good manager. Producing an exceptional product and knowing your buyers will quickly empty your house, he says. Benson sells mainly to owner/operator retail outlets. He avoids dealing with large chain-store operations because of several bad experiences. "The (chain-store) people I had to deal with were completely ignorant about producing live plants. If a production problem arose that caused a delay in delivery or required a price increase, it was inexplicable to these people. They'd either refuse to pay the necessary price increase or refuse the delivery," Benson says.

He finds operators of independent stores more understanding of occasional production problems. Benson also recommends dealing directly with manufacturers in buying everything from specialty greenhouse and ventilation systems to production supplies. Whenever possible, buy in bulk. "The idea is to buy smart – not cheap. In this way it's possible to reduce your costs by up to 25 percent," he says. "I'll never become a millionaire in this business, but I can stay well in the black."

$22,000 and Growing

A love of growing plants and dealing with people has turned into a profitable business for full-time high school chemistry teacher Bill Reidel and his wife, Faith. Their greenhouses are located in southeastern Pennsylvania on Route 222, a major artery to the scenic Pennsylvania Dutch country.

"My parents relocated from Pennsylvania to Virginia about 15 years ago and started a greenhouse bedding plant business. When we would go down to visit, I'd find myself helping out in the greenhouse," Bill says. The experience was invaluable. He learned how and when to start each species.

He picked up the management skills needed to develop a retail trade and he realized business growth doesn't happen overnight.

"Five years before we put up the first greenhouse (erected in 1985), I decided to raise field-grown mums and try selling them along the highway that fronts our property. I planted 500 chrysanthemum cuttings in late May and by mid-September we were potting and selling them. In a few weekends, we sold out," Bill says. The second year, Bill doubled his first year's planting and in the third year he again added 500 plants. Each year ended with a "Sold Out" sign. It was during the fourth year of selling mums his customers were notified he would have greenhouse-grown bedding plants available in the spring.

"We broke even in the first year of our retail bedding plant business and since then we've been in the black," Bill says. Staying in business and making a profit takes plenty of hard work and commitment. Looking for ways to increase cash flow is a must. The longer or more intensively you keep a house producing, the greater the cash flow. The couple's 3,300 square feet of productive area can produce $12,000 or more in bedding and potted plants and additional $7,000 to $10,000 worth of poinsettias. When sales of field-grown mums are added in, a good season could gross in excess of $30,000.

Both Bill and Faith go out of their way to please customers with individual attention that will be remembered long after the sale. Customers unsure of what variety to plant often come in with diagrams of their flower beds. "We study the diagram, ask about growing conditions, and then make our recommendations," Bill says. These are repeat customers, Faith notes.

"This is a people business. If you don't like dealing with people, you won't be successful," remarks Bill. Offer your customers a good selection of high-quality plants (the Riedels have 30), give customers special attention and before you know it, you'll be adding another house to handle the increased business. The couple recently added 2,500 square feet of greenhouse space.

So far, the Riedels have been able to do all the work themselves. "There's no point in paying someone to do a job you have time to do. (Hired labor) adds to your overhead and reduces the cash flow," says Bill.

Another way to reduce overhead is to avoid heating the greenhouse until the last possible minute. January can be very cold in Pennsylvania. Instead of starting up in January, like most greenhouses do, Bill waits until February 1. "We can grow a quality, salable plant even though we've omitted the entire month of January and save on fuel bills," he remarks. By April 1, all seeding and transplanting has been completed.

The Reidels are open for business from April to June for bedding and potted plant sales, then close during July and August for maintenance, cleanup and starting poinsettias. They reopen the second week of September and stay open through Halloween for sales of potted field-grown mums and carving pumpkins purchased from local farmers. They stay closed until Thanksgiving, then reopen for sales of poinsettias and purchased Christmas trees and wreaths. "December 24th is our last day of the business season and we're glad when it comes. But in a couple of weeks, we're looking forward to February first – the beginning of our next year," Bill admits.

§

Tunnels Of Plenty

Low-cost hoophouses can get your produce to market a month or more ahead of the competition.

by Bob Hofstetter

Dale Haubrich had been growing vegetables for a decade on his 10-acre farm near Nevada, Iowa. And aside from farming organically, he was a pretty ordinary grower. He planted and harvested at ordinary times, and he bit the bullet like everyone else when weather conditions were unfavorable.

But Haubrich realized that as long as he was selling produce at the same time his competitors were, he would always be ordinary. So, in the mid '80s he built six hoophouses, each about 100 feet long, 30 feet wide and 11 feet tall. He made two

300-foot hoophouses by joining the units end-to-end in groups of three. Together, the quonset-shaped structures gave him a grand total of 18,000 square feet of plastic-covered production area.

By late winter, Haubrich was already preparing a seedbed on this nearly half-acre indoor field while other local farmers were still waiting for their ground to thaw. He applied manure with a mechanical spreader pulled by his Allis-Chalmers D-14 tractor. Then he worked the ground to within a few inches of the sidewalls of the hoophouses using a 4-foot Howard rotavator mounted to the tractor's 3-point-hitch. (He could have used conventional plowing and disking equipment, but he wouldn't have been able to get as close to the sidewalls and would have needed much more turn-around space.)

Haubrich direct-seeded spinach and other cool-season species in the hoophouse in mid-February. A few weeks later, he also put in transplants of lettuce, cabbage and other brassicas that he had started in a separate greenhouse.

Transplants of tomatoes, peppers and eggplants followed in early to mid-April. But by then – about the time other local farmers were just starting to direct-seed early vegetables in their fields – Haubrich had already sold $5,000 worth of hoophouse-grown spinach and lettuce to restaurants, grocery stores and other local retail outlets.

Two More Marketing Months

Haubrich learned a valuable lesson that many other growers are discovering, too: Hoophouses are a low-cost way to turn ordinary produce into high-value produce. While they cost a bit more than lean-to growing structures they offer a lot more flexibility.

For starters, they don't have to be placed against a building. You can build one almost anywhere you have some flat ground. They consist of little more than a series of steel, semi-circular hoops with wood-framed walls at each end, all of which is anchored to the ground and covered with plastic.

Because of their size and shape, hoophouses can act like a giant "row cover" over an entire portion of a field. They help your soil warm up earlier and stay warm longer, enabling you to tap those vital early and late markets. "In many cases," says Haubrich, "you can get on the market four to six weeks before field-grown produce is available and can extend it for the same period – or longer – in late fall, well after outside crops have been killed by frost."

Hoophouses can be as small and cheap or large and expensive as you need. While you may not be able to build one from scrap materials, you don't need an engineering degree to set one up, either. Many companies that sell greenhouse components also offer hoophouse kits.

The "deluxe" versions of these kits come with the works – frame, covering, heating unit (self-contained, thermostatically controlled), exhaust fans and exhaust shutters. These can cost up to $5,000 for a 96- by 28-foot unit like Haubrich's.

But farmers who only want to grow their own transplants can get by with a much smaller, less expensive unit. I know one farmer who uses his 30- by 14-foot hoophouse strictly for transplant production. He bought the kit three years ago for about $350. It contained hoops, hoop anchors and end-wall framing. He bought glazing and a ventilation system separately for about $150. The ventilation system consisted of four louvered vents and a thermostatically controlled exhaust fan. And he used a single layer of 6-mil, UV-treated polyethylene plastic to cover the house and end walls.

1-Year Pay Back

If you think $500 is too much to spend for a structure that will only be used for transplant production, consider this: Greenhouse consultants say you should be able to produce your own vegetable transplants for about $3 to $4 per hundred in a hoophouse – including everything but labor. I've never seen quality, custom-grown transplants for less the $9 per hundred in my area. (Editor's note: Industry average is now $15 per hundred.)

A hoophouse with 400 to 500 square feet of growing area should be able to produce 10,000 or more transplants per year. At $3 per hundred, those homegrown transplants would cost you $300. If you had to buy them, you'd spend about $900. The $600 savings would easily pay for the hoophouse. It doesn't take much of a mathematician to figure out who's making the profit on purchased transplants.

Permanently installed heating units aren't necessary in a small hoophouse that you're using only for producing transplants. The structure will generally see its heaviest use in March, April, June and July. You will need some type of portable heating unit for starting transplants early, and many farmers use portable kerosene space heaters when outside temperatures drop below 50 F. Figure on using anywhere from 30 to 60 gallons of kerosene early in the season to heat a 30- by 14-foot hoophouse.

Haubrich doesn't use supplemental heat in his hoophouses, because he doesn't need the rigid climate control he'd need if he were growing transplants. His technique is what I like to call "tunnel growing." He uses conventional field-prep and planting methods, only they take place beneath a cover rather than in an open field.

His hoops are 4 feet apart and are covered with a single layer of 6-mil, UV-treated polyethylene. "I didn't purchase factory-made end walls for the houses. I framed them out myself using 2x4s," says Haubrich, who drip-irrigates his vegetables. "The end walls aren't in place very long, only when temperatures are low in the early part of the season and again when temperatures drop in mid- to late fall. The rest of the time the houses are open on both ends."

'Natural' Disease Control

Keeping his end walls open also helps Haubrich avoid pockets of warm and cold air. Warm, still air creates perfect conditions for plant disease, and cold air can put stress on plants, slowing their growth. For additional air circulation, Haubrich sometimes rolls back the glazing over one or two hoops (about 4 to 8 feet) at each unit juncture. If you're going to keep your hoophouse enclosed, you will need a small, portable fan inside to help keep the air moving.

Knowing when and how to change his hoophouse environment takes careful management and a good deal of experience. Since Haubrich doesn't have thermostatically controlled heating and ventilation, he has to monitor air temperatures and movement several times a day. Even with the end walls removed, temperatures in summer can rise quickly and the air can become still. When that happens, Haubrich has to create a draft and vent that hot air quickly through the roof.

Special "greenhouse" varieties aren't necessary with Haubrich's tunnel-growing methods. When Haubrich compared these to standard varieties, he says he found no noticeable difference in yield. Such varieties would be useful if you use your hoophouse more like a greenhouse – that is, keeping it closed year-round and controlling the environment artificially. That's an important consideration. Seeds for some greenhouse varieties cost 10 times more than similar hybrids used for field growing.

Haubrich believes most any vegetable crop can be highly productive in a hoophouse. He also feels that, since the plants are isolated from the elements, most all of the harvest is of number one quality. His records bear that out: Haubrich's hoophouse-grown tomatoes yield four times more marketable fruit than field-grown tomatoes.

Hoophouses offer other cropping possibilities. They lend themselves well to herb production, especially perennials like thyme, sage, oregano and mint, because they don't have to be replanted every year. They can tolerate cold weather, too. And because they're protected from cold, they'll break dormancy earlier and come into production sooner.

Hoophouses probably could even be used for strawberries and raspberries, if you could find a way to introduce bees for pollination. One idea I hope to try is using a hoophouse to produce day-neutral strawberries, the kind that bear fruit a couple of times a season. In a hoophouse, they would probably start producing fruit a month earlier than day-neutrals normally do in my area (mid-May instead of mid-June). They would likely continue bearing later into fall, too.

Diversity, quality and timely marketing are the keys to successful vegetable production. A hoophouse can help you accomplish all three of those goals. It can provide space to start as many different varieties as you want. And it can give you the head-start you need to get those crops to market when their price is highest.

Practice Makes Perfect

Get Good Before You Get Big

A "practice garden" may be the way to start your market garden if you have limited growing experience. Enrich just 1,000 square feet and use it to practice gardening during the first year. At the same time you can be upgrading an adjacent half-acre or 1-acre future expansion garden using compost and cover crops.

Set up the practice garden as a miniature of the larger market garden that you are planning for the future. This will give you a chance to practice with growing techniques and cultural requirements for the following year of market gardening. This will give you enough yield to feed your family, and some to sell as well. If you like the membership gardening idea, you can contract with two or three families in your neighborhood who will buy what you don't need from your garden.

If you like farmers markets or card table sales, you can start small, only one day per week. This will give you a chance to learn the trade without the risk of having to sell enough food to make your living during this first practice year. You will probably make enough money to cover all your expenses with a little bit left over.

This first year will relieve a lot of stress because you aren't doing this for a living. Look at it as if you were enrolling for a semester at college. That would cost you anywhere from $3,000 to $6,000, so this practice garden is a pretty cheap semester if you only spend a few hundred dollars. Do a self-designed semester study plan like in an adult learning program. Assign yourself books to read, people to interview, papers to write and set up a schedule.

In fact, if you are pursuing a college degree through an Adult Degree Program, anyway, why not use this practice garden as your topic for the semester. You can even stretch this exercise out to three semesters, one to plan, one to implement and one to review. Why, you might even use it as a master's degree thesis. This way you will have a faculty advisor to turn to for assistance and guidance. It will also give you someone breathing down your neck, putting pressure on you to do a really good job.

This practice year will also give you the time you need to shop around for good equipment and supplies. If you buy a truck that will fit your marketing plan, use it as your family car. Then all the expense doesn't have to be borne by the market garden. Give your family and friends a chance to ease into your new commitments rather than all at once. It provides a smooth transition from being a non-gardener to becoming a market gardener.

CHAPTER 8:

The Best Defense Is A Good Offense

For Weed, Disease and Pest Control

The three best ways to achieve efficient and effective weed, disease and pest control are early detection, careful identification and speedy treatment. - Andy Lee

Every year I talk to gardeners who haven't kept up with disease and pest problems, or with the weeding. Often their last resort is to plow the crop under. This means time wasted in planting and early care of the crop, and time wasted in tilling them under. The result is money lost because the product never gets sold, not to mention the hours of hard work and stress.

In 1991, Connie Koeller, owner of Abundance Garden in the Intervale, had a fungal infection called septoria leaf spot on 600 tomato plants. To combat the problem she spent over $200 for copper-sulphur spray. Each spray application took two hours, and she had to do it six times. Plus, she spent 24 hours pruning off infected leaves.

At $10 per hour this excessive spraying and pruning cost her nearly $600. To aggravate matters, while she was tending the tomatoes the weeds in her other crops got ahead of her. She had to hire extra help to get the weeds back under control. This cost her another $400. To top it all off, the yields from the tomato plants were reduced more than 50 percent, causing an even greater loss of income.

The secret to successful weed-disease-pest control is healthy soil and a thriving ecological system in your garden. Walk through your garden daily, looking for signs of trouble. As soon as you spot a problem, identify it and deal with it immediately. This early detection of problems is important so that you can handle them in a timely manner before you suffer a crop loss. Handling a little problem that has grown up into a big problem can increase your work load and stress levels by major degrees.

This is important in your backyard market garden because of the constraints on your time. Most of the problems will appear during the harvesting and marketing season, when you has even less time. Fortunately, many problems that can become a major disaster later in the season can be avoided with careful management. If the problem can be detected in its early stage, the control is less time consuming, easier, and cheaper. And, it will increase your profits.

An example is cabbage looper infestation on cabbage and broccoli plants. Look for holes in the leaves, and little dark green worm droppings inside the plant. You will be able to see these signs long before you see the well-camouflaged pale green cabbage loopers. As soon as they are spotted, a simple spraying of *Bt.* on a regular basis will keep them under control.

I'll use weed control as another example. When the weeds are less than one inch high, a scuffle hoe pulled or pushed across the surface can knock them out very quickly. Three 4- by 50-foot beds can be weeded with a diamond scuffle hoe in 30 minutes or less when the weeds are this small.

Once the weeds are more than 4-inches high, however, the scuffle hoe is not effective. Then you have to use a rotary tiller or weed by hand. Hand-weeding takes three to six hours for the same three beds. If there are 50 beds in the garden, hand-weeding the whole garden could take a week.

Sometimes, diseases and pests can be very difficult to identify correctly. Anytime you see a problem that you aren't familiar with, take a sample to your Cooperative Extension Service for classification and treatment suggestions. If the treatment suggestions you receive from the Extension agent are for chemical applications, politely ask them to recommend organic controls, too. There are a growing number of Extension agents who take organic gardening seriously. They will be only too happy to share their knowledge and expertise with you.

Many diseases can be stopped by keeping insects under control. When I first started out as a gardener I had a laid back attitude about diseases and pests. In my eagerness to share nature's bounty with everyone, I left pests alone, thinking there was more than enough produce for all of us. Since becoming a market gardener, however, I've had to adopt a more intensive protocol to prevent severe crop losses. Otherwise, the garden's economic sustainability is questionable.

Insect pests and diseases may not be a frequent problem for you, but every gardener must contend with weeds. Some weeds, in manageable amounts, are OK. They are nature's way of filling a vacuum by covering bare soil to protect it from the elements. For the commercial gardener, however, the problem is compounded. Too many weeds will ruin the market gardener's chance for a fair profit.

Weeds compete with vegetable crops for moisture and nutrients. Some weeds exude toxic chemicals that inhibit tuber formation in root crops. Other weeds harbor pests and diseases. Some of these insects and diseases can overwinter in dead weeds left in the garden. That's why it's a good idea to remove the weeds from the garden at the end of the season.

It's important to keep weeds around your garden edges mowed if you aren't going to till them under. This will prevent them from setting seeds, some of which will blow into your garden beds. Often you can use a regular lawnmower to keep them mowed. If the ground is too rough or rocky for a lawnmower, buy a string trimmer (weed whacker), a brush cutter or a goat.

It's OK to till weeds under with the crops. Just be sure to do it *before* they set viable seeds. Till thoroughly to break up the heavy growth so that soil organisms can completely consume the bits of weed stems before it's time to plant again next year. Otherwise, you'll have a whole new generation of pests and diseases to deal with next season.

The only way to prevent weeds from taking over your garden is to nip them early, and stay after them until they are under control. It will take more than one season to accomplish this, especially if you are plowing up part of an old cow pasture or part of your lawn. In the pasture, you will have weeds to contend with, in the lawn you will have grasses. I'll take weeds over grasses any day. Once grasses are established they can be a dickens to eradicate.

If you are turning part of your lawn into a market garden there are several ways to kill the grasses so that you can till. One is with herbicides such as Roundup, which I don't recommend. Another way is to use the organic herbicide Sharpshooter, manufactured by Safer Inc. This is a completely safe control, but not always effective on hardy perennial grasses. It will take more than one spraying, and it's darned expensive.

Tilling the sod under will not be totally effective, especially with heavy perennial grasses. It will take at least three passes with a good rotary tiller to prepare a seedbed. Even then, a follow-up tilling and timely cultivation will be necessary, because grass roots regrow.

If your sod is quackgrass or crabgrass, it may be a mistake to use the rotary tiller to turn the sod. These grasses have underground stems called rhizomes, that are up to three feet long. Rhizomes have a joint or node every few inches. When the tiller breaks the root apart, it will resprout at each joint. It's better to kill these grasses with plastic mulch, or a foot-thick layer of organic mulch such as straw or leaves.

Leaving the organic mulch on the ground for a whole year is best. This will completely smother out the perennial grasses, and enrich the soil at the same time. When you pull back this heavy layer of mulch you will find a damp soil, thriving with soil life such as sow bugs and earthworms. This organic matter will help solve nutrient imbalances, and will decompose the sod so that wireworms, grubs and other sod loving pests aren't such a problem.

Since weeding will take so much of your time, it's a good idea to use all the tools available to eliminate as much weeding as possible. One of the tools is plastic mulch. I used to think that plastic mulch should be banned from the face of the earth. It is petroleum based, and there isn't any good way to get rid of it after the season is over. You either have to burn it, or landfill it. Either way is detrimental to the environment.

After using plastic mulch for a few years, though, I have modified my judgment and have learned to be more tolerant. It may be the lesser of several evils. For one thing, it is inexpensive, easy to install and provides almost 100 percent control of weeds. This eliminates hours and days of manual labor for cultivation. If you are mechanized, even with a walk-behind tractor, this will save gallons and gallons of fuel by eliminating repeated trips over the field. It will also eliminate intensive cultivating and tilling that help destroy soil structure.

The plastic warms the soil, allowing the plants to maintain peak production over a longer season. You will be able to plant fewer plants to obtain a good yield. The plastic retains moisture. This cuts down on the amount of irrigation water you will need. It provides habitat for earthworms and other beneficial soil life. It creates a barrier between the plants and soil-borne fungal diseases. All of these reasons add up to a very powerful argument for the continued use of plastic mulch. Straw, leaves and grass clippings can also be used as a mulch to smother weeds. Consider them as another tool in your weed-control lineup.

CHAPTER 9:

A Plea for the Earth

THIS WE KNOW.....the Earth does not belong to man, man belongs to the Earth. All things are connected, like blood which connects one family. Whatever befalls the Earth befalls the children of the Earth. Man did not weave the web of life – he is merely a strand in it. Whatever he does to the web, he does to himself.

- Chief Seattle, 1854

In 1854, Chief Seattle predicted that if we didn't learn how to manage our waste we would suffocate in it. Nearly a century and a half later, his prophecy appears to be chillingly correct. Our Planet Earth is suffering an ecological and biological breakdown. Earth's present condition is analogous to a harried businessperson suffering a breakdown of the central nervous system preceding a stroke or a heart attack.

Of key importance in this breakdown of earth's life support systems is the destruction of the final fragile layer of topsoil, the only thing lying between humanity and starvation. It is so important to our very existence and to the continuation of life on this planet yet our farm soils are disappearing at an alarming rate.

Thousands of acres of soils that were once fertile and productive are now biologically dead, barren and wasted. They have had too many chemicals applied to them, combined with inappropriate tillage practices and the non-renewal of organic matter.

Desertification is no longer a problem confined to the African Continent. We are seeing vast areas of major food producing regions of the American West becoming non-usable due to loss of topsoil and salt build-up caused by excessive irrigation. In 1963, over 1 million acres of farmland had been lost to desertification in the United States. By 1993, this emerging American desert will encompass more than 7.5 million acres. This is land that was once fertile and productive and is now a bitter, salt-laden wasteland. Even a section of Maine, just west of Freeport, has become a tourist attraction because of a newly formed 300-acre desert. It's on land that used to be a sheep farm. This Desert of Maine comes complete with sand storms and 20-foot high sand dunes.

Tillage, particularly moldboard plowing and rotary tilling, can be disruptive and destructive when not properly managed. This is especially true when improper or excessive tillage coincides with chemical fertilizer, herbicide and insecticide programs. I can remember as a child following my father as he plowed the fields. I was able to pick a can of fishing worms in a furrow not more than 100 feet long. Today, the soil in that same field, after almost four decades of moldboard plowing and chemical farming, won't yield a can of earthworms from an entire acre. It will take a massive effort of composting and soil regeneration to bring this field back to life and healthy productivity.

A farm should be a safe and fun place to live and work and play. We should learn to think like Stuart Hill, professor of entomology at McGill University in Montreal. He encourages us to imagine what it would be like to live in the soil.

Imagine being a plant's root system, an earthworm or a beneficial nematode. Consider the soil environment you would like. Would you prefer a loose and fluffy soil, easy to move around in, or would you prefer a tightly packed hardpan home?

Would you prefer your meals in bits and pieces from various areas of the organic matter and humus in the soil, sort of like a smorgasbord buffet? Or would you like to get your meals in chemical form through straight applications of chemical N-P-K, like an intravenous feeding tube?

There are nearly 2,000 synthetic chemical compounds that can be used on garden crops. There are 400 pesticides alone, each having a particular use, and particular side effects, some of them disastrous. Parathion, for example, kills honeybees. So does Sevin, the most widely used of the general use pesticides. Diazinon kills earthworms. So does Vapam. Do you want to do that to your soil and to the valuable soil life on which your crops depend for nutrition?

Hundreds of millions of pounds of chemical insecticides are used yearly on U. S. crops. Since 1945, pesticide use on food crops has increased by 3,000 percent, yet the portion of those crops lost annually to insects has *increased* by 50 percent. Compare that to Sweden where pesticide use has *decreased* by

50 percent between 1985 and 1990, yet Sweden's farm yields have remained at the same level.

Insects possess an enzyme system called the "mixed-function oxidases" (mfo's) that gives them the ability to detoxify and become resistant to many synthetic insecticides. This problem for chemically oriented vegetable growers is so big that at least one pesticide manufacturer now sells a "chemical booster" (Butacide 8 E.C. piperonyl butoxide - registered to Fairfield American Corporation). This acts to break down the insect's immune system, allowing the chemical pesticide to work.

Conventional vegetable growers now have the paradox of having to use two very strong chemicals to kill a pest. That pest may not have even been there in the first place if the crops were healthy. Look at a good organic supplies catalog such as the one from Necessary Trading. There are less than a dozen standard botanical poisons that can do almost anything the long list of synthetic poisons can do, usually without the long lasting ill effects of many of the chemical pesticides.

Certainly, the organic vegetable grower does suffer losses to insects. These crop losses are expensive. But, what is the true cost of trying to eliminate every suspected pest?

Healthy soil is the best way to decrease pesticide use and increase yields. In tests at the University of Connecticut researchers found that using compost fertilizer instead of synthetic fertilizers increased crop yields. Tomatoes increased 10 percent, broccoli 27 percent and peppers 100 percent.

Fortunately, more and more people are getting concerned, even angry, about the dismal future of Spaceship Earth, and are willing to do something about the eco-crisis. Public awareness is growing in quantum leaps. If we voice enough concern publicly, our lawmakers will make changes to begin a worldwide regeneration of our farmlands. This is the first step in the renewal of health for humanity.

America is the best-fed nation on earth, for the least amount of money. The average American family only spends 11 percent of its income for food. Compare this to many countries where consumer food budgets are 25 percent and greater.

For nearly two generations, the American food supply system has worked, for two basic reasons. First, the supply side, which includes farming, transportation and distribution, is making money at it. Second, the demand side, consumers, has enjoyed increasingly unlimited choices and cheap prices.

Our American grocery stores and supermarkets offer a cornucopia of choices. Anytime of year it is possible to get almost any type of vegetables, fruit or meat desired. The produce is almost always blemish-free, relatively inexpensive and is available in seemingly unlimited quantities. Our national food supply system employs millions of people. This includes farmers, truckers, warehouse and distribution crews and supermarket and food store personnel.

In my estimation it is highly unlikely that any American citizen will starve to death for lack of something to eat. Either we have income with which to buy food, or we have access to social support services that will feed us. It is understandable then that we take pride in calling America the land of plenty. When we scratch below the surface of this apparent cornucopia, however, we don't like what we see. What is the problem?

Begin with the source of our food. The vast distance our food travels before reaching our table is the one of the root causes of our concerns. Nearly 90 percent of our fresh fruits and vegetables come from California, Florida and the other southern and southwestern states. A significant portion of our food comes from Mexico, with smaller percentages coming from off-shore locations such as Jamaica, Cayman Islands, and Latin America.

> It is ludicrous to cart stuff about all over the world, so that someone may make a 'profit' out of doing so, when that stuff could much better be produced where it is wanted.To suggest that it should be so produced is no crime against humanity. – Lord Northbourne, 1940

Most states of our union produce only a tiny portion of their food needs. This leads to a lack of agricultural jobs and ownership opportunities for residents in these regions. This contributes to the declining quality of life in non-food producing regions.

In those states where food production is big business, the trend is to monocropping. Huge fields contain only one type of fruit or vegetable. Monocropping leads to heavy infestations

314

of crop-devouring pests and diseases. The agribusiness solution to this increasing threat has been to use more chemicals to combat the problems. The result is an alarming rate of soil erosion and farm-caused pollution. Livestock, major providers of essential organic matter, have disappeared from the mega-farm vegetable fields. Natural soil life, necessary for the conversion of organic matter to nutrient rich humus, has been poisoned into oblivion.

Where intensive chemical cropping is practiced the soil is becoming barren – biologically dead. The only way the farmers can produce crops on this land is by continuing massive infusions of chemical fertilizers. The food thus produced is poor and lifeless, unable to supply our bodies with the minerals and vitamins we need. Annually we, as a nation, spend $370 billion dollars for food. Those Americans who can afford to are now routinely supplementing their diet with chemically derived vitamin pills and food supplements. For this we spend another $38 billion. We are literally stuffing ourselves with food that doesn't feed us.

In the short term, the price we pay for food is kept low as a result of the mining of this soil resource in the food growing regions. Government subsidies are required for the huge investment in irrigation water, transportation networks, and cleaning up our environment. Farmers need large bank loans to purchase the huge, heavy duty equipment to farm these mega-fields. Housing demand in some of the food-growing regions is now escalating land prices beyond the ability of farming, even mega-farming, to pay. Drought is a recurring nightmare for many farmers in the food-producing regions, creating more demands for subsidized water supplies.

Growing food in one location and shipping it extreme distances to another location for consumption is not natural and it is not sustainable. We call this agribusiness. It is the removal of resources from one region, and the disposal of these resources in another region.

Fresh food does not travel well. As soon as a fruit or vegetable leaves the vine it begins to decay. That's nature at work. Farmers know that to keep the food from spoiling in transit will require special care in crop planning and handling.

Mega-farmers choose varieties that yield well and ship well. Flavor and nutritional value are secondary or even ignored. Chemicals and synthetic compounds are used to increase

315

yields and for the control of weeds, diseases and pests. Chemical fungicides are used to control molds and diseases that would otherwise shorten the shipping and shelf life of the food. Use of chemicals is especially alarming in foreign countries that do not control deadly poisons such as DDT.

Foods that cannot be shipped fresh are preserved, usually with chemical preservatives to keep food from spoiling in transit. Food dyes are used to enhance color. Flavor enhancers are used to trick consumers into thinking the food is fresh and healthy.

Long distance shipping is expensive, and it takes a long time for food to travel from one coast to the other. Food is picked before it is ripe so that it won't spoil in transit. Food that is immature has little flavor and little nutritional value. Industry standards established by wholesale buyers and brokers demand special waxed boxes in myriad sizes and shapes. These containers are hard to dispose of because they can't be recycled and they are darned expensive.

Packing, warehousing, transporting and distributing are all energy consumptive; transportation over extreme distances is particularly so. Trucks and trains are expensive to build, maintain and operate. Fuel consumption on highways and railways uses up our resources incredibly quickly. For long distance shipping of food, we are spending many more calories in energy than the food contains.

Before this shift to mega-farming began in the forties and fifties, most Americans knew how to produce some or all of their own food. Or at least they knew the farmer who produced the food for them. Now, most of us have no connection to the land at all. We don't feel connected to the food that we are eating, or the farmers who grow it for us. A trip to buy groceries at the supermarket is now a joyless occasion, one to be gotten through quickly, so we can turn our attention to more pleasant tasks.

Americans may be the best fed people in the world, but we are also the least nourished by the food we eat. Nationally, cancer and heart disease are the biggest killers, and they are often related to a nutritionally deficient diet. We have become a product of what we eat. We are eating food that is laced with poison, placed there for the very purpose of making that food available to us in a convenient and inexpensive way. We are breathing air and drinking water that has been polluted by farm chemicals.

Each year, the fragile layer of topsoil that feeds us is becoming thinner and thinner. When farmers use plows to scratch and stir the soil they set in motion a chain of events that is neither natural nor sustainable. Erosion, caused by wind and rain, begins to occur. Organic matter and humus degenerates rapidly when exposed to harsh sunlight and drying winds. Microbial life in the soil is uncovered and exposed, interrupting its life cycle. Minerals and nutrients, lacking their humus cover, are subjected to leaching, volatilization and erosion.

Heavy rains, winds and baking sun harden the earth's surface, causing crusting. The soil becomes unable to receive and retain the water from heavy rainfall. It becomes runoff, dirtying and polluting nearby waterways, creating massive erosion, resulting in the condition described by author Edward Faulkner as, *...watching the farmer's fortune wash downstream.*

Labor-intensive organic gardening and farming practices address these problems, but by themselves, they are not the whole answer. Extensive labor requirements, marketing difficulties and severe crop losses often negate any gains in soil health or food value from the organic farming models. The organic farmers, even as they improve their soil, often face financial hardships.

We are all in this mess together. Consumers realize that farmers don't like these chemical- and energy-intensive farming practices, either. Farming is no longer fun in the major food-growing regions where fields have become battle zones, pitting humans against nature in the struggle for survival. Missing most of all is the quality of life that we Americans once enjoyed, when the community was part of farming and the farmer was part of the community.

Chapter 10:

Eco Farming:

The Next Step

Gross and excessive food transport from one region to another should be against the law. It's doing a hell of a lot more harm to us and the environment than many of the things that are currently considered criminal. – Andy Lee, 1992

American farmers, myself sometimes included, have failed miserably if we ever intended, as we so pompously believe, to create successful and sustainable agricultural models for the world to replicate. Our country has indeed, as stated by Dr. Joseph Nichols, become the best fed and least nourished nation on earth. Fortunately, the arena in which change can happen now exists. Farmers want to improve their standard of living and consumers want to improve their dietary options. In a 1988 Harris Poll, 86 percent of the respondents voiced dissatisfaction with the food we are eating. If we farmers can appeal to this vast number of Americans to support us, then we can change the way America grows and distributes its food.

We can begin by developing, testing and demonstrating models of community supported food production that are environmentally sensitive, economically sensible and socially just. Each of us can take a small step to create these systems. Combining our efforts will achieve gigantic results. These models will be the first giant step in ending America's hunger for safe, flavorful food. With these models we can fulfill our yearning to be connected to the land that grows our food and to the farmers who steward the land.

The issue is not to make food cheaper, but to make food more valuable. We can use good food as a tool to combat our increasing health care costs and to enhance our quality of life.

Modern agribusiness often ignores the concept of the integrated or whole system. Conventional farmers focus on one element of the food chain as an isolated target, ignoring the ecological and economic consequences of chemically dependent monocropping.

A "whole" sustainable food production system is a model that regenerates and improves the soil each year. It supports the labor requirements of the farmers by providing decent living wages. It provides safe, flavorful and nutritionally valuable food for the farmers and for consumers. Most importantly, it works within its ecological surroundings to lessen the deterioration of our environment. These new models of sustainable food production that I envision need to be fully integrated. They need to include *soil, plants, livestock, nature, farmers and consumers.*

This needs to be more than just a few specialty growers who are demanding and receiving premium prices for gourmet varieties in their local community. It needs to be an entirely new force of sophisticated food growers. They need to be trained, equipped and capitalized to satisfy the buyer's needs for flavor and price, while sustaining the farm, the farmer and the environment for the future.

Food producers need a food production system that identifies and solves the six major conflicts of agriculture: Land, water, capital, skills, tools, and markets.

These are conflicts because they are absolutely necessary to make a living as a farmer. Yet the acquisition of these components often pits the farmer against an economic and social system that is more appropriate for industry than for stewardship of the soil and the soul.

When farmers have sufficient capital, they can obtain land, water and tools. Capital comes from the marketplace. When a market garden serves a local community, that community shares the responsibility of helping to capitalize that market garden.

Markets are available wherever there are people. It is necessary to grow the food where the people live, and this can be done in almost every bioregion of the world. Growing food near the population will reduce the complex and costly array of brokers, shippers and distribution or warehousing facilities.

When more small-scale growers produce food at the local level it increases the pool from which consumers can choose their diet. Then, more consumers will rely on local producers for a

319

larger portion of their food supply. The only way to reverse the trend of "mega-farm, mini-flavor" is to educate the public to buy locally, and educate farmers to produce for the local marketplace.

The Obtainable, Sustainable Integrated Garden Farm System

I would like to help create a new food production model. We can call it the *obtainable, sustainable, integrated garden farm*, The integrated garden farm I envision will have four components; the land, nature, the gardener and the families who will eat the food grown there.

The gardener provides the labor and skills needed to grow the optimal amount of food on small parcels of land. The land needs to be economically productive, without demanding excessive yields that deteriorate the life force of the soil. The consumers become shareholders, co-partners, paying the costs of the garden, and reaping fresh and flavorful produce on a daily or weekly basis. They bring capital to the gardener, and harmonious energy to the garden.

We can divide the garden activities into four categories:

1. Vegetables and fruits

2. Cover crops and compost

3. Small livestock

4. Habitat for beneficial wildlife

These will rotate each year. The animals, cover crops and compost provide the fertility and help build soil tilth and structure. This ensures extra high yields and nutritionally superior food. The livestock and vegetables provide food for the gardener and the member/shareholders. This nutrient rich diet will enhance the health of the shareholder community. Inviting the bees, earthworms, beneficial insects and native birds into the garden helps insure a balanced ecological system that provides for the health and bounty of the garden.

This plan offers vast potential as a model for profitable and sustainable food production at almost any level, on one-quarter acre or hundreds of acres. It can serve a community of one family, or hundreds of families. This can be a one-person part-time food production system, or it can be made larger to provide employment for several farmers. It can provide meat, honey, eggs, chicken, turkey, vegetables, berries, flowers and herbs for 10 families on less than a half acre. Or, it can provide these things for dozens, even hundreds of families on larger land holdings. A goal might be to feed 40 families on one acre of land, while providing a decent living wage for the full-time farmer, and regenerating the land and creating a harmonious ecological system.

The integrated garden system is *obtainable* because it can start on a very tiny amount of land with a small group of people. The gardener can start part-time, and expand gradually as capital, skills, and membership levels increase.

The system is *sustainable* because it grows most of its fertilizer, requiring fewer and fewer outside inputs each year. The compost to enrich the system comes from livestock manures and plant debris, combined with compostable waste from the community. The garden sustains the farmer with a living wage, and the shareholder with healthful food.

This system is *integrated* because it produces more than just vegetables. The system includes consumers in the internal workings of the garden. They become co-partners, sharing the risks and the rewards with the gardener. They provide the start-up capital the gardener needs to get established.

By integrating the natural ecosystem we make sure that the native bird population can be included. Building homes and maintaining forage for the birds will encourage them to reside in the garden. They are valuable as pest predators, and friendly companions for the humans who toil there.

The *integrated garden system* is Eco-Farming at its best. Its design is gentle on the land, similar to a natural ecosystem that includes the plant, animal and mineral kingdoms. These rotations of livestock, cover crops and vegetables are an ongoing solution to the problem of exhausted soils, weed-disease-pest infestations and unhealthy food. A healthy soil grows healthy plants that are more resistant to pests and disease. People who eat these healthy plants will be better able to withstand disease, and will be healthier and stronger, more able to contribute to and support the community in which they live.

Putting It Together In The Sustainable Food System

Let's look at the emerging sustainable agriculture models. Do they protect and enhance the value of the soil? Do they offer a living wage and decent livelihood to the farmer? Do they provide good food at a fair price to the population? If not, why not? How can we improve these models to fulfill the requirements of being obtainable, sustainable and economically productive?

First, consider the land, the heart of the system. Let's stop thinking of it as just dirt and recognize it as a living system, one that supports itself while it grows food to support us. We can adopt ways to make the soil more fertile and less erosion prone. We can grow plants that are more resistant to diseases and pests. We can enable the soil to provide healthy food for the sustenance our bodies require.

The fastest way to reclaim land and make it continually sustainable is with compost. Compost is more than just a soil amendment, though. The composting process itself is an economical and practical alternative to landfilling the organic fraction of our waste stream. In the short-term, the greatest economic value of this compostable material lies in the effort it takes to get rid of it through landfilling, incineration or other means. Its true long-range value lies in the regenerative benefits it can provide to the soil. Organic materials currently entering our landfills are compostable, rich in protein, carbon and trace elements. We urgently need these beneficial amendments in our farm soils.

Landfilling costs us all money, either directly in hauling and "tipping" fees, or indirectly in higher taxes and damage to our environment. Let's redirect these compostable organic materials. Give them to local farmers and pay them to turn the material into nutrient-rich compost. By avoiding landfill costs, municipalities will save money. Some of the savings can be passed on to the farmers as contract service fees for providing the alternative to land filling. Paying farmers to provide this alternative waste disposal adds to their economic base and enriches their fields. It helps restore their ability to remain in business as food providers for the nation. Most importantly, it allows waste *from* the community to become food *for* the community.

Next, let's look at the skills of the farmer. We can help establish college level continuing education programs that enable farmers to get the information they need about sustainable farming practices. Schools all over America are beginning to add sustainable and alternative agriculture classes to their curriculum. We need more of them.

Capital for the *integrated garden system* comes from the eco-partners who receive their food from the garden. The crops sell to a membership group of families in the local community. Each member pays a proportionate share of the garden's expenses, and receives an equal share of the harvest.

Members pay their share over a 10-month period beginning in January. Payments in the winter months are lower, as families get more of their food from grocery stores. Payments in the summer months are higher, as families get almost all of their food from the gardens. This pays the start-up and ongoing costs of the market garden, including the gardener's salary for the season. Food storage in freezers and root cellars will continue the supply of food into the winter months. The garden can be perpetuated by saving the seeds of the healthiest plants from each year's crop.

From this integrated garden system each shareholder will receive much of their meat and produce needs for the year at a cost similar to conventional food prices. The superior flavor and nutritional value of the organically grown food is free. It's the reward for the families who join in and provide philosophical and financial support to the farmer and the garden.

An Action Plan For The Integrated Garden Farming System

The centerpiece of the integrated garden system is the boxed raised bed gardening method. It has been a standard for centuries, and has been further developed by garden writer Jeff Ball in the early 1980s. The heavy board sides on the raised beds provide the foundation for trellises, growing tunnels, and livestock fencing.

Jeff Ball talks about this gardening method in his book *60 Minute Gardening* (Rodale Press, 1983). The system is very well displayed in Jeff's *Yardening* video series, published by National Gardening Association, Burlington, Vt.

The boxed raised bed garden method relies on super fertile soil, double dug beds and complex planning and planting schemes. The method uses plastic tunnels, high-rise trellises, drip irrigation, and intensive plantings, for super yields of produce. This garden can provide some of the meats and all of the fresh vegetables a family can eat, on less that 1,000 square feet of land per family per season. In this instance I am referring to the national average family size of 2.65 persons.

One-third of the garden contains vegetables, berries, herbs and flowers. Another third contains grain-producing cover crops that also provide compostable biomass. The remaining third of the garden has portable fencing for livestock pens.

A significant percentage of the feed requirements for the livestock (up to 30 percent) can be grown right in the garden. This includes mature cover crops, excess vegetables and fruits, spent garden plants and weeds from the garden beds. Even kitchen scraps from the garden members make good animal feed.

Pigs and chickens, unlike humans, do not recognize non-crop plants as weeds or kitchen scraps as garbage. They eat everything, including weed seeds and pest insects. Bedding for the animals can be straw from mature cover crops such as cereal grains or leaves from the yards of the community.

The garden system operates from early spring to late fall. Piglets are purchased at 20 pounds weight in May. They are fed out to 220 pounds and harvested in October. Day-old chicks are raised to 4-5 pound size, and harvested as fryers and broilers after eight weeks. After butchering and packaging, the meats can be held in the family's freezer for use in the winter.

Because livestock is only grown in the summer months, housing needs are minimal. Pigs and chickens live in small huts that can be positioned at bed ends for easy access to the fenced bed areas. Throughout the season, the pens are rotated weekly for even distribution of manures and for weed-disease-pest control.

In the *integrated garden system* we can use a rotating plot system. The pig pen this year will be in cover crops next year. This year's cover-cropped beds will be next year's vegetable beds, and so on.

The key to the super fertility of the garden beds is the livestock manure. One feeder pig will produce nearly 2.25 tons of nutrient-rich manure in six months. A laying hen will produce only 100 pounds of manure per year, but it is high in available nitrogen. Chicken manure is an extremely fertile activator for the compost pile.

Nearly 100 percent of the value of this animal manure can be recovered. Most of it can be collected in a few minutes each day and delivered to the compost piles. Manure and urine that can't be collected will remain on the soil, providing nutrients for next year's cover crops.

The compost, high in available macro and micro nutrients, will be a valuable soil amendment for the following year's vegetable and cover crops. Because compost is so valuable, it deserves special attention from the gardener. Composting in the *integrated garden system* takes place in a series of bins designed to fill one of the boxed raised beds.

In a 4- by 50-foot boxed raised bed there is room for 12 compost bins, each measuring 4-feet square and 4-feet high. Gather the materials in alternating bins, using eight of the 12 bins for raw materials. As decomposition occurs, the material will shrink, allowing the total from eight bins to be combined into only four bins. Turn the material every month with a pitchfork. The process continues throughout the summer. By fall, four bins will be brimming with nearly 10 cubic yards of finished compost. This is enough to lay a 1-inch layer on the 2,400 square feet of land that is to be used for vegetable production next year. Thanks to the super fertile soil, this 2,400 square feet of land can provide all of the vegetable needs for 10 families.

Spread the compost on the growing beds in the fall and cover it with leaf or straw mulch for the winter. By spring planting time, the earthworms will carry most of the compost into the soil, adding more than 5 percent organic matter to the top 6-inch layer. This gives the super fertility required for successful intensive vegetable production.

In the spring, the leaf or straw mulch that is still on the surface can be raked off the beds and put in the compost bins to start another round of compost making. The seeds or transplants can go directly into the soil without plowing or rotary tilling. This elimination of tillage is a giant step forward in decreasing labor requirements and in promoting excellent soil health.

Through the growing season, the garden's soil is never bare to the sun, wind or rain. It is always protected, either by mulch, food plants, or cover crops. Erosion, compaction, crusting and soil degeneration is negligible in these protected beds. Even the livestock sections of the garden are protected by bedding and leaf mulch during most of the year.

You may be starting the *integrated garden system* on land that needs immediate soil improvements. In this case, you may need to bring in compost materials and soil amendments. Asking the garden members to bring in leaves, yard waste and kitchen waste will be a big first step in getting enough raw materials to make good compost.

Fertility and tilth can also be enhanced dramatically by adding earthworms to the soil. It's possible to increase the earthworm population a great deal by simply mulching the soil with leaves or straw for a season or two. Sometimes, that takes too long. A faster way to increase the garden's earthworm population is to grow them as a "crop" in one of the raised beds.

To do this, dig out about six inches of soil from one of the boxed beds. Install a wire screen, then put the soil over it to refill the bed. Then seed the bed with a few thousand earthworms. The screen will keep worms from escaping. The following year, the bed can be used for vegetable production by removing the wire screen. Or, you can leave this one bed in the rotation as an "earthworm nursery".

To provide food for the earthworm nursery, install rabbit hutches above the boxed raised bed. The gardener moves the hutches along the bed weekly. As the rabbit manure and food bits fall to the ground the earthworms eat them. Three hutches, containing two rabbits each, will fertilize the whole bed in a season. This will create a super rich soil that will exceed all expectations for vegetable yields in the future.

Earthworms have a 90-day reproduction cycle. In healthy soil with plenty to eat, they are astonishingly prolific. By the end of the first summer, the 2,000 or 3,000 "seed" worms will have multiplied to many thousands, enough to seed every bed in the *integrated garden system.*

It's a simple matter to sift through the soil above the screen wire and take out the earthworms. Save the super rich castings to fertilize plants, or for mixing potting soil. After taking the earthworms out of the propagation bed, remove the screen and store it for use in another season. If you leave the screen in place, any earthworms that are trapped above it during the winter will freeze unless you cover them with at least two feet of straw or leaves.

In the fall, after seeding the rest of the garden beds with earthworms, cover the beds with leaf mulch to protect the worms and the soil. The worms will burrow several feet deep to survive the winter and will continue to multiply rapidly in following years.

Natures Living Mulch – The Cover and Smother Crop For Natural "Green" Manure

Cover crops in the *integrated garden system* play several important roles. They provide a portion of the feed for the livestock and serve as a living mulch to protect the soil. Their vigorous root growth tills the soil and makes thousands of tiny channels for soil life to use for habitat and migration routes. Their top growth provides biomass that chokes out weeds and enriches the soil. The flowering cover crops will provide pollen for bees and birds. Beneficial insects will live in the cover crops and prey on insect pests.

During winter, the cover crops will form a soil-protecting mulch on the surface. This layer of biomass provides food for the earthworms until the ground freezes and the worms enter dormancy. When the soil thaws in spring, the worms will awaken from dormancy and burrow to the surface to resume feeding on the mulch. As they eat the mulch, their excrement will fertilize the soil throughout the top 6-inch layer.

This fertile layer of soil is the real secret of how this tiny garden can feed so many people. Here is just one example of how this is true. In poor soil, it might take 500 tomato plants to yield 1,000 pounds of fruit, enough for 10 families for the season. In super rich soil fertilized with animal manures and compost, it might take only 100 tomato plants to yield the same 1,000 pounds.

In the boxed raised bed method it is very easy to add season extenders such as plastic mulch, floating row covers and high-rise trellises, which will enable the gardener to gain even higher yields. Under ideal circumstances it is possible to gain up to 20 pounds of yield from one tomato plant. Then the 1,000 pounds of tomatoes needed for 10 families could be grown on only 50 plants.

True, these season extenders are not natural products. They come from synthetic materials. However, their ability to shade the soil, protect the plants against light frosts and certain insect pests, and decrease labor inputs often outweighs their negligible detrimental impact on the environment. Some growers may choose to forego the use of these synthetic materials altogether. In this case, their yields won't be the highest possible but will still be well beyond yields achieved with conventional cultural methods.

Yields of many flowering plants can be further enhanced if beehives are at the edge of the garden. More thorough pollination results in more harvestable yields per plant. The honey produced by the bees is a desirable natural sweetener for the garden members.

Using boxed raised beds can end most of the annual tillage and cultivation required in the standard garden. Mulches and cover crops combined with the animal grazers will all but eliminate weeds. Active soil life, spurred on by a good diet and optimal living conditions, will till the soil better and more gently than any mechanical equipment yet designed.

Because the vegetables grow on trellises and mulched beds there is less chance for soil borne fungal diseases to harm the plants. Trellises also help increase yields by raising plant foliage upward for greater photosynthesis. This gives vegetables better flavor as well.

Plastic mulch warms the soil and decreases evaporation of valuable irrigation water. The soil moisture can be maintained at the optimum level with very little effort from the gardener. Earthworms thrive beneath the plastic mulch, and will bring their super rich castings to the surface in astonishingly high amounts. If the plastic mulch only remains on the surface for six months or less it will have no detrimental effects on the soil.

For those gardeners who don't want to use plastic mulch, they can get excellent results by using organic materials such as straw or leaf mulch. The list of benefits of using organic mulches is almost endless. Organic mulches act like a slow-release compost. Over time, mulches will adjust pH in almost any soil. It is a fertilizer and soil conditioner, contributing major and micro nutrients and trace elements to the soil.

These mulches eliminate most of the weeding normally required in the garden, and decreases irrigation needs dramatically by helping the soil retain moisture and by limiting evaporation. It protects the soil from compaction and drying, and provides unlimited nourishment for valuable soil life. Organic mulches, when applied properly, can moderate soil temperatures, thereby providing an optimal micro-climate for your garden plants. Finally, using organic materials is an excellent way to recycle the organic fraction of our waste stream, both from the home and from our communities.

A Challenge to Growers Everywhere.

With careful planning and honest effort, the *integrated garden system* can accomplish the goal of feeding families from tiny parcels of land. These tiny parcels of land are available in backyards and vacant lots all over America. The *integrated garden system* can be economically sustainable. With fewer plants giving greater yields, the gardener can work fewer hours and spend less money.

The idea is elegant, simple and obtainable. The animals provide the manure and grazing that benefits the land. The green manure cover crops protect the soil and the soil life, and help the micro-organisms assimilate and metabolize the healthy nutrients provided by the livestock. The vegetables and meats provide food for the gardener and the garden members.

In turn, the families provide the economic stability for the garden and the gardener. They can also help with the gardening chores. This connection with the soil will soothe the spirits, and assuage the craving most of us have to be part of the food production cycle. Social interaction and group sharing of management and gardening tasks becomes a rewarding byproduct of this gardening experience. This gives the family members an excellent chance to touch the soil and to know the farmer who grows their food. The gardener will become part of the community that eats the food, and will share gladly with the community of supporters.

This connection to the soil and the farmer who grows our food, though hard to measure in economic terms, helps provide the core happiness that we all crave. The *integrated garden system* is truly socially just, environmentally sensitive, and economically sensible.

The result is to form the perfect loop. You can use waste from the community to fertilize the land where the food is grown for the community. You can organize a local group of consumers to join in partnership with the you. Together, you can enjoy the bounty of the *integrated garden system* and the balanced ecosystem the garden will help form.

These ideas have only scratched the surface. There are many benefits and an equivalent number of challenges in this gardening method. As you go forward with the planning and implementation of this system there will be joys, delights, rewards and surprises. Some are tangible, others intangible, with all being satisfying and fulfilling. It is gentle on the land, easy on the gardener, and responds immediately to the needs of people searching for local access to flavorful, wholesome and safe food.

Let's work together to design a model – many models – so we can learn and improve. Let's create and demonstrate a food production system that is truly sustainable. One we can all take pride in. One that will allow our children and their children to inherit a legacy of agricultural pride, integrity, joy and fulfillment.

I invite each of you to start now to design your *integrated garden system*. We can each design a system that fits our personality, climate zone, gardening site and market area. We can share information and work toward the optimal plan for this obtainable and sustainable food production system. Send your questions, suggestions and experiences to me. Once we have worked out the problems and developed a truly complete system, we can publish our findings. Our experiences will enable gardeners, farmers and educators all over the world to replicate our successes. Within just a few years, cities and towns everywhere can have one or more of these *integrated garden farms*. Eco-farming can truly be the agriculture of our future.

Afterword

The purpose of *BACKYARD MARKET GARDENING* isn't to teach you how to become a successful market gardener, your customers and your own experiences will do that. My hope, instead, is that I have been able to teach you how to *think* about creating a back yard business.

Shortly after I finished the manuscript for *BACKYARD MARKET GARDENING* I was invited to be the keynote speaker for the Vermont Natural Organic Farmers Association conference in Middlebury. The text of my speech displays my frustration with the "system" that surrounds food production and distribution in this country today. This system is founded on volume, convenience and price. It totally ignores the needs of small scale farmers, and grossly overlooks the wants of today's health conscious consumers.

Yet, in spite of the sad state of our national food industry, I feel great hope for America's market gardeners and small-scale farmers if we can only learn to think locally when we design our marketing plans. Here is the text of my keynote address to Vermont's organic farmers.

"Ward Sinclair is a market gardener over in Dott, Pennsylvania. He recently wrote that when he started his farming business nearly a decade ago, he had ten self-styled commandments for being successful. Well, he's been at it a good number of years now, and he's learned a few things. As a result, his list of ten commandments has become a list of two suggestions.

"That's sort of the way I feel when I think about the future of farming here in Vermont. I can only offer one good suggestion to help you be successful. *Get close to your customers!* Do whatever it takes, whatever you can do, to eliminate the middlepeople. Go directly to your friends and neighbors when you need customers. They are close, they know who you are and they will pay you what your crops are worth.

"My vision of a sustainable agriculture is that every household, in every community in Vermont will have access to safe, fresh, affordable, locally grown food at least 6 months each year. And, that in the providing of this service, Vermont's farmers will receive fair wages, fair treatment and a respectable livelihood.

"The public mania to 'Buy America' we are hearing and seeing these days is a direct manifestation of people's frustration and anxiety. Americans are tired of being pushed around by partisan political interests and by market forces that are well beyond our control. We need to take back our power and we need to take back the responsibility of feeding ourselves. We need to turn to local self-determination to set our own new policies. We can then turn to local self-reliance to carry out these new policies.

"Buying local food can become part of the Vermont ethic within the next five years. Just like with recycling. Five years ago nobody was doing it, now we all feel guilty if we don't recycle. We need the same thing to happen with food. Within five years every household in this state should feel compelled to buy local produce when it is available.

"Right now, Vermont is a colony for the rest of the country. We export 80 percent of the milk we produce, but we import 95 percent of everything else we eat. Our challenge is to convince and encourage our friends and neighbors to buy from us, instead of from the supermarkets. While our neighbors are spending their money at the supermarkets our local farmers are going out of business, currently at the rate of two farms per week.

"This is not healthy, it is not sustainable and we cannot let it continue. The one bright report from the statehouse in the last two years is that sales of higher-value specialty crops is increasing at 15 percent per year. That's good news. We can build on the specialty market and turn our farm failures around.

"There are 500,000 people in Vermont. They spend $900 million annually for food. Almost all of that food comes from somewhere outside our state. If all of us in this room can get only 1 percent of the Vermont market we will split a pie worth $9 million every year. That's $130,000 annually for every certified organic farmer in this state. And that's only 1 percent of the total market. Imagine if we can get 2 or even 3 percent? Every one of us could triple our annual plantings and we'd still have to add farmers to help us grow all that stuff.

"I've heard it said, by farmers here in this room, that you can't sell all the organic food you can grow. Or at least you can't sell it profitably. If that is true then let's find out why! Why aren't our friends and neighbors buying from us? All we need is one out of each hundred households. That's a 1 percent market share. Is that asking too much?

"Before we see more farmers apply for food stamps, and before we let more farms go bankrupt, we need to find out why our neighbors aren't buying from us. If we are doing something wrong, then what is it? That's our first challenge. If we need to change our ways, let's do it. Let's adapt to the marketplace of the 90's. Let's find out what we are doing right, or can do better, and do a lot more of it. That's our biggest challenge.

"My one suggestion to you right now, is to stop driving by your market to get to a market. Driving long distances to sell food to city people is not the answer to our problem. I'm sure of it. Sell your food to your neighbors. Let's stop competing against each other for a tiny piece of the pie and set our sights on that $9 million market share this year.

"I don't have all the answers, but I think collectively we can make a difference. We need to create a "Buy Local Because" program. We know the reasons, and there are lots of them, why people should buy from us. Now we need to tell them. We need to encourage them to want to buy from us. One family at a time, like ripples on a pond surface, we need to get our neighbors to become our customers. First in a one mile radius, then two miles out, then three. Eventually we will be able to touch and serve every household in the state. Then our dream for a sustainable agriculture in the state of Vermont will start to become a reality. Dreams can come true if we work while we dream."

This speech was written specifically for vegetable growers in the state of Vermont. I do feel, however, that much of what I said is true nationwide, even world-wide. We need to stop hauling our food past our neighbors on our way to market. It only takes from 100 to 200 families to support each vegetable grower, if the grower is getting retail prices for their produce and doesn't have to truck everything hundreds of miles to market. Surely you can find that many families in your own community to support your backyard market garden. Good luck, and remember, *dreams can come true, if we work while we dream.*

Appendix 1

The Intervale Foundation
128 Intervale Road
Burlington, Vt 05401
802-660-3508

Andrew W. Lee, Executive Director

The Intervale Foundation is a 501(c)(3) non-profit educational organization whose mission is to discover and demonstrate models of community farming that are agriculturally sustainable, environmentally sensitive, economically sensible and socially just. Our goal is to help stimulate a 10 percent annual increase in production and consumption of locally grown food in Chittenden County, Vermont. Intervale Foundation projects have been awarded the *Environmental Achievement Award* by the Renew America Foundation.

Commonly shared problems that often exist in communities include declining agricultural land base, decreasing job and ownership opportunities for the farm community, pollution from farm chemicals and long-distance transportation of food, increasing community solid waste stream, declining landfill space, increasing environmental health costs and non-availability of locally grown fruits, vegetables, meats, poultry and dairy products.

The Foundation's community farming projects demonstrate how municipal and private land can be reclaimed with compostable materials from the community waste stream. The land can then be used for producing food and to provide jobs and agricultural ownership opportunities for local residents and farmers.

The 30 acre farm is located in Burlington's Intervale, a 820 acre flood plain along the Winooski River. The land is rented from the city of Burlington. Programs operating on the site are:

Intern Training: This program began in 1990 with 4 students from the University of Vermont. The purpose is to provide hands-on training to complement the student's academic training. Students receive a salary and up to 15 credit hours for the summer-long program. Intern graduates are now managing community supported farms and market gardens that sell produce in the Burlington area. This program provides skills training that leads to increased job and ownership opportunities, creates a greater supply of locally grown food in the area and continues the agricultural heritage of the region.

Burlington Small Farms Business Incubator: This program is designed to provide land, shared equipment, irrigation, training and marketing assistance to organic food producers. Six new market gardeners will participate in the Intervale in 1992 as well as five vegetable growers from outside the city. This program creates job opportunities for low-skilled and semi-skilled workers, ownership opportunities for agricultural entrepreneurs and demonstration models for other farmers in the state. The end result is to provide excellent, high quality food for the area's residents and keep more of our food buying dollars in the local economy.

Intervale Community Farm: This is a 150-household community supported agriculture (CSA) farm that provides food for more than 300 people from less than four acres. ICF serves as a training ground for interns and demonstrates how other farmers in other communities can utilize vacant urban/rural fringe farm land. CSA is a system wherein the shareholding families provide the capital required to pay the farmer and staff to grow the food, thereby eliminating most of the marketing and capitalization worries of the farmer. Shareholders enjoy fresh, flavorful and healthy produce at a reduced cost. They also have a chance to connect in a meaningful way with the land and the farmer that feeds them. This helps to create a complete system which nourishes the land, the farmer and the consumer. Other positive aspects of this program are to provide free or low-cost food for families in need and for the local emergency food shelf. Nearly 3 tons of food are donated annually.

Home Garden Education Center: This is a 16-week Discover Gardening course that teaches beginning and intermediate gardeners how to grow a major portion of their food needs. The season-long program offers skills training in seeding, transplanting, soil improvements, composting, weed-disease-pest control, harvest and succession planting, basic fresh food preparation and winter storage. This project also includes appropriate technology research and transfer.

The Native American "Three Sisters" garden offers a model representation of an agriculture that has been practiced in the region for centuries by indigenous peoples.

A new feature of the Home Garden Education Center is the "Giving Away Gardens" program which coordinates volunteer efforts to go to the homes of low-income residents in Burlington and help them build and manage a garden in their own backyard.

Burlington Compost Project: Through this project, leaf and yard waste from nearly 8,000 homes and business is diverted from the landfill and is turned into nutrient-rich compost which is used to reclaim and fertilize land for growing organic fruits and vegetables. Ten acres of land have been reclaimed and are now in food production. An additional 20 acres is being readied for organic certification. Over 7500 tons of leaf and yard waste have been diverted from landfills since 1987, at a savings of more than $300,000 in avoided landfill costs. Our latest effort is to develop a food waste composting facility that will compost food scraps from area restaurants, supermarkets and the hospital cafeterias. These waste generators will in turn be purchasing organic vegetables from our local farmers.

The benefits of these alternative agriculture programs have been:

1. Provide on-the-job training for unskilled workers and ownership-livelihood opportunities for agricultural entrepreneurs.

2. Increase local food supplies with fresh, organically grown produce that is tasty and nutritionally valuable.

3. Retain a larger percentage of our food buying dollars in the local economy.

4. Provide ecologically sound models for farm land regeneration by using the organic fraction of the solid waste stream as fertilizer and soil amendment.

5. Demonstrate models of economically sensible food production and distribution systems.

These programs have been successful in teaching us how to use composted materials from the city waste stream to reclaim and fertilize worn out city-owned farm land that has been in chemically dependent crop production for decades. The sustainable agriculture methods now being practiced will allow this land to continue indefinitely to provide healthy and contaminant-free food for the community without adverse impact on the economy or the environment.

Programs are administered by a board of directors with the aid of executive director Andy Lee. The programs have been supported by grants and donations from Gardener's Supply Company, Perry Restaurant Group, Burlington's Community Economic Development Office, Seventh Generation, Chapters Publishing, Vermont Agency for Natural Resources and State of Maine.

These community farming projects serve as models for other communities, to show how public/private enterprise joint ventures can be used to solve food supply problems. Program components are being transferred to interested people through workshops, field days, classes and in written materials that are made available through appropriate alternative agriculture resource centers.

Composting waste from the community to provide food for the community is an idea whose time has come. These Intervale Foundation models can be learned and replicated by municipalities, agricultural entrepreneurs, displaced farmers and concerned educators throughout the country and the world.

Appendix

Suppliers

A. M. Leonard Inc. (hand tools and supplies)
Box 816
Piqua, OH 45356

Market Farm Implement (catalog $3)
RD 2, Box 206
Friedens, PA 15541
814-443-1931

Country Home Products (weed trimmer, brush mower)
Box 89 Ferry Road
Charlotte, VT 05445

Crop King Inc. (greenhouses and supplies)
Box 310
Medina OH 44258

Cook's Garden (specialty seeds, books)
Box 65
Londonderry, VT 05148
802-824-3400

Gardener's Supply Co. (supplies, tools, greenhouses)
128 Intervale Road
Burlington, VT 05401
802-863-1700

Johnny's Selected Seeds (seeds, tools, supplies)
Foss Hill Road
Albion, ME 04910

Mellinger's (tools, supplies)
2360JF Range Road
North Lima, OH 44452

Necessary Trading Co. (tools, supplies, fertilizers)
328 Main Street
New Castle, VA 24127
703-864-5103

Stuppy (greenhouses, supplies)
Box 12456
North Kansas City, MO 64116

Vey Sales (Red Dragon torch)
1153 Cornell Street
Pittsburgh, PA 15212

Book Publishers

New World Publishing
3701 Clair Dr.
Carmichael, CA 95608
(*The Grower's GREEN BOOK, A Guide To Profitable Marketing*, by Eric Gibson)

Acres USA
P.O. Box 9547
Kansas City, MO 64133

agAccess
P.O. Box 2008
Davis, CA 95617

American Botanist
Box 532
Chillicothe, IL 61523

The Stephen Greene Press
Viking/Penguin Inc.
40 West 23rd St.
New York, NY 10010-5201

Garden Way Publishing
Schoolhouse Road
Pownal, VT 05261

Good Earth Publications
Box 4352
Burlington, VT 05406
Phone : 802-985-8184

Rodale Press
33 E. Minor Street
Emmaus, PA 18098

Periodicals and Newsletters

Growing For Market
Fairplain Publications
P.O. Box 365
Auburn, Kansas 66402

The Natural Farmer
NOFA
RFD 2
Barre, Mass., 01005

Lamb's Quarterly
Susan Sides
Box 57
Fairview, NC 28730

Avant Gardener
P. O. Box 489
New York, NY 10028

The Business of Herbs
PO Box 559
Madison, VA 22727

Healthy Harvest III
Potomac Valley Press
Washington, D.C. 20250

Hortideas
Rt 1
Gravel Switch, KY 40328

Whole Earth Review
Box 428
Sausalito, CA 94966

Organic Gardening
Rodale Press Inc
33 E. Minor St.
Emmaus, PA 18098
Rural Enterprise

N80 W12878 Fond du Lac Ave
P.O. Box 878
Menomonee Falls, WI 53051

Small Farms Today
c/o Ridge Top Farm
Route 1 Box 237
Clark, MO 65243

The NEW FARM
Rodale Institute
222 Main St
Emmaus, PA 18098

Country Journal
P.O. Box 8200
2245 Kohn Road
Harrisburg, PA 17105-8200

New England Farm Bulletin
and Garden Gazette
Box 147
Cohasset, MA 02025

Harrowsmith Country Life
Ferry Road
Charlotte, VT 05445

National Gardening
180 Flynn Avenue
Burlington, VT 05401

Informational Services

Institute For Alternative Agriculture
9200 Edmonston Road
Suite 117
Greenbelt, MD 20770
301-441-8777

Bio-Dynamic Farming and Gardening Association
Box 550
Kimberton, PA 19442
215-935-7797

Ecology Action
c/o John Jeavons
5798 Ridgewood Road
Willits, CA 95490

Office For Small Scale Agriculture
Howard ("Bud") Kerr Jr., Director
USDA/CSRS.SPPS
Aerospace Building Room 342
14th and Independence Ave SW
Washington DC 20250-2200

Natural Organic Farmers Association
The Natural Farmer
RFD 2
Barre, MA 01005

New England Small Farms Institute
Judith Gillan
Box 937
Jackson St.
Belchertown, MA 01007

Agriland Concepts Inc
"Land Preservation Through Profitable Agriculture"
4 Hilltop Road
Farmington, CT 06032
203-658-7498

USDA Plant Hardiness Zone Map
USDA Ag Research Service
Miscellaneous Publication #1475 January 1990
USDA
Washington, D.C. 20002

Alternative Farming Systems Information Center (AFSIC) (USDA)
National Ag Library
Beltsville, MD 20705
301-344-3704

The Land Institute
Rte 3
Salina KS 67401
Publications Department

Small Business Administration
1441 L Street NW Room 100
Washington, D.C. 20416

Small Farm Energy Project
P.O. Box 736
Hartington NE 68739

Organic Agriculture Research Institute
P.O. Box 475
Graton, CA 95444
Woods End Agricultural Institute
RR Box 128
Temple, ME 04984

Rodale Institute Research Center
RD 1 Box 323
Kutztown PA 19530

Tilth
4649 Sunnyside No.
Seattle, WA 98103

Appropriate Technology Transfer for Rural Areas (ATTRA)
P. O. Box 3657
Fayetteville, Arkansas 72702
501-442-9834

Bibliography and Suggested Reading List

Ball, J., *60 Minute Gardening*, Rodale Press, Pennsylvania, 1985

Ball, J., *The Self-Sufficient Suburban Garden*, Rodale Press, Pennsylvania, 1983

Bartholomew, M., *Square Foot Gardening*, Rodale Press, Pennsylvania, 1981

Bartholomew, M., *Cash From Square Foot Gardening*, Storey Publishing, Vermont, 1985

Belanger, J.D., *The Homesteader's Handbook to RAISING SMALL LIVESTOCK*, Rodale Press, Pennsylvania, 1974

Carnegie, D., *How To Win Friends and Influence People*, Simon and Schuster, Inc., New York, 1936, 1964

Editors of *Organic Gardening*, *Getting The Most From Your Garden*, Rodale Press, Pennsylvania, 1980

Faulkner, E. H., *Plowman's Folly*, University of Oklahoma Press, Oklahoma, 1943, reprinted in 1987 by Island Press, Washington, D.C.

Faulkner, E. H., *A Second Look*, University of Oklahoma Press, Oklahoma, 1947, reprinted in 1987 by Island Press, Washington, D.C.

Fukuoka, M., *The Natural Way of Farming, The Theory and Practice of Green Philosophy*, Japan Publications Inc., New York, 1985

Gershuny, G., and Smillie, J., *The SOUL of SOIL, A Guide to Ecological Soil Management*, Gaia Services, Vermont, 1986

Harmonious Technologies, *Backyard Composting*, Harmonious Press, California, 1992

Hawkin, P., *Growing A Business*, Simon and Schuster, New York, 1987

Henderson, P., *GARDENING FOR PROFIT, A Guide to the Successful Cultivation of the Market and Family Garden*, Orange Judd Co., New York, 1867, reprinted by The American Botanist, Illinois, 1991

Hunt, M. and Bortz, B., *High Yield Gardening*, Rodale Press, Pennsylvania, 1986

Jeavons, J., *How To Grow More Food Than You Thought Possible On Less Land Than You Can Imagine*, Ten Speed Press, California, 1982

Logsdon, G., *The Gardener's Guide to BETTER SOIL*, Rodale Press, Pennsylvania, 1975

Logsdon, G., *Small-Scale GRAIN RAISING*, Rodale Press, Pennsylvania, 1977

Lorenz, O. and Maynard, D., *Knott's Handbook For Vegetable Growers*, 2nd Edition, Wiley Interscience, New York, 1980

Minnich, J. and Hunt, M., *The Rodale Guide To Composting*, Rodale Press, Pennsylvania, 1979

Mollison, B. with Slay, R. M., *INTRODUCTION TO PERMACULTURE*, Tagari Publications, Tyalgum, Australia, 1991

Mollison, B., *Permaculture: A Practical Guide for a Sustainable Future*, Island Press, Washington, D.C., 1990

Ogden, S. and Ogden, E., *The COOK'S GARDEN*, Rodale Press, Pennsylvania, 1989

Poincelot, R., *Organic No-Dig, No-Weed GARDENING*, Rodale Press, Pennsylvania, 1986

Rodale, R., *Our Next Frontier*, Rodale Press, Pennsylvania, 1981

Rodale, R. and McGrath, M., *SAVE THREE LIVES, A Plan for Famine Prevention*, Sierra Club Books, California, 1991

Sagan, D. and Margulis, L., *GARDEN OF MICROBIAL DELIGHTS, A Practical Guide to the Subvisible World*, Harcourt Brace Jovanovich, Inc., Florida, 1988

Sinetar, M., *DO WHAT YOU LOVE, THE MONEY WILL FOLLOW, Discovering Your Right Livelihood*, Dell Publishing, New York, 1987

The Findhorn Community, *THE FINDHORN GARDEN, Pioneering a New Vision of Man and Nature in Cooperation*, Harper and Row, New York, 1975

Thomas, S., revised by Looby, G. P., *BACKYARD LIVESTOCK, Raising Good, Natural Food For Your Family*, The Countryman Press, Vermont, 1990

Tompkins, P. and Bird, C., *Secrets of the Soil*, Harper and Row, New York, 1989

Wampler, R. and Motes, J., *PICK YOUR OWN FARMING; Cash Crops for Small Acreages*, University of Oklahoma Press, Oklahoma, 1984

Whatley, B. T., *How To Make $100,000 Farming 25 Acres*, Rodale Institute, Pennsylvania, 1987

Wright, M. S., *BEHAVING AS IF THE GOD IN ALL LIFE MATTERED; A New Age Ecology*, Perelandra, Virginia, 1987

Wright, M. S., *PERELANDRA GARDEN WORKBOOK; A Complete Guide To Gardening With Nature Intelligences*, Perelandra, Virginia, 1987

Index

trace elements 36, 100
trellis 63, 270, 281
Tuff-Bilt 92
U-pick 229
U-Pick marketing 199
University of Vermont's
Center For Rural Studies
121
USDA Cooperative
Extension Service 248
Van En, Robyn 112, 113
Vinylflow 274, 277
walk-in cooler 65, 173
washstand 78, 173
Weed Control 48
weed-disease-pest control
306
weeding 81, 309
Whatley, Booker T. 139,
199, 276
Whatley Small Farm Plan
140
wheel hoe 84, 97
wheelbarrow 76, 173, 274
wholesale 206
Wholesale Direct
Marketing 110
wind stress 291
Women With Infant
Children 14
wood chips 41
word of mouth advertising
108, 130
workers compensation 245
Working Hands Farmstand
155
Yardening 323

$24.95

MONEY GROWS IN YOUR GARDEN

Discover how easy and profitable it is to grow and sell vegetables, fruits, flowers, herbs and small livestock from your own Backyard Market Garden.

Learn how others grow and sell:
- 14,000 pounds of food, on less than one-eighth acre – Ohio.
- $150,000 from one-half acre, to fancy restaurants – Calif.
- $40,000 from one acre of oriental raised beds – Oregon.
- $36,000 from 3/4 acre, to city farmers markets – Mass.

Learn how to:
- Earn top dollar, with minimum effort and maximum profits.
- Improve your garden soil for super yields and superb flavor.
- Buy or build tools that speed your work and increase profits.
- Enjoy a guaranteed salary from community supported agriculture or a membership garden.

"BACKYARD MARKET GARDENING is the book that shows you how to do what you can, with what you have, where you are."
George DeVault, Editor, *Noveii Fermer* (The Russian New Farmer)

"Market gardening, as described by An o the soul, the so and the flow of capital."
Jim Hightower, Austin, Texas

"BACKYARD MARKET GARDENING is written by a master farmer who has "walked his talk."
Will Raap, President, Gardeners Supply Company.

The author, Andy Lee, is a consultant and Executive Director of The Intervale Foundation in Burlington, Vermont, and teaches vegetable production and marketing in the University of Vermont's alternative agriculture program.

ISBN 0-9624648-0-5

52495 >

Good Earth Publications

9 780962 464805